Bartolus of Sassoferrato

The medieval jurist Bartolus of Sassoferrato (d. 1357) has long been accorded seminal importance by historians of political thought. This volume provides the first complete English translation of his three most celebrated tracts: *On Guelfs and Ghibellines*, *On the Government of a City*, and *On the Tyrant*, which constituted the first consolidated response by a medieval lawyer to the problem of tyranny in the city republics of central and northern Italy. Crucial sections of Bartolus's academic commentaries on Roman law are also translated in appendices. George Garnett and Magnus Ryan make the writings of Bartolus accessible to an expanded audience, situating his political theory in its original context and explaining his arguments. Footnotes to the translation explain all Bartolus's references to normative sources, legal and otherwise, and a detailed glossary of legal terms and institutions is provided. This translation allows readers to understand how Bartolus mobilized the Roman and canon laws to address immediate political developments, and why he was the most famous and enduringly influential medieval lawyer.

GEORGE GARNETT is Professor of Medieval History in the University of Oxford, Fellow and Tutor of St Hugh's College, and Lecturer at Lady Margaret Hall. He has published widely on the history of law and political thinking from the eleventh century to the seventeenth. Previous publications include *The Norman Conquest in English History, Volume I: A Broken Chain?* (2021), *Marsilius of Padua and 'the Truth of History'* (2006), and an annotated translation of *Vindiciae, contra tyrannos* (1994).

MAGNUS RYAN is an associate professor in the History Faculty at the University of Cambridge and Fellow of Peterhouse. His previous publications include, as co-editor, *Maitland: State, Trust and Corporation* (Cambridge, 2003), and numerous contributions on medieval political thought and legal history.

CAMBRIDGE TEXTS IN THE
HISTORY OF POLITICAL THOUGHT

General editor
QUENTIN SKINNER
Queen Mary University of London

Editorial board
MICHAEL COOK
Princeton University
HANNAH DAWSON
King's College London
ADOM GETACHEW
University of Chicago
EMMA HUNTER
University of Edinburgh
GABRIEL PAQUETTE
University of Maine
ANDREW SARTORI
New York University
HILDE DE WEERDT
Leiden University

Cambridge Texts in the History of Political Thought is firmly established as the major student series of texts in political theory. It aims to make available all the most important texts in the history of political thought, from ancient Greece to the twentieth century, from throughout the world and from every political tradition. All the familiar classic texts are included, but the series seeks at the same time to enlarge the conventional canon through a global scope and by incorporating an extensive range of less well-known works, many of them never before available in a modern English edition, and to present the history of political thought in a comparative, international context. Where possible, the texts are published in complete and unabridged form, and translations are specially commissioned for the series. However, where appropriate, especially for non-western texts, abridged or tightly focused and thematic collections are offered instead. Each volume contains a critical introduction together with chronologies, biographical sketches, a guide to further reading and any necessary glossaries and textual apparatus. Overall, the series aims to provide the reader with an outline of the entire evolution of international political thought.

For a list of titles published in the series, please see end of book

BARTOLUS OF SASSOFERRATO

Three Tracts on City Government and Related Writings

TRANSLATED AND EDITED BY

GEORGE GARNETT
University of Oxford

MAGNUS RYAN
University of Cambridge

CAMBRIDGE
UNIVERSITY PRESS

CAMBRIDGE
UNIVERSITY PRESS

Shaftesbury Road, Cambridge CB2 8EA, United Kingdom

One Liberty Plaza, 20th Floor, New York, NY 10006, USA

477 Williamstown Road, Port Melbourne, VIC 3207, Australia

314–321, 3rd Floor, Plot 3, Splendor Forum, Jasola District Centre,
New Delhi – 110025, India

103 Penang Road, #05-06/07, Visioncrest Commercial, Singapore 238467

Cambridge University Press is part of Cambridge University Press & Assessment,
a department of the University of Cambridge.

We share the University's mission to contribute to society through the pursuit of
education, learning and research at the highest international levels of excellence.

www.cambridge.org
Information on this title: www.cambridge.org/9781316519899

DOI: 10.1017/9781009019583

When citing this work, please include a reference to the DOI 10.1017/9781009019583

First published 2024

A catalogue record for this publication is available from the British Library.

A Cataloging-in-Publication data record for this book is available from the Library of Congress

ISBN 978-1-316-51989-9 Hardback
ISBN 978-1-009-01145-7 Paperback

For
Peter Linehan
and
Quentin Skinner

Contents

Preface

F. W. Maitland pronounced that those brought up in the English common law tradition were peculiarly ill-equipped to tackle the medieval
civilians and canonists, 'and they are not to be tackled by the untaught'.
This attempt to induct English-speaking readers into the mysteries of
Bartolus's political thinking began when GG was given some teaching
remission by the Oxford History Faculty in order to translate Bartolus's
three political tracts. The aim was to produce a new set text for the Faculty's Further Subject in Scholastic & Humanist Political Thought.

Over many long evening symposia, the editors went through the draft
translation line by line with Hugo Tucker in order to correct and clarify.
They both wish to acknowledge Hugo's relentless and meticulous rigour,
without which these translations would be much fuller of error than they
now are. We are also grateful to him for his good grace on the numerous
occasions when he remained alone in his conviction that Bartolus was
attempting to mimic in Latin the Greek middle.

Years later, Quentin Skinner suggested to us that the existing typescript
translation might be elaborated into a volume for the Texts in the History
of Political Thought series. We are indebted to him for that proposal, for
his advice on supplementary texts to be included in the Appendices, and
for his forbearance in waiting further years for a finished typescript.

We are grateful to Joseph Canning, Dante Fedele, Serena Ferente,
Yves Mausen, and Alessandra Panzanelli Fratoni for their contributions.
Tim Rood and Elinor Garnett tendered advice on scene-setting in classical dialogues, and Georgy Kantor guidance on late antique Roman local
government. John Hudson commented on all and Caroline Humfress
on large portions of the text. Helen Pike did likewise; she also provided

plentiful sustenance during periods of intense collaboration in Oxford. We also wish to thank Liz Friend-Smith and Chris Jackson for steering this book through Cambridge University Press, and our cartographer Michael Athanson. Papers based on the work have been presented at the Oxford Political Thought Seminar, at the Universidade Nova de Lisboa, and at the Institute of Historical Research. We also thank generations of undergraduates in Oxford and Cambridge who have agonized over the tracts, and pinpointed problems.

GG is one of that dwindling band who were taught about Bartolus by Walter Ullmann. It is fitting that Walter's role in promoting Bartolus to Anglophone audiences should be highlighted here. MR was one of the last pupils of Peter Stein, whose deep knowledge of Roman law extended over its entire history, and who had therefore immersed himself in Bartolus. We hope that both supervisors would have approved of our efforts.

It had long been the editors' intention to dedicate the book to our friend and sometime colleague Peter Linehan, another pupil of Walter's. As Research Fellows of St John's College, Cambridge, we both benefitted in myriad ways from his paternal care. It is a matter of regret and grief that we are no longer able to offer this filial tribute to him in person.

For just as long it has been our desire to make Quentin Skinner co-dedicatee. He has had a great influence on both of us – in GG's case, since he took Quentin's celebrated Special Subject on the monarchomachs, in whose thought the medieval learned law was so central. The emphasis Quentin has laid on that law as a substrate in the political thinking of the early modern period has played a very important part in drawing the attention of a wider audience to Bartolus and his ilk.

We both acknowledge with gratitude the periods of leave allowed to us by our respective colleges and faculties.

GG thinks it right to add that in terms of expertise in civilian and canonist jurisprudence, he has played Pollock to MR's Maitland.

Introduction

Bartolus was born between November 1313 and November 1314 in Sassoferrato, a town in the March of Ancona, and died a citizen of Perugia in July 1357. He received his early education from the Franciscans Guido da Perugia and Pietro di Assisi before beginning legal studies at the university of Perugia in 1327, at the precocious age of fourteen. He moved to Bologna probably in 1330, where he took his doctorate in civil law in 1334. After serving as assessor in the courts of Todi, Cagli, and Pisa, he taught at the university of Pisa from 1339 to 1343 before returning to Perugia, where he remained until his death. In 1355 he took part in an embassy sent by his city to Charles IV, Holy Roman Emperor, while the latter was at Pisa, and was honoured by the emperor with the grant of various privileges, such as the right to legitimize bastards among the students at Perugia, and to bestow full legal capacity on minors. Charles also made him an imperial counsellor and member of his household.[1]

Within a decade of his death Bartolus's commentaries on Roman law, which were the precipitate of his teaching at Pisa and Perugia, together with his legal opinions written for courts and litigants, were already famous among academic and practising lawyers. With the possible exception of Accursius, the thirteenth-century compiler of the standard gloss or *Glossa ordinaria*† to the *Corpus iuris civilis*,† no other teacher of Roman law in the middle ages commanded such respect, let alone affection, in later generations. Few would contest the view that he remains the most

---

[1] F. Calasso, 'Bartolo da Sassoferrato', *Dizionario biografico degli Italiani*, vi (Rome 1964), pp. 640–9; S. Lepsius, 'Bartolo da Sassoferrato', in I. Birocchi, E. Cortese, A. Mattone, and M. N. Miletti, eds., *Dizionario biografico dei giuristi italiani (XII–XX secolo)* (Bologna 2013), vol. I, pp. 177–80.

influential post-antique Roman lawyer. He was the first medieval Roman lawyer to merit a book-length analysis by an historian of political thought, the 1913 study by C. N. S. Woolf, *Bartolus of Sassoferrato: His Position in the History of Medieval Political Thought.* In the index to the final volume of the Carlyles' encyclopaedic six-volume *A History of Mediaeval Political Theory in the West* (1936), Bartolus occupies more space than any other single thinker except Jean Bodin. In modern continental historiography, he looms even larger.

Bartolus's three tracts *On Guelfs and Ghibellines, On the Government of a City,* and *On the Tyrant* were the first free-standing works by a medieval lawyer on the political problems of his immediate time and place; they represent a mobilization of the Roman and canon laws to address political developments which Bartolus regarded as deeply pernicious. To appreciate the quality of Bartolus's response, it is necessary to acquaint oneself with both the intellectual and the political traditions within which he was formed.

Bartolus is the most celebrated representative of a type of medieval intellectual which had evolved in the course of the twelfth century, the professional lawyer. In the most general description available to him he thought of himself and his colleagues as *juristae*, or 'jurists'. Jurists were adepts of Roman law, canon law, or both. Roman law was the great collection of imperial laws and classical legal commentaries, the 'Corpus of Civil Law' or *Corpus iuris civilis*,† compiled at the orders of Emperor Justinian I (527–65) between 529 and 534. By the time Bartolus was born, Roman law had long been a fact of life in the city-states of central and northern Italy, in the kingdoms of Naples and Sicily, in France, and in the kingdoms of the Iberian peninsula.

The phrase 'civil law' or *ius civile* meant the civil law of Justinian's books; canon law meant Gratian's *Decretum*, in circulation in its final form by the mid twelfth century, the collection of papal decretal letters known as the *Liber extra* promulgated as law by Pope Gregory IX in 1234, another decretal compilation promulgated by Pope Boniface VIII in 1298 known as the *Liber sextus* or simply *Sext*, and the *Constitutiones Clementinae* initiated by Pope Clement V but published by his successor John XXII in 1317. Roman law was alive wherever an ecclesiastical court did business, for to study and practise canon law was impossible without a familiarity with Roman law. Conversely, although most of the jurists whom Bartolus addressed in his lectures on Roman law called themselves 'civilians', as students primarily of the Roman *ius civile*, they had to familiarize themselves with canon law too. Together, Roman and canon law formed an amalgam known as the common law or *ius commune*, the law common throughout Western Christendom; it was a whole despite educational specialization on the part of civilians and canonists. Accordingly, and like the rest of his more conventional jurisprudence, Bartolus's tracts are replete with references to canon as well as Roman law, and to the medieval commentaries on both which had become standard by his time.

In these political tracts, written during the last couple of years of his life, Bartolus devoted himself to three main tasks. The first was to analyse legally the factionalism characteristic of the North Italian cities, to decide if and why it was permissible to join a party, and to establish the relationship between such parties and legitimate government. This was the subject of *On Guelfs and Ghibellines*. The second was to find a place for the Italian city-state as he knew it in the typology of constitutions deployed by Aristotle in *Politics*, a schema which had been adopted by the numerous medieval commentators on Aristotle, and to demonstrate that one form of government in particular was best suited to such organizations. In Bartolus's view, this was the *regimen ad populum*, or government by the people, rather than monarchy or aristocracy. Bartolus describes and commends this in the second tract, *On the Government of a City*. The third, which Bartolus accomplished in *On the Tyrant*, was to anatomize tyranny in its most common manifestations and lineaments in the Italian cities of his time.

As Osvaldo Cavallar has argued, the tracts are artfully constructed to flow sequentially, and *On Guelfs and Ghibellines* is not the source of the sequence. Rather, *Tiberiadis*, Bartolus's tripartite treatise on the law of alluvial deposits, the formation of islands, and the shifting of river beds, is.[2] Its title might be translated as 'Tiber river-basin' or 'region'; the whole treatise is, therefore, ostensibly concerned with the river Tiber, and

---

[2] O. Cavallar, ed., 'River of Law: Bartolus's *Tiberiadis* (*De alluvione*)', in J. A. Marino and T. Kuehn, eds., *A Renaissance of Conflicts: Visions and Revisions of Law and Society in Italy and Spain* (Toronto 2004), pp. 30–129, at 31, 54–8. Cavallar's edition is only of the first section – *De alluvione* – of the tripartite *Tiberiadis*, which goes on to deal with the formation of an island in the midst of the river (*De insula*), and with a dry riverbed (*De alveo*): pp. 34–5, 40, 47–9. For the complete work, see Bartolus de Saxoferrato, *Tyberiadis, ... Tractatus de fluminibus tripertitus; ab Hercule Buttrigario ... nunc demum restitutus in lucem prodit* (Bologna 1576; repr. Turin 1964). Only four codices examined by Quaglioni, *Politica e diritto*, p. 89, contain all three political tracts; nine contain some or all of *Tiberiadis*. He does not collate Cambridge, MA, Harvard Law School Library, MS. 75, dated to 1475, an opulent codex which contains the full version of *Tiberiadis* and all three political tracts in their logical order, copied out by the same hand: Cavallar, ed., 'River of Law', pp. 47–8.

thus shares the Italian specificity of the three political tracts. Indeed, in a piece of introductory autobiographical scene-setting, Bartolus presents *Tiberiadis* as prompted by his reflections as he looked out over the valley of the Tiber while making his way to a country villa outside Perugia during the summer vacation of 1355. At the very start of the treatise, he signals that the Tiber eventually flows through the city of Rome, within the territory of which it becomes tidal. In legal terms, at that point it ceased to be a river and became sea.

In the opening sentence of *On Guelfs and Ghibellines*, Bartolus is still musing on the third and final part of the preceding *Tiberiadis*, that concerned with the gradual shifting of the river bed. This further episode of personal reminiscence places him 50 km downstream from the Perugian villa, close to Todi, where he had once acted as assessor. He specifies that the spot was 'within the hundredth milestone of the city of Rome' – in Roman law terms, just within the jurisdiction of the prefect of Rome. As foreshadowed by *Tiberiadis*'s early comment about the ultimate course of the river, *On the Government of a City* has a riparian setting within Rome itself. *On the Tyrant*, unlike its upstream antecedents, does not begin in a particular locality close to the Tiber; but, like *On the Government of a City*, it focuses on Rome, which in that immediately preceding tract is twice said to be stuffed with tyrants 'now'.[3] Towards the end of *On the Tyrant*, however, there is a reference back to the opening 'book', on alluvial deposit, of *Tiberiadis*,[4] the notional source of the jurisprudential stream which flows both through that treatise and all three tracts of the subsequent political one. Whereas the opening of *On Guelfs and Ghibellines* had referred back to the final 'part' of *Tiberiadis*,[5] the final *quaestio* of *On the Tyrant* alluded to its first one. That *Tiberiadis* and the three political tracts together were conceived sequentially is implied by the scribe of the late fifteenth-century presentation copy of them all in sequential order in Harvard Law School Library, MS. 75, which adds this colophon to *On the Tyrant*: 'The treatise on the tyrant, and thus the whole matter of the *Tiberiadis* ends.'[6]

It is to be noted that although Bartolus appears to regard all three political tracts as integral parts of a single work, that is not how they came to be treated by posterity.

[3] Below, pp. 18, 33.
[4] Below, pp. 62–3.
[5] Below, p. 13.
[6] Cavallar, ed., 'River of Law', p. 48; Cambridge, MA, Harvard Law School Library, MS. 75, fo. 8or. For this copy, see above, n. 2.

It is thought that Bartolus died before he could complete *On the Tyr-ant*, and perhaps *On Guelfs and Ghibellines* too. They both just stop. If *On Guelfs and Ghibellines*, the first of the political tracts, is incomplete for this reason, then Bartolus must have continued to revise it after drafting its sequels. A reference close to the end of *On the Tyrant* to Gil Albor-noz's appointment as cardinal-bishop of Santa Sabina, which took place in December 1356, appears to confirm that Bartolus was working on it very shortly before his death.

If mortality had indeed prevented him from putting the finishing touches to these tracts, that may have created a problem in terms of sub-sequent interpretation. Usage over the centuries has dubbed each of the three political tracts a *tractatus*, a treatise. However, a passage in *On the tyrant* suggests strongly that Bartolus conceived of the three tracts as a sequence in an integrated whole, forming a composite response to the problem of tyranny in contemporary Italy, that the three components of this response were not in his view *tractatus* but 'books' (*libri*), and that it was the ensemble of three books that constituted a *tractatus*.[7] At the beginning of *quaestio* VIII, he refers to the more specific actions of a tyrant 'which have been for the most part presented above, in the first book of this treatise'. He cannot mean the first *quaestio* of *On the Tyrant*, for it contains no such matter; and *On the Tyrant* is in any case divided not into books but *quaestiones*. The only matching passage in any of the texts is *quaestio* III of *On Guelfs and Ghibellines*. The strong implication of this passage, therefore, is that Bartolus conceived of all three 'books' as a single 'treatise'. An earlier passage in *On the Tyrant* points in the same direction. At the very beginning, Bartolus says that, 'before proceeding further with the present treatise on the tyrant', he will list the questions he is about to consider. Since he has not yet begun that discussion, the phrase 'the present treatise' and the sense of ground already covered con-veyed by the phrase 'before proceeding further' would most plausibly refer to our hypothesized composite whole, rather than to the specific component *On the Tyrant* which is to follow.

The picture is complicated, however, by an implication in the same introductory passage that Bartolus is *only now* turning to the topic of tyranny: 'I have not dared to broach bitter, distressing, and troublesome subjects, especially when I see tyrannical perfidy extending its sway.' Thereby, it appears, he pursues the theme signalled by the concluding

---

[7] Below, pp. 52–3.

sentence of the immediately preceding tract, *On the Government of a City*. Diego Quaglioni revealed that the opening paragraph of *On the Tyrant* is only to be found in one manuscript; but we, like him, are unwilling to discount it as inauthentic, even if, like him, we register some unease about it. It is in any case the only conceivable objection to the hypothesis that, had Bartolus lived to complete and polish the work, the result would probably have looked much more like the antecedent *Tiberiadis*: an integrated treatise, repeatedly so titled, consisting of three separately subtitled 'parts' or 'books'.

However that may be, the discussion immediately preceding the final sentence of *On the Government of a City* also points to tyranny as a logical terminus; many of the roads travelled by Bartolus in *On Guelfs and Ghibellines* and *On the Government of a City* lead to the tyrant, the proclaimed subject of the final tract.

The conceit serving both to connect the three political tracts together and to frame much of their specific content is the Tiber. The city through which the Tiber eventually flows is the source of all laws, which makes it unique; but in another respect what can be said of the 'Roman river Tiber' might be said of any river. A river is always moving, its water, its content, is constantly renewed, always different. The movement of water means that the river is also forever and almost imperceptibly changing its course. Yet it remains always the same river, perennial and perpetual. These key characteristics are set out in the definition of terms preliminary to the opening part of *Tiberiadis*.[8] In these respects rivers are analogous to artificial entities, such as cities, or lesser groupings within cities, such as factions, as Bartolus observes at the outset of the first political tract, *On Guelfs and Ghibellines*. Indeed, its very opening sentence refers back to the 'third part' – that is, the final part – of *Tiberiadis*, concerned with the shifting course of a river, and specifically of the Roman river. Changes over time are not easy to prove, but can be inferred from their manifest, measurable, but nevertheless intrinsically impermanent, results. In the case of rivers these become visibly obvious as land is eroded and created. In the case of city politics, the constantly shifting changes are much more difficult to determine or measure – they are not susceptible to geometric calculation – and their manifold causes still more so. The problem of proving the existence of a tyranny is also explicitly linked to the difficulties of proof with regard to the deposit of alluvium in *quaestio* XII of *On*

---

[8] Cavallar, ed., 'River of Law', p. 92; *Tiberiadis*, p. 13.

the Tyrant.[9] If Bartolus's main general concern in these tracts is to apply Roman law to the analysis of political change in contemporary North Italian cities, the specific problems of perception, proof, and calibration bulk very large.

During the twelfth century, most cities in Northern and central Italy had developed communal forms of government which by modern standards were oligarchies, but which alert contemporary observers immediately recognized as revolutionary. In his biography of his own nephew, Emperor Frederick Barbarossa, Bishop Otto of Freising noted in 1157 or 1158 with mixed wonder and horror how the inhabitants of Italy, out of love of liberty and concern for the commonwealth or *res publica*,[†] imitated ancient Roman practice by electing consuls instead of having lordly rulers to govern them. There was, in his view, hardly a noble left of sufficient standing to resist the power of these cities, which had extended their rule over the whole of their respective dioceses and thus over the entire land. Without using the precise word, Otto was describing the commune, the institutional manifestation of which was a bundle of offices in a collective organ of government staffed by officials elected for short terms, and accountable to the full assembly of the adult male citizens of the city. In the course of the thirteenth century the original communal institutions were joined in many cities by the *popolo* or 'people', a pressure-group representing those who had been excluded from the original charmed circle of families eligible for communal office in the twelfth century. The commune rapidly became the foundation of civic existence, and proved ineradicable from the political consciousness of North Italians. In *On the Government of a City*, Bartolus adapts the typology of true and perverted constitutions from Aristotle's *Politics*. He brings one particular form of communal government under this schema when he substitutes the phrase *regimen ad populum* for the word *politia*, which rendered the Greek *politeia* in the Latin version of Aristotle's *Politics* in use across Western Europe at the time, and meant the mixed constitution. Bartolus also recasts its antitype, the perverted regime called democracy by Aristotle, into 'a perverted people'.

Party conflict had unsettled the communal and the later communal-popular regimes from the beginning; there never was a Golden Age of civic harmony in Lombardy, Tuscany, the Romagna, the March of Ancona, and elsewhere. The long-standing antagonism between the

[9] Below, p. 63.

(German) Roman emperors and the papacy in the region had exacerbated this endemic tendency towards political fission in the cities, and provided the terminological couplet of Guelf and Ghibelline, labels which had originally described the papal and imperial camps respectively, but which had, as Bartolus explains in *On Guelfs and Ghibellines*, lost all but coincidental identity with these causes by the early fourteenth century, possessing merely local relevance. Party violence undermined the effectiveness of committee-based, elective, and – in that limited sense – consensual government, but the rise of a single ruler as 'lord' or *signore* could extinguish it. The two phenomena were related, since rule by a *signore* was often the outcome of destabilizing factional violence. A straight *coup* had on occasion established the rule of a *signore*; but by Bartolus's time it was more common for strong-men to rise through, and in specious ways to work within, the institutions of legitimate communal and popular government. Elections were subverted and malcontents intimidated, office was bestowed not for a short, fixed term, but for life; powers which had previously been divided between different elected bodies were amalgamated in the hands of one lord, while taxes and other resources of the city were distributed among his clientele. By the time Bartolus reached maturity, such corruptions of the institutions which had framed North Italian civic experience since the mid twelfth century had taken on alarming institutional fixity and could look, on a purely formalistic level, like legitimate government: elections had taken place, extended terms of office had been agreed in public meetings, and the more notable *signori* had traditionally taken pains to buy confirmation of their offices from either emperor or pope in the form of vicariates.†

On the Tyrant is the first attempt by a medieval thinker to analyse the genesis of such regimes, and to measure the developing contrast between the maintenance of the communal veil and the underlying realities which it to varying extents concealed; but the earliest, shortest, and first of the tracts, *On Guelfs and Ghibellines*, already contains the kernel of the later, more elaborate, treatment. Factional nomenclature is mentioned here and there in the jurisprudence of earlier lawyers on banishment and expropriation, two standard tools of thirteenth-century communal government; and the existence of parties usually lurked not far below the surface of such discussions. But Bartolus's *On Guelfs and Ghibellines* provided the first consolidated treatment of the matter. It identified the underlying questions and brought them into focus through one lens, the question of all questions: was a particular set of arrangements, a particular pattern of behaviour, for the common good or not? Before he even reaches this point, Bartolus argues that if there is a Guelf tyrant in a city, a *good* man will become a Ghibelline, regardless of the original, historical, but now superseded associations of these labels respectively with the papal and imperial parties of long ago, just as a *good* man in a city under a Ghibelline tyrant will become a Guelf.

In cities such as Todi, where Bartolus had worked, parity of influence between the two parties was the foundation of the civic peace, and established by statute. As Marco Gentile noted, Bartolus's discussion of how to prove party affiliation therefore answered an urgent and quotidian political need.[10] But that discussion is also embedded in a broader one of political morality; Bartolus is concerned with much more than the question of whether factional affiliation is nowadays determined primarily or wholly by local political context, rather than, as had allegedly once been the case, simply by allegiances to popes and emperors who were at loggerheads. His formal and general position is stated a few lines further on: it is lawful to join a party if this makes it easier to defend the public good, a principle which also justifies resistance to a tyrannical government. It is similarly lawful for a just government to avail itself of a party label if this helps sustain it against attack. An appraisal of the legal authorities which Bartolus invokes in support of his claims here reveals the importance of this political language of the common good, derived ultimately from Aristotle's *Politics*, for the law does not sustain the argument very strongly. A passage from the *Digest*[†] punishes collusion with one litigant against another with the purpose of benefitting from the latter's property; a second provides help against those who conspire to accuse the innocent. The higher-order Aristotelian distinction between action for selfish gain and action for the public good is clearly the organizing principle and definitive criterion here, whereas the legal references provide but distant and imperfect analogues.

This, the third section of *On Guelfs and Ghibellines*, has axial importance, for it reveals the tyrant as Bartolus's ultimate target in a tract ostensibly dedicated to another problem. That is why he refers back to this discussion in the midst of *On the Tyrant*.[11] Bartolus's preoccupation with tyrannical government underlies the distinction between legitimate

---

[10] M. Gentile, 'Bartolo in prattica: Appunti su identità politica e procedura giudiziaria nel ducato di Milano alla fine Quattrocento', *Rivista internazionale di diritto comune*, 18 (2007): 231–51.

[11] Above, p. xv; below, p. 61.

action for the public good, and selfish, illegal action against the public good. A government which acts in the latter way will necessarily be tyrannical, just as a clique seeking to overturn a legitimate government for selfish reasons will *ipso facto* harbour tyrannical ambitions.

The citations from Roman and canon law at this point furnish a parade-ground example of how scholastic legal argument worked. If, Bartolus reasons, it is lawful to assemble one's friends for the protection of one's own property, it must *a fortiori* be lawful to form a group in order to defend the public's property. The *Digest*[†] passage he then quotes merely allows armed defence of one's property against armed aggression; it does not sanction collective action. Yet it is precisely action by a party which Bartolus is trying to justify here. *Digest* 43.16.3.9 permits collaborative resistance to force, but this is in private law (the rubric is *De vi privata*, 'Concerning private force'), and regulates relations between citizens, not between citizens and their government. To extract from Roman law the authority to topple a government is predictably difficult. To do so, Bartolus has to quote a passage which appears to forbid any such undertaking, then alter it by way of an addendum. *Code* 9.30.1 condemns sedition as a stirring up of the common people against the commonwealth, but Bartolus adds the caveat that this is legal if the objective is to depose a tyrant and restore government for the public good. This is one of several passages in these tracts where the law is only made relevant once the question under discussion has been virtually answered by extra-legal means, with the result that the law is sometimes a veneer applied to an argument, the substance of which is derived from other sources.

Again, and to follow Bartolus a little further through this section of the tract, it is lawful to be 'of one faction and one name' in order not merely to oppose but even to depose a tyrannical government, provided that it would be prohibitively difficult to achieve this by recourse to a superior authority, and also provided that one's purpose is to re-establish government for the common good, not to replace one tyranny with another. Two of the three legal authorities Bartolus cites at this point merit examination. The first, *Code* 1.9.14, forbids violent self-help and imposes legal process instead; it is only Accursius's gloss to this passage that allows self-help when no judge is available. The second, *Digest* 42.8.10.16, defines the circumstances in which one of several creditors may unilaterally take what is owed to him when he apprehends the debtor. In formal terms, then, Bartolus's method here is to embed legal passages relating to private law in governmental, public contexts. To exercise a tyranny is to detain the commonwealth by force against the commonwealth itself or against a superior lord, so to proceed against such tyranny for the motive of private gain is illegal. Three passages from the *Digest*† are then cited as examples of when the use of force for private gain is not allowed against another private person. These legal texts only support Bartolus's claim up to a point, because they do not allow or even imply the converse, namely, that it is permissible to resort to such means if one's purpose is to protect the public good. It is no coincidence that here, too, Bartolus appeals to the Aristotelian tradition in quoting Thomas Aquinas's lapidary statement that 'Tyrannical rule is not just, because it is not directed to the common good, but to the private good of the ruler.'

In *On the Government of a City*, Bartolus extends the category of tyranny. Aristotle and his medieval commentators had defined it as the perversion of monarchy, whereas Bartolus notes that all government for the sake of the governors is tyranny, whether by one, by few, or by many. Bartolus's wider ambition in this tract is to subject the tradition of Aristotelian political science to legal scrutiny. In book III of his *Politics*, Aristotle had famously asked what the best manner of ruling was; but Bartolus explains that he will approach the question via the hugely successful book *De regimine principum* by the prior-general of the Augustinian Order of Hermits, Giles of Rome (1243–1316), 'who was a great philosopher and a master of theology' and had, in Bartolus's opinion, treated the matter more clearly than Aristotle.[12] This was sensible insofar as Giles's book was the most widely known work of medieval political science, having been already translated into both French and Italian. Bartolus goes on to say that he will present Giles's 'opinion and follow his reasoning', but without adopting Giles's vocabulary, which was alien to jurists. The intention at this point seems to be to reformulate by reference to the law what Giles and indirectly Aristotle had said: 'I shall use their reasoning and I shall prove it by the laws; afterwards I shall describe my own views.' Bartolus does not mean that he will necessarily confirm by reference to the law what is said by Aristotle and Giles, merely that he will try to find legal analogues for the main points made by his august forerunners before offering his own opinion. The outcome demonstrates that in truth he disagrees with Giles.

Bartolus begins by providing legal parallels for Giles's main propositions. Any good ruler should possess rational discernment, right

---

[12] Below, p. 19.

intention, and perfect steadfastness: so far, Giles. Bartolus cites *Digest* 1.1.1.1, where jurists (but not rulers) must distinguish the licit from the illicit. Thanks to the opening words of the *Institutes*,[†] every lawyer also knew that steadfastness was integral to the very definition of justice, the constant and perpetual will to give to each his right. He continues to provide a legal version of the case Giles sets out against monarchy before relaying Giles's conclusion: an emphatic endorsement of monarchy as the best constitution. Speaking as a lawyer, he does not think Giles's statements are to be understood straightforwardly. There follows a covert tussle with Giles as Bartolus explores the implications of an Old Testament topos in discussions of kingship: Samuel's ominous prophecy of what looks like tyranny for the people of Israel who have demanded a king after the manner of other nations, and thereby, implicitly, rejected God as their ruler (1 *Kings* 8). Bartolus cites only one legal source of no particular consequence here, relying instead on the interpretations of the theological authorities quoted in the Ordinary Gloss to the Bible, in particular their hedging about of Samuel's unsettling predictions by means of the reassuring *Deuteronomy* 17, which portrays a more benevolent ruler. Bartolus uses this biblical exegesis to establish what the 'right of a king' is; that done, he returns to the question 'whether it is advantageous to a city or people to be ruled by a king'.

Here Bartolus makes his most forceful and original intervention. There are three categories of city or people: large ones, larger ones, and the largest. Rome had proceeded through each of these stages, changing its constitution as it did so, a process summarized in the Roman law in a long excerpt from the classical jurist Pomponius which formed *Digest* 1.2.2.[13] This told a story of constitutional change as the Roman people grew and expanded its sway. Bartolus argues that the merely 'large' city or people cannot sustain the expenses and magnificence of a kingly court, citing *Digest* 1.2.2, according to which the ancient Romans expelled their kings when Rome was still in its initial stage of growth. Rule by the few is also inappropriate for a small city where the riches of the rulers will be resented by the rest, and where there is also a danger of division between the rulers.

Bartolus sees the first observation confirmed by recent events in Siena, where Charles IV had disbanded the rule of the Nine, while the repeated

---

[13] The threefold categorization of cities in terms of size in *Tiberiadis*, p. 91, is not tied to Roman historical development in this way.

tensions within Pisa's ruling elite confirmed the second. Bartolus concludes that 'It is most advantageous to a people of the first magnitude to be ruled by the multitude, which is called a government by the people [*regimen ad populum*]', and he refers to the section of *Digest* 1.2.2 covering the period when Rome was ruled neither by its ancient kings nor the senate, but by the people. In this, its first period of conspicuous success, Rome therefore most resembled an average-sized Italian city of Bartolus's time, proving to his satisfaction that such cities 'of the first magnitude' should be ruled by the people, for 'It is evident that this form of government is good, because in that period the city of Rome expanded greatly.' Rule by the people – 'multitude' as he calls it here – excludes, however, the vile and commoner sort, whom Bartolus associates with the mobs hired by would-be tyrants. The best he can extract from the law to justify this limitation is a slew of references to the urban governments of the later Roman empire, which were staffed by dignitaries such as defenders† of cities and decurions;† since such persons were civic officials, rather than the entire citizen body, the contrast here with commoners is far from clinching.

Guided still by the *Digest*'s† account of the growth of Rome, Bartolus thinks that rule by a few good men is appropriate to a people of the second order of magnitude, such as Venice and Florence – which in Bartolus's opinion were therefore not popular but aristocratic regimes – for as Roman power expanded the senate took over government. In this second and 'larger' category of city or people, the danger of division between those who rule is diminished by the fact that they are actually many in number; the majority in the middle can provide a firm foundation for government even when there are some dissenters. The populace will not resent the power of the few, because in such larger cities these few are only few relative to the total population, and are in absolute terms rather numerous. Bartolus indicates the texture of good aristocratic rule by again citing laws regulating late Roman municipal government, particularly injunctions to provincial governors not to allow the rich to oppress the poor, and to distribute honours and burdens according to merit and capacity in the cities subject to them. Again, these legal texts might be accepted as illustrative, but they do not seem to constitute a satisfactory explanation for the stability of aristocratic city government.

Once a city has gained sway over many other cities, however, monarchy is the appropriate form of government, and the reasons advanced by 'Brother Giles' in favour of monarchy in general then apply. There will be an abundance of good men to provide counsel to the ruler. Moreover, *Deuteronomy* 17 clearly describes a king, and implies that he will rule over 'a large people of great standing' capable of holding dominion over other nations. Again the Roman model is authoritative, for once the Romans had entered the category of a 'largest' people, and won their wide empire over other nations, they finally re-adopted monarchy.

Bartolus extracts the further lesson from *Deuteronomy* 17 that kings over the very largest peoples should not accede by succession but election; the emperor ('who is universal king', as we shall see shortly) is elected by the princes and prelates of Germany; canon law states this unequivocally and also denounces hereditary succession to ecclesiastical offices. Rule over smaller kingdoms can pass by succession, which Bartolus terms a 'human constitution', whereas election is a more divine and noble mechanism. He could thus acknowledge the positive aspects of monarchy propounded by Giles whilst vindicating the *regimen ad populum* of – in Bartolus's terminology – 'large' Italian cities like Perugia, which are the smallest category he considers here, as well as the elective monarchy of the universal Roman empire.

On the Government of a City ends with a brief discussion of the worst form of government. Since Bartolus has already argued that all government for the private utility of the rulers is tyranny, the question for him now is which of its three manifestations is worst, tyranny by the one, the few, or the many? His conclusion is that where many are involved in rule some vestige and memory of the common good survives, whereas the fewer the rulers, the worse their tyranny.

The final sentence of *On the Government of a City* – 'And because today all Italy is full of tyrants, let us investigate those matters concerning the tyrant which are relevant to jurists' – effects the transition to its sequel, *On the Tyrant*. According to Pope Gregory the Great, the tyrant is someone who rules unlawfully in the commonwealth. Canon lawyers had adopted this definition in the generation before Bartolus, whereas thinkers in the Aristotelian tradition had focused instead on the criterion of the common good. Rule by one person against the common good was tyranny, and a variety of further characteristics such as the deployment of foreign bodyguards, the fomenting of discord between citizens, the waging of unnecessary wars, could be extracted from Aristotle's *Politics*. For Bartolus, tyranny consists primarily but not solely in the usurpation of jurisdiction, which he defines as 'the power introduced by public law with the necessity of stating law and establishing equity in the capacity of a public person'. There can therefore be tyranny in a household because the father exercises a type of royal right or jurisdiction, as a string of Roman law citations demonstrates at this point in his tract. By the same token, there can be no tyranny over a neighbourhood because the neighbourhood itself is not a subject or carrier of jurisdiction, only the city to which it belongs.

The engine-room of *On the Tyrant* is its second half, starting in *quaestio* VI. Here Bartolus subjects the quotidian political realities of contemporary Northern Italy to legal analysis, and concludes that most of the means of gaining rule over cities and their dependent settlements are examples of 'tyranny without title': fear, duress, force of arms, the use of the vile and commoner sort to propel oneself into power, the prevention of exiles from participating in one's election, the occupation prior to an election of the city's fortifications or those of its dependent settlements. The list is long, and familiar to anyone versed in medieval Italian politics.

The surprise is that Bartolus also condemns as tyrants those with an apparently unimpeachable title, in the form of an imperial or papal vicariate.[†] By his time the more sophisticated Italian *signori* had not merely been elected by the peoples of their respective cities, but had paid for appointment as imperial or papal vicars too. Appointment by one or other of the universal powers of empire and papacy was the second of what Italian scholars call the 'twin roots of the *signoria*', the first being election by the people of a city. Although, therefore, Bartolus de-couples modern Guelf and Ghibelline affiliations from loyalty to the church or empire respectively, his assumption in the three tracts that the superior should deliver a city from tyranny demonstrates that, for him, the two universal authorities were not simply an irrelevance. Where emperor or pope, whom Bartolus characterizes as 'universal lords', are compelled to accept the worse for fear of the very worst, the recipients of such grants are no less tyrants than if they had dispensed entirely with the cosmetics of just title. They still rule by denying the legal holders of jurisdiction their rightful exercise of that jurisdiction, and against the common good – the context implies that Bartolus means the common good only of the relevant city at this point, not that of the universal bodies of empire or church – by fear and duress. Such tyrants may be imperial or papal vicars, but they remain tyrants.

The lawyer needed to know what followed from this. In *quaestio* VII Bartolus explores the legal validity of acts undertaken in the city's name during the rule of a tyrant lacking title. The chief strength of Bartolus's

discussion, unparalleled in medieval jurisprudence or Aristotelian commentary, is his treatment of fear. Roman law was helpful on this, fur-
nishing the interdict *Quod metus causa* ('What on account of fear') for
restitution of what had been lost or renounced as a result of intimidation,
and the classical jurists had left behind rich discussion about when the
claim or presumption of fear was valid. The combination of administrative and private law is the most striking and, for the newcomer, often the
most alienating characteristic of the political theory of the medieval lawyers; Bartolus's politicization of fear in private law is no exception. *Digest*
4.2.21 nullifies the grant of a dowry made under duress; *Digest* 5.1.2 nullifies the judgment of a praetor if he has forced himself as judge upon the
litigant. In the context of a people cowed by superior force into accepting
a tyrant as its ruler, we might have less difficulty in accepting the second
passage as proof that 'jurisdiction should be transferred voluntarily', for
the first is hardly a comfortable fit, whereas the praetor was at least a
public official. To raise a mob is also a contravention of the Julian law on
public force (*Lex Iulia de vi publica*†): applied to the ruler of the city, who
has just been elected thanks to such a mob, this furnishes a criterion by
which to decide whether acts conducted under his rule do or do not bind.

As in *On Guelfs and Ghibellines*, but now with greater urgency, Bartolus confronts the problem of proof, for, as he suggests in *quaestio* VI, such
a ruler might be deemed to have been elected by the greater part of the
citizenry, and therefore appear legitimate. Bartolus emphatically denies
this, because the mechanics of the election have definitive importance
for him. If a crowd of retainers, hired muscle, was deployed to intimidate
the citizens at the time of the election, *Code* 12.1.6 applies, debarring
the low-born and those of mean condition from municipal office. The
legal backing is once again furnished by passages from Justinian's *Code*
on the decurions† of late Roman municipal government, and, once again,
the fit is far from snug, because Bartolus is talking about intimidation of
the electorate by such people, whereas the law prohibits them from actually governing.

Bartolus's response is to scour the Roman and canon laws for instances
in which formally faultless transactions are rescinded once intimidation
or duress can be demonstrated or reasonably assumed. His innovation
here is not the application of private law concerning matters like dowries
to the relations between rulers and ruled – medieval and most early modern law-based political theory would have collapsed without that habit of
mind – but to subject daily reality to the searching question of legitimacy

without fetishizing the formalities. An election is a constitutive process but becomes an empty formality if conducted under the shadow of an armed, sectarian mob. Appointment as a papal vicar[†] is a constitutive act, but becomes an empty formality if extorted by Taddeo Pepoli, tyrant of Bologna, from a powerless Pope Clement VI.

Some passages in Roman law were surprisingly amenable to Bartolus's agenda. The Julian legislation on the use of force both in private and in public contexts, discussed in book 48 of the *Digest*,[†] helpfully condemns all who alone or as a group seek to prevent judges and magistrates from operating normally. It similarly punishes those who impose illegal taxation. *Code* 1.2.16, which is about church appointments made during a preceding period of schism, provides Bartolus with a standard by which to assess the legal effects of transactions conducted under a tyrant, for canon law associates the schismatic office-holder with the tyrant, and even the *Glossa ordinaria*[†] to the Roman law contains some discussion of the matter, which Bartolus dutifully quotes. The Julian law on treason (*Lex Iulia maiestatis*[†]) is obviously useful in condemning anyone who, without a command from the emperor, wages war, raises a levy, or prepares an army, although it is Bartolus who adds 'if he raised an army against a city without an order from the superior'. Even within the standard normative framework Bartolus assumes in these tracts, in which the emperor or pope are present as notional superiors, the tract on the tyrant in particular shows repeatedly how difficult it was to identify a tyrant in a legally conclusive fashion, and to decide the legal consequences of such an identification.

This brings us to the final question. How far has Bartolus advanced what can usefully be done with the Roman and canon law to give clear lineaments to tyranny, and to analyse its consequences? It would be a grotesque injustice not to acknowledge the immense progress Bartolus made in these respects, for where consequences are concerned, the tract provides a lot: above all, the section on rescission of contracts made under a tyrant's rule is replete with usable distinctions. But how does one legally anchor the distinction, all-important as we have seen, between action prompted by the desire to protect the common good on the one hand, and selfish action on the other? What does the common good look like in the concrete situations which Bartolus describes in such profusion? Bartolus as a lawyer enjoyed and still enjoys the reputation of commendable practical-mindedness, and it is this, perhaps his greatest strength, which rules out any facile answers for him here. His pragmatic sobriety leads him to state that 'There is virtually no government which will not on occasion appear tyrannical to some people.' In the same spirit, he runs through the famous Aristotelian characteristics of tyrannical behaviour mentioned above, and notes that such tactics are often necessary if a good, non-tyrannical, government is to survive. As he explains, many of the practices listed by Aristotle as marks of tyranny were legitimate tools of government in fourteenth-century Italy. By comparison, Giles of Rome's pieties on all this appear rather insubstantial, and these are indeed some of the most refreshing pages of Bartolus's generally fresh and alert tract. They nevertheless underline the fact that the most important of the answers Bartolus the lawyer brings to this hitherto almost exclusively Aristotelian philosophical debate beg further fundamental questions.

Bartolus's engagement with medieval Aristotelian political science foregrounds a vocabulary which inevitably presents false familiarities to the unprepared modern reader, for whom it almost naturally implies a self-contained political society. Particularly in *On the Government of a City*, the basic categories of analysis such as monarchy, aristocracy, and *politia* – even when the last is replaced by *regimen ad populum* – might seem to invoke Aristotle's *polis*, the highest of all human associations with no political authority above it. Bartolus had no such organization in mind, so it is to this, the broader normative framework accepted by a particular kind of *ius commune* political thinker, that we must now turn.

We have seen that, according to *On Guelfs and Ghibellines*, tyrants who rule by force detain the commonwealth 'against the commonwealth itself or against a superior lord'.[14] Further on, it is only permissible to join a party in order to topple a tyrannical government if this same end cannot be achieved by recourse to a superior. In *On the Government of a City* Bartolus observes that in contemporary Italian cities regalian rights do not belong to the *podestà*[†] or other officers, such as the papally appointed rectors, 'but to the cities they rule, or to another superior, or to the fisc'.[15] As these examples show, the existence of a superior to the city is regularly assumed, just as, later in the same tract, it is the business of a city's superior to reform its government, although the implication here that the city can be its own superior hints at a more complex scenario. Most obviously in *On the Tyrant*, it pertains to the superior to rescue the people from servitude, so it is the superior's duty to depose a tyrant.

---

[14] Above, pp. xx–xxi; below, p. 9.
[15] Below, p. 23.

The superior alluded to in these passages can be either of the two universal powers recognized by Bartolus as legally supreme over all Christians: the Roman emperor and the pope. The former undoubtedly has the higher profile in these tracts, as across Bartolus's jurisprudence generally, and was embodied for him, as for Italians ever since the mid tenth century, by the rulers of Germany. According to patristic theologians, Rome, as the last in the sequence of great empires prophesied in the Old Testament book of Daniel, would be the final empire to rule mankind before the Apocalypse. The Roman law itself emphasized the eschatological and universal character of the empire, and although there were fourteenth-century Roman lawyers who dismissed both as humbug, Bartolus was not one of them. For him, the divinely instituted universal authority of the Roman empire was the servant of the universal Roman church; to deny the universality of the empire was therefore to flirt with heresy. Accordingly, the Roman empire was the normative framework for everything he wrote, despite its near paralysis in northern Italy, where cities had been vying with each other for pre-eminence ever since the late eleventh century, when the decay of imperial power in the region became precipitous.

Bartolus's most detailed statement of the universal authority of the Roman empire, including its relation with the authority of the papacy, occurs in his commentary on the law *Ad reprimendum*, promulgated by Emperor Henry VII at Pisa in April 1313, in which the emperor declared that all rebels against the emperor were guilty of high treason. Bartolus's comments on this constitution (excerpted below in Appendix II) anchor the Roman empire securely in a biblical, prophetic scheme.[16] Although as a matter of fact – *de facto* – there are those who do not obey, by law – *de iure* – they should. The objection that the emperor's summons has no authority in the lands ruled directly by the church is of no force because, since Christ's advent, the empire has devolved to the church. It has since been granted by the church in the person of the pope to the emperor, and the church must of course last until Christ's return. The legal superstructure thus becomes an eschatological one.

For a lawyer of such fastidiousness, it was natural to appeal to the authority of the emperor for the resolution of difficulties in Italy, as we have seen Bartolus occasionally doing in his tracts. But the ineluctable fact, which conditioned all his jurisprudence, was that many cities and towns across northern Italy nowadays failed to acknowledge imperial authority.

---

[16] Below, pp. 82–4.

Our sins, he laments in the preface to an earlier treatise, *On reprisals*, have merited that the Roman empire has lain prostrate for a long time, and that kings, princes, 'and even cities, especially in Italy, recognize no superior in temporal matters, at least *de facto*'.[17] Now that there is no superior able to rectify injustices, Italian cities resort to self-help by exacting reprisals from each other's citizens.

Bartolus returned to this issue repeatedly in the course of his academic commentaries on Roman law, to which we must now turn. 'You know', he told his students in his lecture on *Code* 2.3.28,[18] 'that the cities of Italy generally do not possess *merum imperium*,† but have usurped it.' In explaining in another lecture (on *Digest* 39.2.1) 'how what I see comes about, that nowadays all the rulers of cities and *castra*† throughout Italy exercise the rights pertaining to *merum* and *mixtum imperium*†', he mentions the obvious mechanisms of imperial grant and legitimate custom, but adds 'or perhaps they use it *de facto*'.[19] Bartolus is famous for the next step in his argument: the *de facto* exercise of imperial powers by a city not acknowledging the emperor's authority is a reason for accepting its right to use such powers. In his own words, 'If [the city] proved that it has been exercising *merum imperium*, then [the claim] is valid' (*Code* 2.3.28).[20] The strictly legal or *de iure* objection that this was still usurpation could therefore be ignored. Whenever the authority of the emperor was required for a particular procedure to be valid, the city itself could now claim to act as its own superior, as *civitas sibi princeps*, 'a city which is emperor unto itself', always provided that it could prove that it had been using these powers already under certain circumstances, and for a certain period of time. That done, 'those cities which *de facto* do not recognize a superior ... have *imperium* over themselves'. The most common manifestations in Bartolus's experience of both the *regimen ad populum* recommended in *On the Government of a City* as appropriate in merely 'large' cities – that is, the smallest of the three categories he defines – which Emperor Charles IV himself apparently extolled to Bartolus when they met – and of the aristocratic regime appropriate to cities of the second level of magnitude were in cities which did not normally acknowledge the authority of the emperor.

[17] Bartolus, *Tractatus de repraesaliis*, in *Bartoli a Sassoferrato Consilia, quaestiones et tractatus* (Basle 1588), fo. 327va.
[18] Below, p. 111.
[19] Below, pp. 88–9.
[20] Below, p. 111.

Much of Bartolus's jurisprudence, driven as it was by emerging problems of civic existence in Italy, inevitably focuses on the powers of a city's magistrates in a variety of situations. The materials in Appendix III demonstrate how frequently the neuralgic point was reached when the authority of the generally 'non-recognized' emperor was nevertheless required to validate an act of government. They reveal the frequency with which the fundamental question of legitimate authority irrupted into the quotidian business of governance in a city which usually failed to recognize the authority of the emperor, a question to which 'the city emperor unto itself' provided the answer.

However, a set of broader questions about legislative capacity frames everything Bartolus wrote about civic life, for which it is necessary to turn to his lengthy commentary on a passage excerpted from the *Institutes* of the classical jurist Gaius and included in the very first title of book 1 of the *Digest*[†] under the rubric 'On Justice and Right', the famous law *Omnes populi*, or 'All peoples ...' (*Digest* 1.1.9).[21] Here, Gaius explained that all peoples ruled by laws and customs live under a compound of norms, of which some are common to all mankind and are natural, and others are specific to a particular people or *civitas*. This text was the *locus classicus* for the discussion of statute-making powers in the Italian cities; Bartolus's commentary, excerpted in Appendix II, is so important because in it he locates every echelon of government known to him from his own society within the various categories of office-holders and their jurisdictions as defined by Roman law.

The law *Omnes populi* appears to permit cities to make their own statutes: is this true, and if so, to what extent? Bartolus's answer, developed over several distinctions and sub-distinctions, is that a city possessing all jurisdiction may legislate for itself without explicit authorization by a superior, meaning the emperor (or the pope, in regions where his temporal overlordship was recognized). The emperor might have granted such jurisdiction, or the city might have acquired it by prescription.[†] The point is that only the city itself has it, not subordinate communities in the region belonging to that city, nor subdivisions of the city, such as particular quarters or neighbourhoods, for jurisdiction resides in the whole people or the council which represents it.

21 Below, pp. 69–81.

Almost the same point is made in *On the Tyrant*.²² Bartolus can insist on it partly because the vocabulary employed by Gaius in *Omnes populi* identifies peoples as legislating agents, but then slides from peoples to cities. Guilds and other subordinate collegiate bodies are permitted to pass statutes regulating their internal business, but only the city may pass statutes on the administration of justice. Bartolus then asks about judges. Those in office for life, possessing what he calls 'perpetual jurisdiction', may legislate in this, the fullest, sense. Modern kings fall into this category, as do certain nobles such as counts; but a civic official such as a *podestà*† is in a lower category because he is only appointed for a fixed term. Bartolus is differentiating carefully between a circumscribed, temporary, executive authority, and full legislative power. On his own authority a *podestà* may impose curfews, curtail the export of grain from the city, or prohibit the bearing of arms within its walls, but only for the duration of his term of office. 'Major judges' – in another formulation – such as kings and counts ought to take counsel from experts before legislating, but they are under no legal obligation to do so. The case is otherwise in a city, where the whole people – or the council which represents it – must be involved. If any council members have been exiled without just cause, then a statute passed without their participation cannot bind them to their prejudice – another point he develops in *On the Tyrant*.²³ When the consent of all is required, moreover, all must congregate and give evident signs of consent or dissent in full public assembly; door-to-door procedures are illegitimate.²⁴

Bartolus's city or *civitas* can easily be mistaken for an elemental quantity in his legal theory, as being tautologically related to the people or *populus*.† In fact, the people itself is conceptually prior to the *civitas*. For example, in his lecture on *Digest* 49.1.1.3, Bartolus explains that the judge of appeal will be 'The people itself, or the *ordo* [that is, the echelon of government] which appoints that officer, because this is the only superior to the people itself, and is emperor unto it.'²⁵ When discussing the relaxation of sentences of infamy, which was an imperial prerogative, Bartolus argues that 'Since every city in Italy nowadays – and particularly in Tuscany – recognizes no lord, it has within itself a free people and has in itself *merum imperium*,† and has as much power over its people as the

---

²² Below, pp. 39–40.
²³ Below, p. 44.
²⁴ Below, p. 79–80.
²⁵ Below, p. 102.

emperor has over everything.'[26] Ever since the mid thirteenth century at the latest, lawyers had become used to the idea that a king might recognize no superior in temporal affairs and thus become 'emperor in his own kingdom'. Bartolus was the first to apply that principle of non-recognition to a city, and express it so effectively in the instantly memorable formula of *civitas sibi princeps*. But the city itself is best taken as shorthand for the true actor or agent in such situations, which is the people.

This people was a corporate body or corporation, a concept rendered by the term *universitas*.† The corporate people of a city such as Perugia elected a council and acted through it, a relationship which Bartolus felicitously captured with the apophthegm 'The council represents the mind of the people.'[27] Numerous lawyers before Bartolus had explored the multifarious questions arising from corporate legal status, including liability for corporate debt, culpability for collective misdemeanour, the birth and death of corporations, the means by which corporate bodies could bind themselves, the relationship between a corporation and its members, and many more; but his contributions contain peculiarly arresting formulations which betray a highly developed political sensibility. *Civitas sibi princeps* was one; the contention that the commonwealth could be detained illegitimately against the commonwealth itself another, for it opens a conceptual space between one abstraction and its even more abstract self. The most intriguing example relates to the personhood of corporations, including of course the corporate people. As he epitomizes the point in *On the Government of a City*, the 'whole city is one person and one artificial, imaginary man'.[28]

Lawyers had attributed personhood to a variety of corporations since the mid thirteenth century at the latest; Pope Innocent IV, whose commentary on the *Liber extra* Bartolus cites so frequently, had famously emphasized that such a corporate person was fictitious, not real. Bartolus elaborates on this fictiveness by explaining that corporate persons are represented persons: 'What belongs to a corporation does not belong to its individual members, because a corporation is a represented person in itself.'[29] In the case of the *populus*† of an Italian city, the organ which performs this act of representation is the ruling council: 'Thus elected,

---

[26] Bartolus on *Dig.* 48.1.7; below, p. 96.
[27] *Bartoli a Sassoferrato in primam Digesti Veteris partem commentaria* (Turin 1574), fo. 17vb; *Dig.* 1.3.32.
[28] Below, pp. 20–1.
[29] *Dig.* 47.22.1.2; below, pp. 92–3.

xxxiii

this council then represents the whole people.'[30] Bartolus's source here is Accursius's *Glossa ordinaria*† to *Cod.* 8.52(53), according to which the council represents not precisely the people but 'its place' (*vicem eius*). In his commentary on *Cod.* 4.32.5, Bartolus again appears to echo Accursius: a council 'represents the place [*vicem*] of the whole people'.[31] At *Digest* 46.1.22 the Roman law itself stated that an inheritance, like a *municipium*,† a subdivision of various corporations known as a *decuria*,† or a business partnership (*societas*), could function 'in place of a person'. Bartolus seems oblivious to the distinction between representing the person of the people and representing its place, so it is probably not significant: he is just quoting Accursius *verbatim*. In another passage Bartolus inverts the relationship in observing that 'The corporation represents one person',[32] thus betraying a certain insouciance towards the relationship between representer and represented.

Representation was not a new concept in jurisprudence, then, but the notion that the corporation is a represented *person* was, apparently, original. In the case of corporate as distinct from individual ownership, the claim that the corporation is a 'represented person' does little work of its own; but in another passage of Bartolus's jurisprudence it does. Bartolus was strikingly hostile to the notion that jurisdiction could inhere in a territory exclusively: for him, jurisdiction always belonged to persons. In his commentary on *Digest* 2.1.1, which is about the jurisdiction of judges, he asserts with brio that the jurisdiction apparently belonging to cities and *castra*† 'coheres with their people and their communities [*communitatibus*] ... because they are represented persons which have jurisdiction, and they themselves appoint the *podestà*† and suchlike, hence jurisdiction inheres in persons and pertains to persons'.[33] That is a lot of persons in a short sentence. It is no coincidence that this is the concluding sentence of his commentary on this passage. Bartolus's represented persons, by 'personalizing' the bearer of jurisdiction, served to keep it in the hands of the people, rather than allowing it to leach into the impersonal abstraction of the territory.

It would be out of place as well as impossible here to attempt an assessment of the influence of Bartolus's general jurisprudence over political debate in the centuries which followed. The precise phrase *civitas sibi*

---

[30] Bartolus on *Cod.* 10.32(31).2; below, pp. 111–12.
[31] *Bartoli a Sassoferrato in primam Codicis partem commentaria* (Turin 1574), fo. 158ra.
[32] Bartolus on *Dig.* 48.19.16.10; below, pp. 99–102.
[33] Below, p. 87.

princeps seems not to have been widely adopted by lawyers after Bartolus. His interpretation of the law *Omnes populi*, moreover, was not universally accepted by his fellow jurists. The distinction between the *de facto* and the *de iure* states of affairs, which plays a far more important role in Bartolus's jurisprudence than in that of his predecessors, famously caught on. His most celebrated pupil, Baldus de Ubaldis (d. 1400), in whose hands the autograph manuscript of *Tiberiadis* ended up,[34] used the distinction routinely in many of the same contexts as Bartolus did. And Baldus was far from alone. Without attribution, *On the Tyrant* was filleted by the French jurist Évrart de Trémaugon in his *Somnium viridarii*, the compendium of political debates commissioned by Charles V of France in 1374 to re-establish concord between ecclesiastical and secular jurisdictions.[35] Because the *Somnium* was quickly translated into French, in anonymous and condensed form some of Bartolus's ideas reached a vernacular readership beyond Italy barely twenty years after the composition of *On the Tyrant*.[36] Later Italian lawyers who wrote mainly for signorial regimes were predictably less forthright in their comments. Baldus, who from 1390 taught in Visconti-ruled Pavia, clearly integrates several of Bartolus's ideas into his own treatment of tyranny, including the important contention that a *signore* who is only accepted by the emperor because the emperor lacks the power to expel him is also a tyrant; but he is understandably more circumspect about signorial rule in general. In the generation after Baldus, Martinus Garatus explicitly condemned Bartolus's contention that there were circumstances justifying the assumption of Guelf or Ghibelline party-labels, for in what was by that time the Visconti Duchy of Milan, those terms had been outlawed as politically divisive. As Diego Quaglioni showed, Garatus referred not to Bartolus on the tyrant, but to Bartolus's contemporary Albericus de Rosate, in asserting that 'the true *princeps*⁺ puts the good of the commonwealth above the private good; and the *princeps* is the image of the divine majesty, who ought not to rage against his subjects and neighbours'. That made it easy to accommodate the dedicatee of Garatus's treatise *On Princes* (*De principibus*), Filippo-Maria Visconti, within the category of princes.

---

[34] V. Colli, 'Collezioni d'autore di Baldo degli Ubaldi nel MS Biblioteca Apostolica Vaticana, Barb. lat. 1398', *Ius commune*, 25 (1998): 323–46.
[35] *Somnium viridarii*, ed. M. Schnerb-Lièvre, 2 vols. (Paris 1993–5), vol. I, ch. 133, 163–70.
[36] *Le Songe du vergier, Édité d'après le manuscrit Royal 19 C IV de la British Library*, ed. M. Schnerb-Lièvre, 2 vols. (Paris 1982), I. CXXXI, i. 217–21.

An episode in the sixteenth century conveys a sense of the busy after-life both of Bartolus's tracts and some of the more eye-catching claims in his legal commentaries. Unsurprisingly, the tracts resurfaced promi-nently in the Huguenot advocacy of armed insurrection after the Saint Bartholomew massacres of 1572 in France. The anonymous author of *Vindiciae, contra tyrannos* routinely deploys the distinction made famous by Bartolus between a tyrant for want of just title and a tyrant who is defined as such by his abusive exercise of power; but Bartolus's influence over this, the most sophisticated of the Calvinist polemics of the time, is endemic rather than merely episodic. First, Bartolus's name remained a rallying-cry: 'Although he was born in an age abounding in tyrants, Bar-tolus himself was not afraid to conclude from this that subjects were not the slaves of a king but were to be considered his brothers.'[37] The phrase 'Bartolus himself' shows that his name still resonated in northern Euro-pean Protestant circles in the late sixteenth century. The same inference may be drawn from the occasional explicit appeal to Bartolus which is not warranted by what Bartolus wrote. For example, Bartolus nowhere asserts that the tyrant of tyrants is the fear in the mind of the tyrant himself, and the *Vindiciae* also blurs Bartolus's distinction between the Julian laws on treason and on public force. As many of Bartolus's own arguments from Roman law in his three tracts show, it is the fate of textual authorities to be taken in vain, by which index Bartolus on the tyrant was certainly an authority.

But there is more to be said. The claim at this point in *Vindiciae* is that subjects are the brothers of their kings – a spirited application of Barto-lus's harmless comment on *Deuteronomy* 17 which occurs not in *On the Tyrant*, but in *On the Government of a City*. Elsewhere, *On Guelfs and Ghibellines* is cited, on one occasion to buttress the vital contention that although sedition is not always unjust, it is so when directed at the wrong goal.[38] Bartolus is also mentioned alongside Giles of Rome during a dis-cussion of the latter's list of the differences between kings and tyrants.[39] Clearly, in the mind of this later author, to think of Giles was to think of Bartolus too. Equally clearly, all three of Bartolus's tracts served as a reservoir for authoritative arguments about tyranny. Although, then, his citations of the tracts are sometimes of questionable relevance, the author

---

[37] *Vindiciae, contra tyrannos: Or, Concerning the Legitimate Power of a Prince over the People, and of the People over a Prince*, ed. and trans. G. Garnett (Cambridge 1994), p. 107.
[38] *Vindiciae*, p. 49.
[39] *Vindiciae*, pp. 145–6.

of *Vindiciae* appreciated their essential unity as parts of a composite, extended, analysis of tyranny. Most significantly, it was natural for him to link arguments from Bartolus's tracts with passages in Bartolus's commentaries on Roman law. For example, we have seen that in *quaestio* IX of *On the Tyrant*, Bartolus says it is the duty of the superior to depose a tyrant.[40] In *Vindiciae*, this is combined with a further point extracted from Bartolus's commentary on *Digest* 4.3.1: 'For the superior is the whole people, or those who represent it.'[41] Bartolus's general jurisprudence is therefore as much a part of the fabric of argument as his specific three tracts on tyranny.

Closer to Bartolus's own time and place, *On the Tyrant* might well have changed political vocabulary. Andrea Gamberini recently observed that in 1354 it was still a rational tactic for the Milanese propaganda machine to portray Archbishop Giovanni Visconti, uncle and predecessor as lord of Milan of the brother-rulers Matteo, Galeazzo, and Bernabò Visconti, as a tyrant.[42] He is so described in the inscription on the sarcophagus housing his remains together with those of the thirteenth-century archbishop Ottone Visconti in the *Duomo* of Milan. The word had some entirely respectable antecedents, and formed part of the active vocabulary of signorial regimes. But, as Gamberini plausibly claims, the appearance and speedy diffusion of Bartolus's tract rendered the epithet politically toxic, with the result that the next generation of the most influential and best informed pro-signorial pamphleteers – precisely such as those serving the Visconti in the pen-war against republican Florence – avoided it. It may therefore justly be claimed on behalf of Bartolus's three tracts – revealingly termed by him on one occasion a (single) treatise, consisting of several books[43] – that they achieved what Thomas Aquinas's *De regno* and its continuation in the shape of Ptolemy of Lucca's *De regimine principum* had not.

---

[40] Below, p. 56.
[41] *Vindiciae*, p. 156.
[42] A. Gamberini, 'Orgogliosamente tiranni: I Visconti, la polemica contro i regimi dispotici e la risignificazione del termine *tyrannus* alla metà del Trecento', in A. Zorzi, ed., *Tiranni e tirannide nel Trecento italiano* (Rome 2013), pp. 77–93.
[43] Below, pp. 52–3, discussed above, pp. xv–xvi.

Translators' Note

In his address 'To the Readers' at the beginning of his translation of Thucydides' *History of the Peloponnesian War*, Thomas Hobbes wrote:

> For I know, that meere Translations, have in them this property, that they may much disgrace, if not well done; but if well, not much commend the doer.

This is a general truth; but it is particularly apposite in the case of Bartolus of Sassoferrato's prose, which is crabbed and terse. It is technical, dense, and allusive because Bartolus wrote for a learned audience which he took to be equally well-versed in the authorities he had in mind. For those not familiar with this frame of reference it can often seem opaque. His style was honed in his commentaries on the *Corpus iuris civilis*,[†] which by definition were focused on particular points in the text, and were not intended to be read sequentially, just as modern footnotes are not. He made little effort to adapt this style when he attempted to write these and a few other sustained, if also very succinct, jurisprudential tracts of his own. Every point had to be explored and if possible justified by reference to authorities in Justinian's *Corpus*, or more rarely the *Corpus iuris canonici*,[†] to their respective standard glosses, and to commentaries by other lawyers.

The standard system of reference was to quote the rubric, usually in abbreviated form, followed by the incipit – the opening few words – of the law being cited. To a modern reader, this does nothing to assist the fluency of Bartolus's exposition of his own arguments, more especially because the incipits being in Latin, and therefore inflected, means that as quoted they usually made little grammatical sense on their own account,

still less so when spliced into Bartolus's prose. Learned medieval readers could adjust, because they would immediately recognize the allusion
from the incipit. We have had to substitute the modern conventional
numerical system of reference. The frequent appearance of these numbers in our translation serves to highlight just how much more staccato
Bartolus's original Latin is.

   This was a characteristic of Bartolus and most other medieval commentators[†] which came to provide an easy target for humanists who
esteemed fluent Latin prose of the sort written in the two centuries on
either side of the institution of the Principate as the standard of purity.
Indeed, Bartolus and his ilk became a favourite butt of abuse: 'with regard
to cultivated letters and knowledge of antiquities and histories, they were
as well equipped with those faculties as is a toad with feathers, and have
as much use for them as a sottish heretic has for a crucifix'.[1] Like Peter
Lombard and John Duns – 'Dunce' – Scotus, they were to be categorized
as 'men of the night',[2] supposedly consigned to darkness by the coming
of the neoclassical dawn. It should, however, never be forgotten that Bartolus and those for whom he wrote did not see mellifluous antique prose
as a model. The *Corpus iuris civilis*[†] was not written in it, because the vast
majority of its contents originated much later. The still more barbarized
style of the medieval commentators on the *Corpus* was the conventional
one for jurisprudence throughout the high and later middle ages, and in
many circles well beyond. Paradoxically, this was the fashion in which
practitioners of the *ius commune* applied the law of ancient Rome to the
problems of the modern world. That it proved obnoxious to those who
thought classical Latin the only acceptable Latin does not mean that it
was not a very effective means of communicating complicated legal analysis concisely to learned medieval (and early modern) audiences. We can
only aspire to reproduce the style in English translation, expanding no
more than is necessary to convey Bartolus's meaning. To the extent that
our translation appears to make few concessions to readers, it accurately
reproduces one characteristic of the original.

   Bartolus may, however, have been softening towards his intended audience when he decided to ape a literary device deployed at the opening of
classical dialogues. At the start of *Tiberiadis*, his tripartite treatise on the
law of alluvial deposits, the creation of islands, and the shifting of river

---

[1] Rabelais, *Pantagruel* II, x.
[2] F. W. Maitland, *English Law and the Renaissance* (Cambridge 1901), p. 6.

beds, the fount from which the political tracts are presented as flowing,[3] he set a lengthy autobiographical scene. On a journey to a country villa near Perugia during the summer vacation of 1355, he had been prompted to reflect by a view of the Tiber meandering through the Umbrian countryside below him.[4] That night, in a dream, he had a vision of an unidentified man who urged him to write up those reflections.

There is no evidence that the scene-setting at the start of *Tiberiadis* depends in a textual sense on Cicero's *De legibus*, but it is striking that Cicero's dialogue also takes place beside a river and its tributary, and on a small island in the middle of the latter.[5] It may be that Bartolus had it in mind as a model. Given Cicero's prominence as an interlocutor (*De legibus* is one of very few extant classical dialogues which purports to be autobiographical), and the dialogue's concentration on the laws of Rome, it would have been a particularly apt one. Whatever Bartolus's initial literary aspirations, however, a plunge into a torrent of customary rebarbativeness followed precipitately.

A further source of inelegance arises from the fact that the extant texts of these three terse political tracts are palimpsests, in the sense that they bear signs of cumulative revision, some possibly by Bartolus himself, but much more likely by later unidentifiable hands. Given the date at which he wrote them, he had little time left to make any changes himself. Indeed, *On the Tyrant* and *On Guelfs and Ghibellines* may be incomplete because he died before he could finish them. The large number of manuscripts of all three are much later than the period when Bartolus wrote. In this respect the surviving autograph of the opening part of *Tiberiadis*[6] – that concerned with alluvial deposit – is quite exceptional. Revision, almost certainly by other jurists, scribes, or owners seeking to clarify, to elaborate, or to amend, is likely to have compounded the infelicities in the originals. Amongst the numerous variant readings recorded by Diego Quaglioni in his edition, many of them created by copyists' errors, we have had to make judgments about what in our view is most likely to have been Bartolus's intended meaning. We have attempted to justify our preferred readings in the notes. Though we have occasionally differed from

---

[3] Above, Introduction, pp. xiii–xiv.
[4] Cavallar, ed., 'River of Law', pp. 30–129, at 84. The date is given in the text.
[5] *De legibus*: 1.5.14; 2.1.1–2; 2.3.6–7.
[6] Biblioteca Apostolica Vaticana, MS. Barb. Lat. 1398, fos. 157r–170v; Cavallar, ed., 'River of Law', pp. 38–9; Colli, 'Collezioni'. Some thirty manuscript copies of *Tiberiadis* survive, many of them only preserving one or two parts of the tripartite work.

Quaglioni on these questions, we wish to pay tribute to the exemplary nature of his edition, without which this annotated translation would have been far poorer than it is. On the few occasions when Bartolus's elliptical and condensed prose required, we have added a few words by way of expansion; these amplifications are in square brackets.

Given Bartolus's style, it may be impossible for any translation of his works, however accurate, 'much [to] commend the doer'. But we hope that this one will make it easier for those who currently know little of Bartolus not only to understand his thought on politics, but also to appreciate how covertly central it remained in legal and political thinking well beyond the medieval period. 'Political philosophy in its youth is apt to look like a sublimated jurisprudence.'[7] The 'abstract vesture' in which he clothed his current fourteenth-century projects long outlived them. He is one of those arid, technical, dense, and apparently dull late medieval thinkers who wrote with 'a significant dullness'. His thought remains 'bone of our bone'.[8] 'Grotius and Gentilis and Bodin not merely quote Bartolus, but are what they are largely because of him.'[9] These remarks were made over a century ago. Their force is still insufficiently appreciated. *Habent sua fata libelli* ('books have their fates').

---

[7] F. W. Maitland, 'Introduction' to O. Gierke, *Political Theories of the Middle Age*, trans. F. W. Maitland (Cambridge 1900), p. viii.

[8] J. N. Figgis, *Studies of Political Thought from Gerson to Grotius*, 2nd edn (Cambridge 1916), p. 2.

[9] J. N. Figgis, *The Divine Right of Kings*, 2nd edn (Cambridge 1914), p. 343.

Abbreviations

Auth.	*Authentica ad Codicem Iustiniani*
C.	*Causa*; subsection of *Decretum*, pt. 2
CCSL	Corpus Christianorum, Series Latina
Clem.	*Clementinae* or *Clementis Papae V Constitutiones* in *Corpus iuris canonici*, ed. A. Friedberg, ii
Cod.	*Codex Iustiniani*
D.	*Distinctio*; subsection of *Decretum*, pt. 1
Decretum	*Decretum Gratiani* or *Concordia discordantium canonum*, in *Corpus iuris canonici*, ed. A. Friedberg, i
Dig.	*Digestum Iustiniani*
Extra	*Decretales Gregorii P. IX seu Liber extra*, in *Corpus iuris canonici*, ed. A. Friedberg, ii
Extrav. Comm.	*Extravagantes communes*, in *Corpus iuris canonici*, ed. A. Frieberg, ii
Feud.	*Libri feudorum*
Inst.	*Institutiones Iustiniani*
MGH	Monumenta Germaniae Historica
Nov.	*Novellae Iustiniani*
q.	*quaestio*; subsection within a *causa* in *Decretum*, pt. 2
Quaglioni, *Politica e diritto*	D. Quaglioni, *Politica e diritto nel trecento Italiano: Il 'De tyranno' di Bartolo da Sassoferrato (1314–1357), con l'edizione critica dei trattati 'De Guelphis et Gebellinis', 'De regimine civitatis' e 'De tyranno'* (Florence 1983)
Sext.	*Liber sextus decretalium Bonifacii P. VIII*, in *Corpus iuris canonici*, ed. A. Friedberg, ii

Glossary

Terms included in the Glossary are marked with a † elsewhere in the book.

affectio ('sympathy', 'persuasion', 'inclination', disposition', or 'tendency'): in classical Roman law the intention to establish a contract of partnership (*societas*) was termed *affectio societatis*. It denoted the consent among the partners (*socii*) that constituted the contractual relationship between them. Bartolus uses *affectio* to mean a favourable disposition or inclination, hence the state of mind which moves someone to be a member of a particular faction. We translate this as 'sympathy'.

antianus (Latinization of the vernacular *anziano*, 'elder', therefore synonymous with the senator of a *municipium*, *q.v.*): used by Bartolus to mean either a member of a municipal council – cf. *decurio* (*q.v.*) – or a governing official – cf. *prior* (*q.v.*) – or both.

Authenticum (*lit*. 'the authentic', 'real', or 'genuine thing'): a Latin translation of most of Emperor Justinian's 168 *Novels* (*q.v.*) or *Novellae*, new constitutions promulgated mainly in Greek (with a few in Latin) between 534 – the date of the completion of the original *Corpus iuris civilis* (*q.v.*) – and *c.* 556, when the *Authenticum* was devised for teaching purposes. It was one of a number of private collections of *Novels*: there is no evidence of an official collection from the Justinianic period. In the medieval West, the *Authenticum* was, after its rediscovery in Bologna *c.* 1100, deemed to be the entirety of Justinian's *Novels*. It was termed *Authenticum* because it superseded the previous version known in the West, the *Epitome Juliani* (a summary of 122 *Novels* produced by Julianus, a sixth-century Constantinopolitan law professor). The *Authenticum* was considered thenceforth

xliii

to be the authentic collection of Justinian's supplementary constitutions. It is arranged in a roughly chronological order, not thematically. Of the 134 constitutions included, the medieval civilians
glossed only 97. They were divided into nine 'collations', in imita-
tion of the nine books of the *Code* (*q.v.*), which, until the rediscovery
of the final three books (*Tres libri* – books 10–12) in the later twelfth
century, were thought to constitute the entire collection. Individual
constitutions from the *Authenticum* – *authenticae* – were sometimes
added to, or interpolated into, the *Code* at relevant points, with the
texts occasionally doctored. Together with the *Tres libri* of the *Code*,
the *Authenticum*, the *Libri feudorum* (*q.v.*), some of the constitutions of modern Western Roman emperors, and the *Institutes* (*q.v.*)
formed what became known as the *Volumen parvum* (*q.v.*), the fifth
and final part of the *Corpus* in medieval manuscripts and early modern printed editions. There is no modern edition of this medieval, or
Vulgate, version of the *Corpus iuris civilis* (*q.v.*).

castrum: in the *Corpus iuris civilis* (*q.v.*) this term has purely military sig-
nificance; the glossators (*q.v.*) understood it according to the political geography of contemporary Italy, where a *castrum* (vernacular:
castro) was a fortified, nucleated settlement. According to Bartolus,
such a settlement must depend on a city (*civitas*), and unlike a *civitas* cannot have jurisdiction or appoint its own magistrates. Those
exceptional Italian *castra* which did exercise jurisdiction were by
this definition *civitates*. For the creation of *castra* within the *contado*
(*q.v.*) of Perugia in the late thirteenth and early fourteenth century,
see Blanshei, *Perugia 1260–1340*, pp. 38–9. The inhabitants of a *castrum* might form a *universitas* (*q.v.*).

Code: Justinian's (second, revised) compilation of previous imperial
constitutions, promulgated in November 534, and arranged in
twelve books, divided into titles. Constitutions might be edicts –
proclamations – or rescripts – replies to petitions – in addition to
other types of imperial text. Initially, only the first nine books of the
Code were widely known to medieval civilians. In the later twelfth
century, the final three began to receive attention. These, thenceforth known as *Tres libri codicis*, often shortened to *Tres libri*, covered
matters of public law. They were kept separate from the rest of the
Code, and grouped instead with the *Authenticum* (*q.v.*), the *Libri feudorum* (*q.v.*), some constitutions of modern Western Roman emperors, and the *Institutes* (*q.v.*), to form the *Volumen parvum* (*q.v.*), the

final part of the *Corpus* in medieval manuscripts and early printed editions.

collegium ('college', 'collegiate body', or 'collegiate association'): clubs or associations were formed for many purposes, public and private, including representing the collective interests of particular trades and crafts. It was this purpose which particularly interested Bartolus, who often uses the term to mean guild. In ancient Rome certain *collegia* were subject to vigilant official oversight: if not sanctioned by authority, and therefore illicit, they would be dissolved. Like corporations (*universitates*, *q.v.*), but unlike partnerships (*societates*), *collegia* had a legal personality distinct from their individual members, which meant that medieval lawyers could designate them fictive persons (*personae fictae*, *q.v*).

commentator: a medieval civilian who wrote subsequent to the widespread acceptance of Accursius's *Glossa ordinaria* (*q.v.*).

consuetudo ('custom'): in the sense of *mos maiorum* (the 'practices of ancestors'), custom played a fundamental role in classical Roman jurisprudence. Roman jurists also tended to categorize local variants of Roman law as customs. Such customs were considered to derive their authority from the will of the people of the locality, expressed through acceptance in actual practice. They were unwritten. A custom could be legally valid if it supplemented, but did not contradict, the written law. In a passage on which Bartolus laid great stress (*Dig.* 1.3.32), the second-century AD jurist Julian stated that written laws bind because they have been accepted by judgment of the people; therefore what the people has approved without any writing should also bind all. The people could declare its will by its actions as well as by voting; and laws might be repealed not only by vote of the legislator, but also by the tacit consent of all through desuetude – that is, by a sustained practice contrary to the written law. This key statement appeared to be in some tension with a law of Emperor Constantine excerpted in the *Code* (8.52(53).2) which, while acknowledging the authority of custom, declared that it could be valid only to the extent that it did not override either reason or written law. Medieval civilians were forced to resolve this tension as they applied texts from the *Corpus* to the analysis of problems in the Roman empire of their own day. The issue was more pressing than it had been in antiquity because individual cities and kingdoms within the still notionally universal empire evidently observed their own written laws and unwritten customs, restricted to their individual territories, and in some cases failed to acknowledge the superiority of the emperor. Medieval jurists reached very different conclusions on how to resolve the apparent discrepancies between the text of Roman law and local practices.

contado (vernacular for *comitatus*, 'county'): used to signify the immediate hinterland over which a city exercised jurisdiction. Perugia's *contado* in the early fourteenth century covered about 1300 square kilometers. In 1351 thirty-three subject communes from the *contado* participated in the ceremonies in honour of Perugia's patron saint: Beneš, *Urban Legends*, p. 116.

Corpus iuris canonici ('Corpus of canon law'): by Bartolus's time the *Corpus* consisted of Gratian's *Concordia discordantium canonum* ('Harmony of discordant canons'), alternatively (and almost universally) known as *Decretum*, which reached its final form *c.* 1140–50, and later collections of decretals, which were papal judgments in the form of letters. These collections were: the *Liber extra* (short for *Liber extravagantium*, i.e. 'the book of those things which wander outside [the *Decretum*]'), commissioned by Pope Gregory IX in 1234; the *Liber sextus* ('Sixth Book'), commissioned by Pope Boniface VIII in 1298; and the *Constitutiones Clementinae* ('Clementine Constitutions'), promulgated by Pope John XXII in 1317.

Corpus iuris civilis ('Corpus of civil law'): Emperor Justinian's compilation, consisting of the *Code* (*q.v.*), the *Digest* (*q.v.*), and the *Institutes* (*q.v.*), subsequently supplemented by the *Novels* (*q.v.*). The whole *Corpus* was conceived as having no contradictions either within or between its constituent parts. Despite ostensibly drawing on historic materials, it was treated as a single coeval and co-eternal statement of law. The Vulgate version known to Bartolus consisted of five volumes. The first three were the three parts of the *Digest*: the *Digestum vetus*, the *Infortiatum*, and the *Digestum novum*. The fourth volume was Books 1–9 of the *Code* (*q.v.*), and the fifth was the *Volumen parvum* (*q.v.*), consisting of the three remaining books (10–12) of the *Code*, the *Authenticum* (*q.v.*), the *Libri feudorum* (*q.v.*), certain constitutions of modern Western Roman emperors, and the *Institutes*. The whole was first termed *Corpus iuris civilis* in 1583, but the neologism soon became conventional.

decuria (a group of ten men, or tithing): originally there were three tribes in Rome, each of which was divided into ten *curiae* (courts, or territorial entities), each in turn composed of ten *decuriae*. In origin *decuriae* were military units, but they also had other functions. The senate was divided into *decuriae*, as were many professional bodies and administrative organizations. The latter might in practice have more than ten members.

decurio, cf. *antianus* (*q.v.*); *prior* (*q.v.*): a member of the senate or council of a *municipium* (*q.v.*), the citizens of which also enjoyed full Roman citizenship. *Decuriones* were elected for life, and by Justinian's day the 'honour' was inherited. They decided matters involving the *municipium*, appointed local magistrates, and functioned as a court of appeal relating to fines imposed by municipal officials, in addition to having various civic duties and burdens (*munera*), financial and otherwise.

defender of a city (*defensor civitatis*): originally (in the fourth century AD) appointed as imperial officials to defend the interests of the poor, *defensores* came to be elected to supervise provincial officials. They were obliged to inform the provincial governor about complaints against his officials. Emperor Justinian required all well-to-do inhabitants of a city to undertake the office – that of a minor civil judge – for periods of two years (*Novel* 15). According to Bartolus, a city may be defined as an entity within which the jurisdiction proper to *defensores civitatum* is exercised: *Tyberiadis*, p. 91.

Digest: a collection of thematically arranged excerpts from the writings of thirty-nine jurists, mostly of the second and third centuries AD, but including earlier ones, some dating from the republican period. It was also referred to by Justinian, in Greek, as the *Pandectae*, meaning an 'all-embracing work'. Over one-third of the extracts are by Ulpian, one-sixth by Paulus. In 533 Justinian promulgated the whole compilation of fifty thematic books, subdivided into titles, as law. It was initially rediscovered in the West in the late eleventh century. According to the standard hypothesis, the three segments known to medieval jurists as *Digestum vetus* (books 1–24.2), *Infortiatum* (books 24.3–38), and *Digestum novum* (books 39–50) were consecutively rediscovered over a number of decades, reaching into the twelfth century.

dominus: originally the owner of a thing, as distinct from a possessor or a usufructuary. In classical Roman law *dominium* was an indivisible right of disposal, good against the world. By the thirteenth century, however, civilians had recognized that such a definition simply did not fit contemporary feudal reality, because the feudal lord did not enjoy *dominium* in its entirety; his vassal tenant had rights which appeared to include some (but definitely not all) of the elements of *dominium*. Indivisible classical *dominium* was therefore now divided into complementary aspects. The *Glossa ordinaria* (*q.v.*) of Accursius influentially reproduced an earlier glossatorial distinction: that a feudal lord enjoyed *dominium directum* and his vassal *dominium utile* in the fief which the latter held of the former.

Glossa ordinaria (literally 'Ordinary Gloss'): the standard gloss, a commentary on the entire *Corpus iuris civilis* (*q.v.*) by the glossator (*q.v.*) Accursius, written in the mid thirteenth century. It rapidly superseded prior glosses, and came to be accepted as the standard one, and was routinely copied in manuscripts of the *Corpus*. The same term was conventionally used for what became the standard gloss on the *Decretum* (*q.v.*), by Iohannes Teutonicus, supplemented by Bartholomeus Brixiensis, and on the *Liber extra* by Bernardus Parmensis.

glossator: a medieval civilian who wrote prior to the widespread acceptance of Accursius's *Glossa ordinaria* (*q.v.*).

imperium; *merum imperium*; *merum et mixtum imperium* ('command'; 'pure command'; 'pure and mixed command'): in classical Rome *imperium* was the highest form of public authority, the supreme power of the Roman people, in terms of both command and jurisdiction; it could also mean military command. *Merum imperium* was complete criminal jurisdiction: in the words of the jurist Ulpian, '*Merum imperium* is to have the power of the sword [*gladii potestas* or *ius gladii*] to threaten wrong-doers; it is called *potestas*' (*Dig.* 2.1.3). The *potestas* or *ius gladii* was capital jurisdiction. *Merum imperium* did not include civil jurisdiction; if this was exercised too the *imperium* was said to be *merum et mixtum*. Whether *merum imperium* belonged exclusively to the emperor (*princeps*, *q.v.*), who in antiquity had enjoyed proconsular *imperium maius*, or was in some way also held by lesser magistrates, either by delegation from the emperor or in their own right, was fiercely debated amongst medieval civilians.

Institutes: a textbook for law students issued by Justinian alongside the *Digest* (*q.v.*) in 533, and given equal status with it and the *Code* (*q.v.*). Modelled on earlier juristic examples of the genre, it consists of four books, subdivided into titles. In the middle ages it was grouped with the *Tres libri* of the *Code* (*q.v.*), the *Authenticum* (*q.v.*), the *Libri feudorum* (*q.v.*), and some constitutions of modern Western Roman emperors to form the *Volumen parvum* (*q.v.*), the fifth and final part of the *Corpus* in the medieval and early modern periods, the so-called Vulgate version.

ius gentium ('law of nations'): originally Roman civil law (*ius civile*) could not, by definition, apply to 'foreigners' (*peregrini*), only to Roman citizens, so a different body of rules and conventions was taken into account in cases involving *peregrini* – for instance, in commercial transactions. This was to be labelled the *ius gentium*, the law common to all civilized peoples, Roman and non-Roman alike: 'what natural reason established among all men is equally observed by all mankind, and is called the law of nations [*ius gentium*], as the law which all nations employ' (*Dig.* 1.1.9, cf. *Inst.* 1.2.1). With the opening to Roman citizens of institutions based on *ius gentium*, and the eventual abolition (in AD 212) of the distinction between citizens and *peregrini*, the *ius gentium* became what was common to all legal systems. In the *Corpus iuris civilis* (*q.v.*) the *ius gentium* is that category of *ius naturale* common to humans, not to all animals.

Lex Iulia de ambitu (*lit.* 'Julian law on going about', i.e. canvassing): discussed in *Dig.* 48.14.1, concerned with electoral corruption.

Lex Iulia de vi privata ('Julian law on private force'): discussed in *Dig.* 48.7, concerned with force used against a private individual which constituted a private delict, and was prosecuted by a penal action brought by the injured person.

Lex Iulia de vi publica ('Julian law on public force'): discussed in *Dig.* 48.6, concerned with violent crimes which were deemed to damage the *res publica* (*q.v.*), and which were therefore prosecuted by the state in a criminal trial.

Lex Iulia maiestatis ('Julian law of majesty', i.e. treason): discussed in *Dig.* 48.4, concerned with crimes 'committed against the Roman people and its security'. By Justinian's time this had been elided with *perduellio*, the crime of one who 'is inspired by a hostile mind against the *res publica* [*q.v.*] and the *princeps* [*q.v.*]' (*Dig.* 48.4.11).

Libri feudorum ('Books of Fiefs'): a compilation of treatises on the customs regulating fiefs, vassals, and litigation in the courts of feudal lords in twelfth-century Lombardy, especially Pavia and Milan. By the mid thirteenth century it was being appended to some manuscripts of the *Authenticum* (*q.v.*) as a 'tenth collation'. Accursius completed the *Glossa ordinaria* (*q.v.*) to this text which thereafter was routinely included in manuscripts of the *Volumen parvum* (*q.v.*) and thus became a constituent part of the *Corpus iuris civilis* (*q.v.*).

municipium: originally any city in Italy (other than Rome) that had not been founded as a Roman colony; the term was later extended to cities in the provinces. A *municipium* was so called because it consisted of *municipes*, individuals who undertook civic duties (*munera*) in it – that is, its citizens. *Civitas* became a synonym, Rome being the only *urbs* (the one city in the empire with no local self-government). By concession of Rome, all *municipia* enjoyed privileges of local government and jurisdiction; their local laws and customs were allowed to persist, within the overall framework of Roman law and administration (cf. *consuetudo*, *q.v.*). What the greater part of a municipal court or assembly enacted was deemed to be done by them all (*Dig.* 50.19.1). To variable extents, municipal citizens came to enjoy some of the rights of Roman citizens too. In AD 212 Emperor Caracalla issued the *Constitutio Antoniniana de civitate* (*Dig.* 1.5.17), by which all free inhabitants of the empire were granted Roman citizenship, and thereby the right to use Roman law. This meant that all citizens of *municipia*, while remaining municipal citizens, were also full Roman citizens; and that all cities in the empire henceforth enjoyed the status of *municipia* while retaining their privileges of self-government. The little recorded in the *Digest* (*q.v.*) about *municipia* preserves detail from centuries before its compilation; this material from a period when they enjoyed varying degrees of autonomy is therefore particularly germane to Bartolus's interest in self-governing cities.

Novels: the constitutions of Justinian issued (mainly) after AD 535, the date of his initial promulgation of the *Corpus iuris civilis* (*q.v.*): see *Authenticum*.

partialitas: a term which does not appear in the *Corpus iuris civilis* (*q.v*) or the *Glossa ordinaria* (*q.v.*), and which Bartolus uses synonymously with *pars* ('part') to signify a faction.

paterfamilias: the head of a Roman household, who enjoyed *patria potestas* ('paternal power') over his male and female descendants, and potentially their spouses. It lapsed at his death, when the males became independent – *sui iuris* ('of his own right'). He might also formally renounce it, thereby emancipating descendants of both sexes. He ceased to have it over his female descendants if they contracted one type of marriage, in which the woman passed into the 'hand' of her husband, thereby becoming part of the husband's agnatic family.

l

But in a second type of marriage, in which the woman did not pass into the 'hand' of her husband, she remained in the power of her own *paterfamilias*, or if there were none, she was *sui iuris*, though married in this second sense.

Peace of Constance: a peace agreed in 1183 between Emperor Frederick I Barbarossa and the Lombard League of North Italian cities. The imperial privilege – *Pax Constantiae* – in which it was embodied would become the foundational charter of the rights and liberties of many such cities in the later middle ages, including some which had not been members of the league. The Bolognese glossator (*q.v.*) Odofredus de Denariis (d. 1265) wrote a commentary on the treaty sometime between 1234 and 1250. Another was composed by Bartolus's pupil, Baldus de Ubaldis (d. 1400). The league had been established in 1167 to resist resurgent imperial influence in northern Italy. In the Peace, the emperor conceded that the cities could enjoy certain *regalia* and their own customs, appoint their own consuls, and legislate for themselves; but their consuls had to be invested by the emperor or his representative. No one who had not sworn fealty to the emperor could become a consul. Appeal could be made to the emperor in cases involving more than a certain sum. However, the appeal would be heard not at the imperial court, but where it had originated, by the emperor's local representative, and in accordance with local laws and customs. Vassals of the emperor who received investiture from the emperor swore fealty to him; anyone else who was a citizen of one of the cities of the league must also do so. And all members of the league who swore fealty to the emperor were obliged to make a supplementary declaration that they would assist the emperor in maintaining his estates and rights in Lombardy both within and outside the territory of members of the league. If any member of the league defaulted on its obligations under the Peace, the others would compel it to observe them. When the emperor entered Lombardy, he would receive his customary dues; but he undertook not to stay too long in any city or diocese to its detriment. Disputes between the emperor and a vassal about a fief were to be settled in the presence of the vassal's co-vassals in the place where the dispute arose, although it was also agreed that if the emperor happened to be present in Lombardy, the matter might, if he so wished, be brought before him.

persona ficta ('fictive person'): the law of persons (*ius personarum*) was, according to the influential second-century jurist Gaius, one of the three categories of law in classical Rome, the other two respectively concerning things (*res*) and actions (*actiones*). The distinctions between the three were not impermeable. *Persona*, for instance, was used of slaves to denote them as human beings, though imperfect human beings who were also chattels (*res*). And certain entities, although not human in nature, were considered to function in the place of persons (*personae vice fungitur*) – that is to say, akin to persons in the sense that they could bear legal rights and duties. This was said to be true of inheritances, *municipia* (*q.v.*), *decuriae* (*q.v.*; groups of, notionally, ten men), and partnerships (*societates*) (*Dig.* 46.1.22), and also of other types of associations of individuals, known as colleges and corporations (*collegia, q.v., universitates, q.v.*). The rule that 'if anything is owed to a *universitas*, it is not due to its members', and conversely 'what the *universitas* owes, the members do not owe' (*Dig.* 3.4.7.1), reveals that a *universitas* (or *collegium*) was a corporate body, distinct from its individual members. In that respect it had legal personality. It therefore differed from a partnership (*societas*), the partners (*socii*) of which were individually liable for its debts, without regard to its funds, and the claims of which on its debtors were claims of its partners. A *societas* therefore did not have legal personality (though it was also said to 'function in the place of a person' (*Dig.* 46.1.22)). The term *persona ficta*, however, was unknown to classical and late antique Roman law. It was an invention of the canonists of the thirteenth century – most famously, Pope Innocent IV – and was borrowed from them by medieval civilians. It was applied by canonists to churches and religious orders, and by civilians to other collectivities – most importantly for Bartolus's purposes, to cities. He termed such a corporation 'a kind of represented person' – represented because it was not itself a person, but represented or acted in place of a fictive person.

podestà (vernacular for *potestas*, 'power'): the chief executive of a city, originally appointed for a fixed term. The first had been appointed or recognized by the emperor, Frederick Barbarossa, in a number of cities in Lombardy and Emilia in the 1160s. City communes also appointed such officers. Usually a *podestà* was not a native of the city he ran. He was often a lawyer, who presided over the judiciary, and exercised police powers. He might also act as commander of the commune's military.

populus: the *populus Romanus* (or *populus Romanus Quiritium*) was the collectivity of all Roman citizens. As a collectivity, it could own, and be a creditor or debtor, but the jurists did not attribute legal personality to it. For Bartolus, each city within the Roman empire was also a *populus*, its citizens also being Roman citizens by force of Caracalla's *Constitutio Antoniniana de civitate* of AD 212. Bartolus defines each *populus*, or *civitas*, or *municipium* (*q.v.*), as a corporation (*universitas*, *q.v.*). As a *universitas*, it is a single person by fiction of law (*persona ficta*, *q.v.*). As a fictive person it does not die, and it cannot act or will for itself, but must do so through real persons, who represent what is deemed to be its single collective mind or will.

postliminium (*lit.* 'beyond the border'): a Roman citizen captured in war became the property, the slave, of his captor, along with his possessions. If he returned to Roman territory (from 'beyond the border') his liberty and possessions would be restored, subject to certain conditions. For instance, if he had been ransomed, *postliminium*, signifying his restoration, was suspended until the ransomer's lien had been paid off. Bartolus argues that in his own day *postliminium* applies between individual cities which do not recognize a common superior, but is inoperative between those that do.

prescription, long-term prescription (*praescriptio*; *longi temporis praescriptio*): in post-classical and Justinianic Roman law, it was possible to become owner (*dominus*, *q.v.*) of something by enjoying unchallenged possession of it for a specified period of time, based upon a legal transaction made in good faith which was intended to transfer ownership. Thereby mere possession was transformed into *dominium*. This was termed *usucapio* – the acquisition of *dominium* by use. Originally the required duration was two years. The *dominium* thereby acquired was *dominium* by Quiritary (=Roman citizen) right, which meant that *usucapio* was not applicable to provincial, as distinct from Italian, land, or available to *peregrini* (free inhabitants of Rome's dominions who were not Roman citizens). Under the emperors Severus and Caracalla, a parallel institution, *longi temporis praescriptio*, was created for these categories of land and people. Initially this did not give the holder *dominium*, but merely prevented the person originally entitled to the land or thing from asserting his claim, because of his inactivity over a specified period of time. But with Caracalla's abolition in AD 212 of the distinction between citizens and *peregrini*, and the progressive extinction of those between Italian and provincial land, the difference between the two institutions in effect disappeared, and acquisition of *dominium* by prescription became possible.

princeps ('ruler', 'emperor'): originally adopted by Augustus to mean 'first citizen', this was not an official title for the emperor, who was variously called *imperator*, Caesar, and Augustus. The power of the *princeps* was based on the tribunician power (*tribunicia potestas*) established by Augustus as a symbol of his restoration of the *res publica* (*q.v.*), and on his proconsular *imperium maius*, which gave him authority over all the provinces as well as supreme military command. According to a celebrated text in the *Corpus*, he was master (*dominus*, *q.v.*) of the whole world (*Dig.* 14.2.9). In the post-classical period, he was addressed as *dominus*. The emperor came to be vested with sovereign power by the people and the senate in a *lex de imperio*, which mimicked the practice in republican times of conferring *imperium* on higher magistrates by a *lex curiata de imperio*. Parts of the *lex de imperio Vespasiani* survive from AD 69–70; a law of this sort is mentioned repeatedly in the *Corpus*, though there it is termed a *lex regia* (*Dig.* 1.4.1, *Inst.* 1.2.6, *Cod.* 1.17.1.7; but cf. *Cod.* 6.23.3 for a reference to *lex imperii*). The first two of these passages proved of great interest to the medieval commentators (*q.v.*), for whom they demonstrated that imperial office was in some sense ultimately dependent on the Roman people. The *Glossa ordinaria* (*q.v.*) elaborated this view by reference to *Cod.* 1.14.4, which states that the emperor should declare himself to be bound by the laws, because his authority depends on a law, and that it is a mark of imperial authority to submit to them. Such passages were in apparent conflict with other statements in the *Corpus*: that 'What has pleased the *princeps* has the force of law' (*Dig.* 1.4.1), generally interpreted as an assertion of the emperor's absolute power; and that the emperor is 'absolved from the bonds of the law' (*Dig.* 1.3.1). According to Bartolus, the *lex regia* had become irrevocable with the passage of time, and only the *princeps* could now exercise the legislative power which had at one time been the Roman people's.

prior; cf. *antianus* (*q.v.*); *decurio* (*q.v.*): a 'first citizen', a category of governmental official. In Perugia, *priori delle arti* (of the guilds) replaced consuls as communal officials from 1303; thereafter the seat of the commune was known as the *Palazzo dei Priori*.

procurator: in private law, one appointed to administer the affairs of another, the principal. In public law, procurators, first appointed by Augustus, were eventually put in charge of all sorts of aspects of imperial administration.

pupillus ('ward'): The male descendant (*filiusfamilias*) of a Roman citizen – typically a son – below the age of puberty (*impubes*) ceased to be under the power of his male ascendant (*paterfamilias, q.v.*) – typically his father – as a result of the death of the *paterfamilias*, and became legally independent (*sui iuris*). But as *impubes*, he still had to be under guardianship (*tutela, q.v.*), hence a ward. A *pupillus* could not alienate his property or undertake any obligation without the authority of his guardian (*auctoritas tutoris*).

res publica: the sum of the rights and interests of the Roman people as a whole. It is therefore distinct from the emperor, from the fisc (the imperial treasury), and from other public entities, such as *municipia* (*q.v.*) or colonies, though these are sometimes also called *res publicae*. In accordance with this convention, Bartolus applies the term to individual cities. We have adopted the translation 'commonwealth' in order to avoid the antimonarchical implications of the English 'republic' while preserving the sense of a public or common resource.

senatus consultum ('consultation of the senate'): a decree of the senate, issued in response to a request from a magistrate for advice.

status: originally a legal rank or condition, Bartolus applied the term to institutions and groups of persons within individual cities. It signifies different things according to context: position, or standing, or stability, sometimes just government, or those who conduct government.

syndic: originally, a representative of a private or public corporate body.

tutor; tutela; tuitio ('guardian', 'guardianship'): a guardian was appointed for a male descendant of a Roman citizen (*filiusfamilias*) who was made independent (*sui iuris*) by the death of his senior male relative (*paterfamilias, q.v.*) while still below the age of puberty (*impubes*). A female descendant who was *sui iuris* had to have one throughout her life, in order to authorize certain legal acts for her. In the case of an infant male (below the age of seven), the *tutor* also administered the property of his ward (*pupillus, q.v.*), because the ward was deemed incapable of speech – the literal meaning of *infans*. Once the child was considered capable of speech, the *tutor*'s role was to supply judgment by authorizing the ward's formal transactions. For any legal act in which a ward of this age might incur a detriment, the authority of his *tutor* was a necessity. Without it, he therefore remained incapable of expressing a legally valid will, unless the transaction was of a sort from which he could only benefit. The *tutor* was deemed to stand in the place of the owner (*in loco domini*, *q.v.*), because the owner, as ward, could not act autonomously. This institution of Roman private law was routinely applied to analysis of the relationship between ruler and ruled in the middle ages.

universitas ('corporation'): a group or association of persons or things. In public law, it might be used of a *civitas*, *municipium* (*q.v.*), or a college (*collegium*, *q.v.*) of a public character; in private law, of partnerships (*societates*) and private colleges. The medieval civilians defined a *populus* (*q.v.*) as a *universitas*, and treated it as a single person by fiction of law (*persona ficta*, *q.v.*) It was therefore distinct from its members, who were real, individual persons. Like a single person, the *universitas* or people was deemed to possess a single mind, and to act as a unity; because it was a fictive person, it did not die.

vicar, vicariate: a delegation, originally by emperors but subsequently also by popes, of broad governing powers over regions or cities to an official – the vicar – who stood in the place of the delegator. Many Italian *signori* paid for such appointments to legitimate their rule. As a personal privilege, the office was in principle not heritable – *Sext.* 5.12.7 – and was terminated by the death of the delegator. Both limitations were challenged by various *signori* during the fourteenth century.

Volumen parvum ('Small Volume'): the fifth and final part of the Vulgate edition of the *Corpus iuris civilis* (*q.v.*). It comprised the *Tres libri* of the *Code* (*q.v.*), the *Authenticum* (*q.v.*), the *Libri feudorum* (*q.v.*), some constitutions of modern Western Roman emperors, and the *Institutes* (*q.v.*).

Biographies

Accursius (*c.* 1182–1263), glossator,[†] pupil of Azo, taught at Bologna, author of the *Glossa ordinaria*[†] on the *Corpus iuris civilis.*[†]

Azo (*c.* 1150–before 1233), glossator,[†] studied and taught at Bologna. He wrote an apparatus of glosses to all parts of the Roman law; his most influential work was a commentary on the *Code*[†] known as *Summa codicis.*

Charles IV (1316–78), king of the Romans 1346, king of Bohemia 1347, king of Lombardy 1355, Roman emperor 1355, king of Burgundy 1365.

Cinus of Pistoia (1270–1336), commentator,[†] poet. He held offices in several cities before teaching at Siena, Perugia – where Bartolus was a pupil – and Naples. His most influential work was a commentary on the *Code,*[†] the *Lectura codicis* (1314).

Clement VI (1291–1352), pope 1342.

Frederick I Barbarossa (1122–90), king of the Romans 1152, Roman emperor 1155. He promulgated several pieces of legislation at the Diet of Roncaglia (1158) which were included in the *Libri feudorum.*[†]

Frederick II (1194–1250), king of Sicily 1198, king of the Romans 1212, Roman emperor 1220, and king of Jerusalem 1225. He was deposed from all his dignities by Innocent IV at the First Council of Lyons in 1245 in the decree *Ad apostolicae dignitatis.*

Gaius (*fl.* AD 130–80), jurist and frequently quoted author in the *Digest.*[†] He wrote the passage excerpted at *Dig.* 1.1.9 *Omnes populi*, or 'All peoples', which was the *locus classicus* for medieval discussions of statute law. Bartolus set out some of the central points of his theory of legislative capacity in his commentary on it.

lvii

Giacomo, third-born son of Taddeo Pepoli (*c.* 1315–67), lord of Bologna jointly with his elder brother Giovanni, papal vicar.[†]

Gil Alvarez Carrillo de Albornoz ('Lord Giles') (1310–67), archbishop of Toledo (1338–50), cardinal-priest of San Clemente (1350–6), cardinal-bishop of Santa Sabina (1356–67), made papal legate for Italy by Innocent VI in 1353, in which capacity, in 1357, he promulgated the law code for the Papal State known as the *Constitutiones Aegidianae* or 'Aegidian Constitutions'.

Giles of Rome (Aegidius Romanus, Egidio Colonna) (1243–1316), theologian, prior-general of the Augustinian Order of Hermits, archbishop of Bourges. Lectured on the works of Peter Lombard and Aristotle at the University of Paris, where he had studied under Thomas Aquinas. Author of *On Ecclesiastical Power* (*De ecclesiastica potestate*) and the instantly influential *On the Government of Princes* (*De regimine principum*).

Giovanni, first-born son of Taddeo Pepoli (*c.* 1310–67), lord of Bologna jointly with his younger brother Giacomo, count palatine, papal vicar.[†]

Gratian (late eleventh century–before 1159), canonist, author of *Concordia discordantium canonum* or, more familiarly, the *Decretum*, and according to a recent hypothesis, bishop of Chiusi. The *Decretum* was in circulation in its final form by the late 1140s.

Gregory (I) the Great (*c.* 540–604), pope 590, saint. A prolific author whose *Moralia* or *Morals* provided Bartolus with a working definition of the tyrant.

Gulielmus de Cuneo (Guillaume de Cunh) (d. 1335), from Rabastens near Toulouse, was teaching Roman law at the University of Toulouse by 1314, where he lectured on the *Code*[†] and *Digest*.[†] By the end of 1317, he had left the university to become chaplain to Pope John XXII (1316–34). In 1319 he was made bishop of Bazas, and translated in 1325 to the see of Saint-Bertrand de Comminges.

Henry VII (1273–1313), count (Henry IV) of Luxemburg 1288, king of the Romans 1308, Roman emperor 1312.

Honorius III (*c.* 1150–1227), pope 1216. His decretals furnished 132 passages in the *Liber extra* of 1234.

Hostiensis (Henricus de Segusio) (*c.* 1200–71), bishop of Sisteron 1243/4, archbishop of Embrun 1250, cardinal-bishop of Ostia (hence the name) 1262, canonist; studied Roman and canon law at

Bologna and lectured at Paris. His *Summa* and *Lectura* on the *Liber extra* had enormous influence. He also wrote a commentary on an intermediate collection of Innocent IV's decretals.

Huguccio of Pisa, grammarian, studied at Paris and later taught at Bologna in the 1160s. The fact that they shared a name and both worked at Bologna may be responsible for the long-standing attribution of the *Derivationes*, a major lexicographical work used by Bartolus, to the canonist Huguccio (early twelfth century–1210), bishop of Ferrara, who studied and taught at Bologna and wrote an influential commentary or *Summa* on Gratian's *Decretum*. This attribution has been powerfully challenged by modern historians of canon law.

Iacobus de Arena (d. 1297/98), glossator,† studied at Parma, taught in Padua and possibly in Reggio-Emilia. He wrote additions to the *Glossa ordinaria*† of Accursius, disputations, legal opinions and several short treatises.

Iacobus de Belviso (after 1270–1335), commentator,† studied and taught at Bologna, Naples, and Perugia; said to have participated in Bartolus's doctoral examination in 1334. Author of influential commentaries on the *Libri feudorum*† and the *Authenticum*† as well as of numerous disputations.

Innocent III (c. 1161–1216), pope 1198, studied theology at Paris and perhaps law at Bologna for a short time; died in Perugia. His decretal letters had a vast influence over the growing canon law of the early thirteenth century and established some of the main terms of debate in controversies between the papacy and secular powers.

Innocent IV (late twelfth century–1254), pope 1243, canonist, studied at Parma and possibly Bologna. Author of a highly influential commentary on the *Liber extra* known as *Apparatus decretalium*, as well as commentaries on his own decretals. The latter did much to shape debates between the papacy and secular powers; he deposed Frederick II at the First Council of Lyons in 1245.

Iohannes Teutonicus (c. 1170–1245), canonist, studied and taught at Bologna until 1218, before taking a succession of positions at the cathedral of Halberstadt. His gloss to Gratian's *Decretum* became the basis of the *Glossa ordinaria*† to that text.

Isidore (c. 560–636), bishop of Seville c. 600, saint. Author, among other works, of the vastly influential *Etymologies*.

Julian (P. Salvius Iulianus), jurist, consul AD 148, governor of Upper Germany.

Justinian I (AD 482–565), Roman emperor 527, commissioned the *Corpus iuris civilis.*[†]

Odofredus de Denariis (d. 1265), glossator,[†] studied at Bologna, where he served in various administrative capacities and also taught law. His most famous legal works are his capacious lectures – *Lecturae* – on the *Corpus iuris civilis.*[†]

Paulus (Iulius Paulus) (*fl.* late second–early third century AD), jurist, one of the most frequently quoted authors in the *Digest.*[†]

Petrus de Assisi (late thirteenth–early fourteenth century), Franciscan friar, taught Bartolus prior to his entry to the university of Perugia.

Taddeo Pepoli (*c.* 1290—1347), jurist, lord of Bologna, papal vicar.[†]

Ulpian (Domitius Ulpianus, d. probably shortly before May or June AD 224), jurist, prefect of the Praetorian Guard under Emperor Severus Alexander. One of the most heavily represented authors in the *Digest.*[†]

Further Reading

The *Corpus iuris civilis*
(including selected medieval additions)

The Digest of Justinian, ed. T. Mommsen and P. Krueger, trans. A. Watson, 4 vols. (Philadelphia, PA 1985).

The Codex of Justinian: A New Annotated Translation, with Parallel Latin and Greek, ed. B. W. Frier, 3 vols. (Cambridge 2016).

Institutes of Justinian, trans. P. Birks and G. McLeod (London 1987).

Novellae, ed. R. Schoell and G. Kroll, 6th edn (Berlin 1954).

The Novels of Justinian: A Complete Annotated English Translation, ed. D. J. D. Miller and P. Sarris, 2 vols. (Cambridge 2018).

Libri feudorum: K. Lehmann, *Consuetudines feudorum, editio altera*, ed. K. A. Eckhard (Aalen 1971) (1st edn K. Lehmann, *Das Langobardische Lehenrecht* (Göttingen 1896)). This edition of the Latin text is re-used in: *The Libri Feudorum (the 'Books of Fiefs'): An Annotated English Translation of the Vulgata Recension with Latin Text*, ed. and trans. A. Stella (Leyden 2023).

Emperor Frederick II, Constitution *Ad decus*, in MGH, *Constitutiones et acta publica imperatorum et regum*, ed. L. Weiland, II (Hanover 1896), no. 85, pp. 107–9.

Emperor Henry VII, Constitutions *Ad reprimendum* and *Quoniam nuper*, in MGH, *Constitutiones et acta publica imperatorum et regum*, ed. J. Schwalm, IV, pt. 2 (Hanover 1909–11), respectively no. 929, pp. 965–6, and nos. 931–2, pp. 966–8.

Printed texts of the medieval, or Vulgate, recension of the *Corpus*, with Accursius's 'ordinary gloss', are available only in early modern editions.

The *Corpus iuris canonici*

Corpus iuris canonici, ed. A. Friedberg, 2 vols. (Leipzig 1879–81).
Gratian, *The Treatise on the Laws (Decretum DD. 1–20) with the Ordinary Gloss*, ed. and trans. A. Thompson, J. Gordley, and K. Christiansen (Washington, DC 1993).
Printed texts of the *Corpus* with Johannes Teutonicus's and Bartholomaeus Brixiensis's 'ordinary gloss' are available only in early modern editions.

Roman Law in Antiquity

J. A. Crook, *Law and Life of Rome* (London 1967).
P. J. du Plessis, C. Ando, and K. Tuori, eds., *The Oxford Handbook of Roman Law and Society* (Oxford 2016).
D. Johnston, *Roman Law in Context* (Cambridge 1999).
H. F. Jolowicz and B. Nicholas, *Historical Introduction to the Study of Roman Law*, 3rd edn (Cambridge 1972).

Dogmatic Guides

A. Berger, *Encyclopedic Dictionary of Roman Law*, Transactions of the American Philosophical Society, n.s. 43, pt. 2 (Philadelphia, PA 1953).
W. W. Buckland, *A Text-Book of Roman Law from Augustus to Justinian*, 3rd edn, rev. P. Stein (Cambridge 1963).

Roman and Canon Law (*ius commune*) in the Middle Ages

M. Bellomo, *The Common Legal Past of Europe, 1000–1800*, trans. L. G. Cochrane (Washington, DC 1995).
J. A. Brundage, *Medieval Canon Law* (Harlow 1995).
J. P. Canning, 'The Corporation in the Political Thought of the Italian Jurists of the Thirteenth and Fourteenth Century', *History of Political Thought*, 1 (1980): 9–32.

'Ideas of the State in Thirteenth- and Fourteenth-Century Commentators on the Roman Law', *TRHS*, 5th ser., 33 (1983): 1–27.

'Law, Sovereignty and Corporation Theory, 1300–1450', in J. H. Burns, ed., *The Cambridge History of Medieval Political Thought c. 350–c. 1450* (Cambridge 1988), pp. 454–76.

The Political Thought of Baldus de Ubaldis (Cambridge 1987).

O. Cavallar and J. Kirshner, eds., *Jurists and Jurisprudence in Medieval Italy: Texts and Contexts* (Toronto 2020).

E. Cortese, *Il problema della sovranità nel pensiero giuridico medioevale* (Rome 1966).

La norma giuridica: Spunti teoretici nel diritto comune classico, 2 vols. (Milan 1962–4).

H. Dondorp and E. J. H. Schrage, 'The Sources of Medieval Learned Law', in J. W. Cairns and P. J. du Plessis, eds., *The Creation of the Ius Commune: From Casus to Regula* (Edinburgh 2010), pp. 7–56.

D. Fedele, *The Medieval Foundations of International Law: Baldus de Ubaldis (1327–1400), Doctrine and Practice of the Ius Gentium* (Leyden 2021).

C. Humfress, 'Out of Time? Eternity, Christology, and Justinianic Law', in J. Robertson, ed., *Time, History, and Political Thought* (Cambridge 2023), pp. 36–53.

D. Ibbetson, 'Custom in Medieval Law', in A. Perreau-Saussine and J. B. Murphy, eds., *The Nature of Customary Law: Legal, Historical and Philosophical Perspectives* (Cambridge 2007), pp. 151–75.

E. H. Kantorowicz, *The King's Two Bodies: A Study in Mediaeval Political Theology* (Princeton, NJ 1957).

S. L'Engle, 'Law at Bologna', in F. T. Coulson and R. G. Babcock, eds., *The Oxford Handbook of Latin Palaeography* (Oxford 2020), pp. 865–78.

F. W. Maitland, 'Introduction' to O. Gierke, *Political Theories of the Middle Age*, trans. F. W. Maitland (Cambridge 1900), pp. vii–lxxx.

K. Pennington, *The Prince and the Law, 1200–1600: Sovereignty and Rights in the Western Legal Tradition* (Berkeley, CA 1993).

M. J. Ryan, 'Corporation Theory', in H. Lagerlund, ed., *Encyclopedia of Medieval Philosophy*, 2 vols. (New York, NY 2010), vol. I, pp. 236–40.

'Freedom, Law, and the Medieval State', in Q. Skinner and B. Stråth, *States and Citizens: History, Theory, Prospects* (Cambridge 2003), pp. 51–62.

'Historicity and Universality in Roman Law before 1600', in J. Robertson, ed., *Time, History, and Political Thought* (Cambridge 2023), pp. 54–66.

'Political Thought', in D. Johnston, ed., *The Cambridge Companion to Roman Law* (Cambridge 2015), pp. 423–51.

'Rulers and Justice, 1200–1500', in P. Linehan, J. L. Nelson, and M. Costambeys, eds., *The Medieval World*, 2nd edn (Abingdon 2018), pp. 586–601.

P. Stein, *Roman Law in European History* (Cambridge 1999).

B. Tierney, *Church Law and Constitutional Thought in the Middle Ages* (London 1979).

Foundations of the Conciliar Theory: The Contribution of the Medieval Canonists from Gratian to the Great Schism, 2nd edn (Leyden 1998).

Religion, Law, and the Growth of Constitutional Thought, 1150–1650 (Cambridge 1982).

W. Ullmann, 'The Delictal Responsibility of Medieval Corporations', repr. in his *Scholarship and Politics in the Middle Ages* (London 1980), ch. 12.

'Juristic Obstacles to the Emergence of the Concept of the State in the Middle Ages', repr. in his *The Church and the Law in the Earlier Middle Ages* (London 1975), ch. 12.

Law and Politics in the Middle Ages: An Introduction to the Sources of Medieval Political Ideas (London 1975).

P. Vinogradoff, *Roman Law in Medieval Europe*, 2nd edn (Oxford 1929).

A. Winroth and J. C. Wei, eds., *The Cambridge History of Medieval Canon Law* (Cambridge 2022).

Works by Bartolus

Bartoli a Sassoferrato in primam Digesti Veteris partem commentaria (Turin 1574).

Bartoli a Sassoferrato in primam Digesti Novi partem commentaria (Turin 1574).

Bartoli a Sassoferrato in secundam Digesti Novi partem commentaria (Turin 1574).

Bartoli a Sassoferrato in primam Codicis partem commentaria (Turin 1574).

Bartoli a Sassoferrato in Tres libros Codicis commentaria (Turin 1574).

Bartoli a Sassoferrato Consilia, quaestiones, et tractatus (Basle 1588).

Tyberiadis, … Tractatus de fluminibus tripertitus; ab Hercule Buttrigario sacrae Lateranensis aulae equite aurato, nunc demum restitutus in lucem prodit (Bologna 1576; repr. Turin 1964).

D. Quaglioni, ed., *Politica e diritto nel trecento italiano: Il 'De tyranno' di Bartolo da Sassoferrato (1314–1357), con l'edizione critica dei trattati 'De Guelphis et Gebellinis', 'De regimine civitatis' e 'De tyranno'* (Florence 1983).

Bartolus, *Tractatus de dignitatibus*, ed. G. Giordanengo, in *Romania*, 187–8 (1989): 214–30.

O. Cavallar, S. Degenring, and J. Kirshner, eds., *A Grammar of Signs: Bartolo da Sassoferrato's Tract on Insignia and Coats of Arms* (Berkeley, CA 1994).

S. Lepsius, ed., *Der Richter und die Zeugen: Eine Untersuchung anhand des Tractatus testimoniorum des Bartolus von Sassoferrato, mit Edition* (Frankfurt 2003).

O. Cavallar, ed., 'River of Law: Bartolus's *Tiberiadis* (*De alluvione*)', in J. A. Marino and T. Kuehn, eds., *A Renaissance of Conflicts: Visions and Revisions of Law and Society in Italy and Spain* (Toronto 2004), pp. 30–129.

Translations of Works by Bartolus

Bartolus on the Conflict of Laws, ed. and trans. J. H. Beale (Cambridge, MA 1914).

E. Emerton, *Humanism and Tyranny: Studies in the Italian Trecento* (Cambridge 1925); includes translations of *De Guelfis et Gebellinis* (pp. 273–84) and *De tyranno* (pp. 126–54).

Bartolus of Sassoferrato, *On the Tyrant*, trans. J. Kirshner, in J. W. Boyer and J. Kirschner, eds., *University of Chicago Readings in Western Civilization* (Chicago, ILL 1986), vol. V, pp. 7–30.

Bartole de Sassoferrato, *Traités sur les Guelfes et les Gibelins, sur le gouvernement de la cité, sur le tyran*, ed. and trans. S. Parent (Paris 2019).

Bartolo da Sassoferrato, *Trattati politici: Sulla tirannide – Sulle costituzioni politiche – Sui partiti*, ed. D. Razzi, trans. A. Turrioni, intro. D. Quaglioni (Foligno 2019).

'Oration on Conferring the Doctorate of Law', ed. and trans. O. Cavallar and J. Kirshner, in their *Jurists and Jurisprudence in Medieval Italy: Texts and Contexts* (Toronto 2020), pp. 117–23.

'Consilium on Citizenship', trans. Cavallar and Kirshner, in their *Jurists and Jurisprudence*, p. 529.

Literature on Bartolus

M. Ascheri, 'The Formation of the *Consilia* Collection of Bartolus of Saxoferrato and Some of His Autographs', in L. Mayali and S. A. J. Tibbetts, eds., *The Two Laws: Studies in Medieval Legal History Dedicated to Stephan Kuttner* (Washington, DC 1990), pp. 188–201.

A. Bartoli Langeli and M. A. Panzanelli Fratoni, 'L'ambasceria a Carlo IV di Lussemburgo', in *Bartolo da Sassoferrato nel VII centenario della nascita: Diritto, politica, società: Atti del L Convegno storico internazionale. Todi – Perugia, 13–16 ottobre 2013* (Spoleto 2014), pp. 271–332.

M. Bellomo, '*Factum* e *ius*: Itinerari di ricerca fra le certezze e i dubbi del pensiero giuridico medievale', in *Medioevo edito e inedito, II. Scienza del diritto e società medievale* (Rome 1997), pp. 63–89.

A. Belloni, 'Bartolo studente e maestro e i suoi commentari', in *Bartolo da Sassoferrato nel VII centenario della nascita*, pp. 559–84.

F. Calasso, 'Bartolo da Sassoferrato', *Dizionario biografico degli Italiani* (Rome 1964), vol. VI, pp. 640–69.

O. Cavallar, 'Il Tevere sfoccia nel Arno: Sigismondo Coccapani e il proemio al trattato Tiberiadis di Bartolo da Sassoferrato', *Rechtsgeschichte – Legal History*, 3 (2003): 223–31.

'Geografia della tirannide: Una proposta di lettura per alcuni degli ultimi trattati bartoliani', in J. Barthas, ed., *Della tirannia: Machiavelli con Bartolo* (Florence 2007), pp. 3–46.

'Il tiranno, i "dubia" del giudice e i "consilia" dei giuristi', *Archivio storico italiano*, 45 (1997): 265–346.

'Personaggi in cerca di editore: Una proposta di lettura per alcuni degli ultimi trattati bartoliani', *Rivista internazionale di diritto comune*, 15 (2004): 97–142.

V. Colli, 'Collezioni d'autore di Baldo degli Ubaldi nel MS Biblioteca Apostolica Vaticana, Barb. Lat. 1398', *Ius commune*, 25 (1998): 323–46.

'La biblioteca di Bartolo: Intorno ad autografi e copie d'autore', in *Bartolo da Sassoferrato nel VII centenario della nascita*, pp. 67–108.

V. Crescenzi and G. Rossi, eds., *Bartolo da Sassoferrato nella cultura europea tra medioevo e rinascimento* (Sassoferrato 2015).

G. Crinella, ed., *Bartolo da Sassoferrato e il Trattato sulla tirannide* (Urbino 2020).

F. Ercole, *Studi sul diritto pubblico e sulle dottrine politiche di Bartolo* (Rome 1917).

J. N. Figgis, 'Bartolus and the Development of European Political Ideas', repr. in his *The Divine Right of Kings*, 2nd edn (Cambridge 1914), pp. 343–72.

M. Gentile, 'Bartolo in prattica: Appunti su identità politica e procedura giudiziaria nel ducato di Milano alla fine Quattrocento', *Rivista internazionale di diritto comune*, 18 (2007): 231–51.

N. E. Hazimihail, 'Bartolus da Sassoferrato and the Conflict of Laws in the Middle Ages', in his *Preclassical Conflict of Laws* (Cambridge 2021), pp. 217–350.

T. M. Izbicki, 'Additional Texts Attributed to Bartolus de Saxoferrato in North American Manuscript Collections', *Manuscripta*, 55/2 (2011): 205–12.

'Manuscript Works of Bartolus de Saxoferrato in the Vatican Library', *Rivista internazionale di diritto comune*, 23 (2012): 147–210.

'Texts Attributed to Bartolus de Saxoferrato in North American Manuscript Collections', in his *Friars and Jurists: Selected Studies* (Goldbach 1997), pp. 381–90.

J. Kirshner, 'Bartolo of Sassoferrato's De tyranno and Sallustio Buonguglielmi's Consilium on Niccolò Fortebracci's Tyranny in Città di Castello', *Medieval Studies*, 68 (2006): 303–31.

'*Civitas sibi faciat civem*: Bartolus of Sassoferrato's Doctrine on the Making of a Citizen', *Speculum*, 48 (1973): 694–713.

S. Lepsius, 'Bartolo da Sassoferrato', in I. Birocchi, E. Cortese, A. Mattone, and M. N. Miletti, eds., *Dizionario biografico dei giuristi italiani (XII–XX secolo)* (Bologna 2013), vol. I, pp. 177–80.

P. Mari, *Il libro di Bartolo: Aspetti della vita quotidiana nelle opera 'bartoliane'* (Spoleto 2021).

'Problemi di critica bartoliana: Su una recente edizione dei trattati politici di Bartolo', *Studi medievali*, 3rd ser., 26 (1985): 907–40.

M. A. Panzanelli Fratoni, 'Bartolo da Sassoferrato e la stampa, ovvero della sua prima fortuna editoriale', in Crescenzi and Rossi, eds., *Bartolo da Sassoferrato*, pp. 253–84.

L. Prosdocimi, '*Ex facto oritur ius*: Breve nota di diritto medievale', in A. Biscardi, ed., *Studi senesi in memoria di Ottorini Vannini* (Milan 1957), pp. 802–13.

D. Quaglioni, 'Intorno al testo del *Tractatus de tyrannia* di Bartolo da Sassoferrato', *Il pensiero politico*, 10 (1977): 268–84.

'"Rebellare idem est quam resistere": Obédience et résistance dans les gloses de Bartole à la constitution "Quoniam nuper" d'Henri VII (1355)', in J.-C. Zancarini, ed., *Le Droit de résistance, XIIe–XXe siècle* (Paris 1999), pp. 35–46.

M. J. Ryan, 'Bartolus of Sassoferrato and Free Cities', *TRHS*, 6th ser., 10 (2000): 65–89.

D. Segoloni, 'Bartolo da Sassoferrato e la *civitas Perusina*', in Segoloni, ed., *Bartolo da Sassoferrato: Studi e documenti per il VI centenario*, vol. II, pp. 513–671.

D. Segoloni, ed., *Bartolo da Sassoferrato: Studi e documenti per il VI centenario*, 2 vols. (Milan 1962).

P. Stein, 'Bartolus, the Conflict of Laws and the Roman Law', repr. in his *The Character and Influence of the Roman Civil Law: Historical Essays* (London 1988), pp. 83–90.

F. Treggiari, *Le ossa di Bartolo: Contributo alla storia della tradizione giuridica perugina* (Perugia 2009).

'Sulle edizioni dei *Consilia, quaestiones et tractatus* di Bartolo da Sassoferrato', *Rivista internazionale di diritto comune*, 27 (2016): 159–84.

W. Ullmann, 'Bartolus and English Jurisprudence', repr. in his *Jurisprudence in the Middle Ages* (London 1980), ch. 9.

'Bartolus on Customary Law', repr. in his *Jurisprudence in the Middle Ages*, ch. 10.

'De Bartoli sententia: Concilium repraesentat mentem populi', repr. in his *The Papacy and Political Ideas in the Middle Ages* (London 1976), ch. 10.

L. Valla, 'L'Epistola contra Bartolum', in M. Regoliosi, 'L'Epistola contra Bartolum del Valla', in *Filologia umanistica: Per Gianvito Resta*, ed. V. Fera and G. Ferraú, 3 vols. (Padua 1997), vol. II, pp. 1531–71. English translation in Cavallar, Degenring and Kirshner, eds, *A Grammar of Signs*, pp. 179–200.

C. N. S. Woolf, *Bartolus of Sassoferrato: His Position in the History of Medieval Political Thought* (Cambridge 1913).

Contexts

L. Andreani, 'Todi nel basso medioevo (secoli XIII–XV): Aspetti di vita politico-istituzionale', in *Todi nel medioevo (secoli VI–XIV): Atti*

del XLVI Convegno storico internazionale. Todi 10–15 ottobre 2009, 2 vols. (Spoleto 2010), vol. I, pp. 51–87.

O. Banti, "'Civitas' e 'commune' nelle fonti italiane dei secoli XI e XII', in G. Rosetti, ed., *Forme di potere e struttura sociale in Italia nel Medioevo* (Bologna 1977), pp. 217–32.

E. Bellini, *L'Università a Perugia negli statuti cittadini (secoli XIII–XIV)* (Perugia 2007).

C. E. Beneš, *Urban Legends: Civic Identity and the Classical Past in Northern Italy, 1250–1350* (Philadelphia, PA 2011).

S. R. Blanshei, *Perugia, 1260–1340: Conflict and Change in a Medieval Italian Urban Society*, Transactions of the American Philosophical Society, n.s. 66, pt. 2 (Philadelphia, PA 1976).

W. M. Bowsky, *A Medieval Italian Commune: Siena under the Nine, 1287–1355* (Berkeley, CA 1981).

M. V. Clarke, *The Medieval City State: An Essay on Tyranny and Federation in the Later Middle Ages* (London 1926).

G. Ermini, *Storia dell'Università di Perugia*, 2nd edn, 2 vols. (Florence 1971).

G. Garnett, *Marsilius of Padua and 'the Truth of History'* (Oxford 2006).

L. Green, 'The Image of Tyranny in Early Fourteenth-Century Italian Historical Writing', *Renaissance Studies*, 7 (1993–4): 335–51.

F. Gregorovius, *History of the City of Rome in the Middle Ages*, trans. A. Hamilton, 8 vols. in 13 (London 1894–1902).

A. Grohmann, *Città e territorio tra medioevo ed età moderna: Perugia, secoli XIII–XVI*, 3 vols. (Perugia 1981).

W. Heywood, *A History of Perugia* (London 1910).

P. Jones, *The Italian City-State: From Commune to Signoria* (Oxford 1997).

P. Lantschner, 'City States in the Late Medieval Mediterranean World', *Past and Present*, 254 (2022): 3–49.

G. Milani, 'Podestà, popolo e parti a Todi tra Due e Trecento: Per una revisione del "paradigma tudertino"', in *Todi nel medioevo (secoli VI–XIV): Atti del XLVI Convegno storico internazionale. Todi 10–15 ottobre 2009*, 2 vols. (Spoleto 2010), vol. II, pp. 351–76.

M. Neri, 'Perugia e il suo contado nei secoli XIII e XIV: Interventi urbanistici e legislazione statutaria', *Storia della città*, 3 (1977): 28–37.

G. Raccagni, *The Lombard League, 1167–1225* (Oxford 2010).

Q. Skinner, *The Foundations of Modern Political Thought*, 2 vols. (Cambridge 1978).

H. C. Thomas, 'The Perugian Nobility, *c.* 1200–1430', unpublished University of Oxford D.Phil. (1982).

B. Tierney, *The Crisis of Church and State 1050–1300* (Englewood Cliffs, NJ 1964).

D. P. Waley, *Siena and the Sienese in the Thirteenth Century* (Cambridge 1991).

D. P. Waley and T. Dean, *The Italian City-Republics*, 4th edn (London 2009).

C. Wickham, *Sleepwalking into a New World: The Emergence of Italian City Communes in the Twelfth Century* (Princeton, NJ 2015).

Note on Scriptural References

References are to the Vulgate translation of the Bible. Bartolus occasionally invokes both the Ordinary and the Interlinear Gloss to the Vulgate; and also the recent *Postilla literalis* of Nicholas of Lyra. These may be consulted most conveniently in *Biblia sacra cum glossis, interlineari et ordinaria, Nicolai Lyrani postilla et moralitatibus* [...], 7 vols. (Lyons 1545).

Como
Adda
Milan
Brescia Vicenza
LOMBARDY Verona
Padua
Treviso
Piave
Trieste
Venice
Pavia
Cremona Mantua
Adige
Piacenza
Po
Parma
Modena
Ferrara
Reno
Bologna
Ravenna
Genoa
STATES
Pistoia
Romagna Rimini
Lucca
Pisa
Arno
Florence
Arezzo
Urbino
Cagli
Ancona
Sassoferrato
OF
Siena
TUSCANY Perugia
Assisi
March
of Fermo
Ancona
Deruta
Todi
Orvieto
Spoleto
THE
Northern Italy
c. 1350
Viterbo
Tiber
Abruzzi
CHURCH
Visconti of Milan
Florence
Genoa
Della Scala of Verona
Venice
Rome
PATRIMONY
OF
Tivoli
ST
PETER
SICILY
Terra
di
Lavoro
Gaeta

0   50 mi

0   50 km

Texts

On Guelfs and Ghibellines

When I had written a literal exposition concerning those matters, and while my mind was occupied with that third part of the *Tiberiadis*,[1] I found myself within the hundredth milestone from the city of Rome,[2] close to the city of Todi. And there I realized that what was written literally about the river and its bed may be said allegorically and morally about what frequently happens in the city of Todi. For our whole life is a river or the water of a river, as is written: 'We all die, and as waters will be spilt upon the ground, which do not flow back', 2 *Kings* 14.[3] And the bed over which these waters run is those things towards which we have sympathies [*affectiones*†], as is written in *Matthew* 6: 'Where your treasure is, there is your heart also.'[4]

Now in that city of Todi I found two sympathies, for some were called 'Guelfs' and some 'Ghibellines'; and in that place there were necessarily as many from one sympathy as from the other, no matter what the public office.[5] Furthermore, it sometimes happens that he who belongs to one

[1] See Translators' Note and Introduction, pp. xxxix–xl, xiii–xiv. This is a reference to the final section of Bartolus's preceding treatise, *Tractatus de fluminibus*, pp. 97–117.
[2] It may not be a coincidence that, according to *Dig.* 1.1.1.4, the jurisdiction of the prefect of the city of Rome began at the hundredth milestone.
[3] 2 *Kings* 14, 14.
[4] Verse 21.
[5] J.-C. Maire Vigueur, 'Échec au podestat: L'expulsion de Comacio Galluzzi podestat de Todi (17 juillet 1268)', in *'Alla Signorina': Mélanges offerts à Nöelle de la Blanchardière*, Publications de l'École Française de Rome, cciv (Rome 1995), pp. 251–83, at 257–8 and n. 26: this arrangement was introduced in 1267–8, reaffirmed in 1275, and, while Bartolus was still in Todi, in 1337; it was not unique to Todi: F. del Tredici, 'La popolarità dei partiti: Fazioni, popolo e mobilità sociale in Lombardia, XIV–XV secolo', in A. Gamberini, ed., *La mobilità sociale nel medioevo italiano, vol. II: Stato e istituzioni, secoli XIV–XV* (Rome 2017), pp. 305–34, at 317–18.

3

sympathy for a certain time changes his course and begins to be of the other; and concerning this many problems arise. So let us examine some. First, whence these terms derived their origin, and concerning their signification.

Secondly, what they mean today.

Thirdly, whether it is legal to have these sympathies.

Fourthly, how to prove that someone is of these sympathies, whether we are speaking of a private individual or of a commonwealth [*res publica*†].

Fifthly, how to prove that someone has changed sympathy.

I

With regard to the first question, it should be understood that at one time great discord arose between the Roman church and Frederick I – called Frederick Barbarossa – who was then emperor of the Romans. From him we have certain laws – as is evident in the *Libri feudorum*† – made while he was still loyal to the church.[6] Afterwards the church deprived him of the empire, as in *Sext.* 2.14.2;[7] 1.6.17.[8] Now in Germany those related to this Frederick on his father's side were known as the lords of Gebello.[9] And as the aforementioned discord lasted a long time, a great part of the Italians adhered to the deposed emperor and were called Ghibellines – in other words, adherents of that lord of Gebello. But others were attached to the church and were called Guelfs – in other words, zealots of the faith.

---

[6] *Feud.* 2.27; 2.53; 2.54(55).

[7] *Sext.* 2.14.2 is the decree *Ad apostolicae dignitatis* promulgated by Pope Innocent IV at the First Council of Lyons in 1245, deposing Frederick II as Holy Roman Emperor and king of Sicily. Bartolus cites this not because he is confusing Frederick I with Frederick II, but because there is no text in the canon law showing that Frederick I had actually been deposed. Frederick I was excommunicated by Alexander III in 1160, who also released those bound by fealty to the emperor from their oaths. It was a matter of debate among later theorists whether absolution of subjects from their fealty to a ruler constituted deposition. See, for Alexander's letter relating his excommunication of Frederick, G. Hödl and P. Classen, eds., MGH, *Briefe vi. Die Admonter Briefsammlung nebst ergänzenden Briefen* (Munich 1983), no. 53, pp. 103–6. For debate, see for example John of Paris (late 1302 – early 1303), *On Royal and Papal Power*, ed. and trans. J. A. Watt (Toronto 1971) ch. 11, sec. 11, ch. 15, sec. 11, pp. 131, 174–5.

[8] *Sext.* 1.6.17 is the decretal *Fundamenta* (Nicholas III, 1278) which refers to the now-dead Frederick II as having been deposed. For further citation of *Fundamenta* in a different context, see below, p. 48.

[9] Waiblingen in Swabia.

4

These points are prefigured in 1 *Kings* 31,[10] and 2 *Kings* 1,[11] where Saul, at one time king and later rejected by God, was beset and killed on Mount Gilboa, which is interpreted to mean the place of fortitude.[12] Thus that same Frederick, sometime emperor, later condemned, trusting in the fortitude of his house of Gebello, was beset and confounded by the Guelfs, that is, the zealots of the faith. For this name 'Zelpha' is found in *Genesis* 30,[13] and is interpreted as the speaking mouth or the gaping mouth,[14] which in the present instance corresponds to the church: for that same emperor was confounded by the words of the sentence of excommunication pronounced by the supreme pontiff.[15] Strictly speaking, therefore, just as Gilboa is interpreted to mean the place of fortitude, so 'Ghibellines' are interpreted to mean those who trust in temporal fortitude – that is, of soldiers and arms. And just as Zelpha is interpreted as speaking mouth, so 'Guelfs' are interpreted as those who trust in prayer and divine worship, as did Emperor Justinian in *Cod.* 1.17.1.[16]

II

With regard to the second question – what the said terms mean today – I say that, as is clear from the above, the aforesaid are terms signifying the sympathies of men. For sympathizers with the position [*status*†] of the church against that enemy of the church are called by one name, and their adversaries by the other. But today these names persist on account of other sympathies. For we see that many who are called Guelfs are rebels against the church, and many others who are called Ghibellines are rebels against the empire. But, as happens in provinces and cities in which there are divisions and factions [*partialitates*†], it is necessary that the said parties be called by some name: so the said names are imposed on them, as more commonplace. In other places other particular names

[10] 1 *Kings* 31, 1–9.
[11] 2 *Kings* 1, 6.
[12] Below, p. 37.
[13] That is, Zilpah: verses 9–12.
[14] Bartolus's source for these interpretations is uncertain; they do not match those given by St Jerome in *Liber interpretationis Hebraicorum nominum*, ed. P. de Lagarde, CCSL, lxxii (Turnhout 1959), pp. 104, 73; cf. Quaglioni, *Politica e diritto*, p. 40 and n. 2, 133 nn. 7 and 11. Isidore of Seville is closer on *Zelpha* ('gaping mouth'), but silent on *Gelboe*: Isidore of Seville, *Etymologiarum sive originum, libri xx*, ed. W. M. Lindsay, 2 vols. (Oxford 1911), 7.6.38, vol. II, p. 282.
[15] Above, n. 7.
[16] *Cod.* 1.17.1 begins: 'We, governing our Empire by the authority of God …'.

come to be used, with which I am not at present concerned; and these are factions, as in *Dig.* 49.15.21.1.[17]

I say, therefore, that today he is said to be a Guelf who adheres to and sympathizes with the position of that party which is called Guelf; and he is said to be a Ghibelline who adheres to and sympathizes with the position [*status*†] of that party which is called Ghibelline. And in this no account is commonly taken of the church or of the empire, but only of those factions which exist in a city or province, as also in *Dig.* 49.15.21.1. And there the Gloss interprets the words 'those who go off [to join one or other side]' when it says: 'Either citizens against citizens, or one city against another.'[18] Again, these factions sometimes arise amongst the aforesaid citizens, and yet no one is rebelling against his lord, whether it be the church, the empire, a king, or a people which rules, as in *Dig.* 49.15.21.1.[19] The facts themselves show that this is true.

From this I infer three things.

First, that if 'Guelf' and 'Ghibelline' are understood exactly as when first coined, an individual cannot be a Guelf in one place and a Ghibelline in another: the reason being that those sympathies, namely with the church and the empire of the reprobate, apply to the whole world universally and uniformly. To say, therefore, that someone can be of one sympathy in one place and of the other in another would be a contradiction in terms, just as one tutor† cannot authorize two wards litigating against each other over the same matter, as in *Dig.* 26.8.15 and the note there.[20] What is written applies: 'No one can serve two masters' – that is, two conflicting masters, *Matthew* 6.[21]

Secondly, I infer that as these names are understood today, one man can be a Guelf in one place and a Ghibelline in another; and this is obvious, because these sympathies relate to different things. Suppose that in

---

[17] *Dig.* 49.15.21.1. Those who join one or other side ('qui in alterutras partes discedent') in 'civil dissensions' are not legally enemies of Rome because neither party is intent on destroying the Roman commonwealth, even though such dissensions gravely damage it. For Bartolus's commentary on this law, see *In secundam Digesti Novi partem commentaria* (Turin 1574), fo. 227vb. There, Bartolus sticks to the vocabulary of the legal text in calling the hostile camps within his own city of Perugia 'partes' rather than 'partialitates', the term he frequently employs in this tract.

[18] See *Dig.* 49.15.21.1, gloss *discedunt*, which Bartolus quotes *verbatim* here, omitting only Accursius's references to *Dig.* 49.15.19.2 and *Dig.* 49.15.24.

[19] The only ruler mentioned in *Dig.* 49.15.21.1 at this point is the emperor.

[20] *Dig.* 26.8.15 in fact allows one tutor to authorize both parties; Accursius's gloss *accipientis* makes the caveat Bartolus mentions.

[21] Verse 24.

one city there is a tyrant, who together with his following [*secta*] is called Guelf, to which sympathy any good man will be opposed because he is opposed to all tyranny: in that territory he is called a Ghibelline. And suppose, in another city not depending upon the first, that there is a Ghibelline tyrant: certainly the same good man will oppose that tyrant, and will there and then be a Guelf, by analogy with what we said concerning a tutor,[†] who may authorize both wards only when they are litigating over different matters, as in *Dig.* 26.8.15.[22]

Thirdly, I infer that a person may be of one sympathy in one respect and of the other in another. For example, in the city of Perugia there are many who wish to be reputed Ghibellines in the first sense in which the names of those sympathies were coined, as if it redounded to their honour that so long ago their forebears were so noble that they were reputed to be of that sympathy. But with respect to the government [*status*†] which now rules the city, they are Guelfs; and for that reason they call themselves Ghibellines by origin, but Guelfs as regards the government [*status*] of the city. Nor is this a contradiction, inasmuch as these names are used in different respects. Such is the case when we say that someone may not be principal and surety in the same respect for the same sum, as in *Cod.* 8.41.28;[23] but in different respects he may be, as in *Dig.* 45.2.11.[24]

III

With regard to the third question – whether it be licit to entertain these sympathies – if many are of one sympathy or if someone is attached to one sympathy, not for the public good, but for his own utility or in order to oppress others, that is simply illicit. And if they combine the one with the other, this will be punishable just like those who form an association for the punishment of the innocent, as in *Dig.* 48.7.6[25] and 47.13.2.[26]

But sometimes there is one party in a city inclined principally to the public good, in order that the city should be rightly and peacefully governed; and yet it cannot resist its adversaries, except under the single name of a faction: then I consider such a sympathy and faction to be

---

[22] Above, n. 20.

[23] *Cod.* 8.41.28 establishes what Bartolus relates here.

[24] *Dig.* 45.2.11: co-promissors may act as guarantors for each other.

[25] *Dig.* 48.7.6 makes liable under the *Lex Iulia de vi privata*† those who dishonestly collude with a litigant so as to profit from any property the litigant may win from his adversary.

[26] *Dig.* 47.13.2 provides a remedy against those who conspire to accuse the innocent.

legal. For as it is legal to assemble one's friends for the protection of one's property, then all the more so in protection of the public's, as in *Dig.* 43.16.3.9.[27] Whenever one party wishes not only to resist, but to depose the others who are ruling, then if indeed they were to rise up against a just government, that would be simply illicit, as in *Cod.* 9.30.1[28] and the note there concerning someone who wished to depose a *podestà*.† But if the government which they wished to depose was tyrannical and of the worst kind, then it is licit to be of one faction and one name for that purpose, subject to two conditions: firstly, that by having recourse to a superior, it would not be possible for that tyranny to be deposed without great difficulty; secondly, that they do this for the public utility, in order to restore the condition [*status*†] of the city. It would be otherwise if they did this in order to install a new tyranny themselves, having expelled the others.

The proof of the first point is that it is licit for anyone to pronounce judgment on his own authority when he does not have access to a judge, as in *Cod.* 1.9.14[29] and the note there; *Dig.* 42.8.10.16;[30] C. 23 q. 2 c. 2.[31] If, therefore, this is licit for individual convenience, how much more so for the liberation of the commonwealth [*res publica*†] which all are allowed to defend, as in *Dig.* 39.1.5.20; 39.1.6.[32] Furthermore, if this is permitted to anyone against a ravager of the countryside or a deserter from the

---

[27] *Dig.* 43.16.3.9 does not explicitly mention assembling a group in establishing that 'Anyone who comes with arms we may repel with arms.'

[28] *Cod.* 9.30.1, 'On the Seditious and Those Who Dare to Assemble the People against the Commonwealth', decrees the severest penalties for those who 'attempt to stir up the populace [*plebem*]' and 'resist the public authorities'. Bartolus refers here to the gloss *tentaverit*: 'For he wanted to depose the *podestà*.' The preceding gloss *plebem* expands: 'Or a *castrum*.'†

[29] *Cod.* 1.9.14 forbids violent self-help against Jews and imposes legal process instead. Accursius's gloss *ultionem* allows self-help in some cases when no judge (and therefore court) is available.

[30] *Dig.* 42.8.10.16 defines the circumstances in which one of several creditors may unilaterally take what is owed him when he apprehends the debtor.

[31] *Decretum*, C. 23 q. 2 c. 2 is an excerpt from Augustine's *Quaestiones in Heptateuchum* (VI. q. 10). It does not justify violence by reference to the absence of a competent judge but merely notes, among other things, that 'just wars are usually defined as those which revenge injuries'.

[32] *Dig.* 39.1.5.20 and the immediately subsequent *Dig.* 39.1.6 are strange authorities in the context. The first compels a procurator† to give security for the payment of a fine when he is acting in defence of another person's rights, the second settles a further point about security arising from the first. *Dig.* 39.1.3.3 and 39.1.4 would provide stronger support for his point: any citizen can serve a notice of new work which is being carried out on public property because it is in the interests of the commonwealth to allow as many people as possible to defend it at law.

8

army, how much more ought it to be permitted against those who ravage the commonwealth itself and its general condition [*status*†], and bring it under the yoke of servitude.

The proof of the second point – that it is not licit for one's own utility – is that those who hold the commonwealth under the sway of tyranny detain it by force against the commonwealth itself or against a superior lord, not against some private individual. Therefore another person[33] who seeks to bring to an end such tyranny for his own utility uses illicit force, as in *Dig.* 43.16.1.30;[34] 43.16.12;[35] 43.16.18.[36] It is licit, then, for the public utility; and if he came to take action, so that uproar or tumult erupt in the city, he would not fall under *Cod.* 9.30.1, because he would be acting licitly, as has been said.[37] In support of this position I invoke the blessed Thomas Aquinas, in his *Summa theologiae*, IIa IIae, q. 42, art. 2 ad 3, where he says this: Tyrannical rule is not just, because it is not directed to the common good, but to the private good of the ruler.[38] And therefore disruption of this regime does not constitute sedition, unless perhaps when the regime of a tyrant is disrupted in so inordinate a fashion, that the subject multitude suffers more harm from the consequent disruption than from the rule of the tyrant.'

So I say that to assume the said names, although they signify division and faction, is nevertheless licit if it is done for a just and due end. For the apostle Paul 'knowing that one party was of the Sadducees and the other of the Pharisees, cried out in the council: "Men and brethren, I am a Pharisee and the son of a Pharisee"', *Acts* 23.[39] Yet I have seen many perish when they mounted sedition against tyrants, although they

---

[33] From the available variants we prefer *alius* to Quaglioni's *aliter*, because Bartolus's preceding comment expresses no contrasting or alternative state of affairs to which *aliter* could meaningfully relate.

[34] *Dig.* 43.16.1.30 allows someone who gained possession by force to use the usual legal remedy against forceful dispossession if another person then ejects him.

[35] *Dig.* 43.16.12 gives another example in which the principle outlined in the previous citation applies.

[36] *Dig.* 43.16.18 makes a tenant who prevents a buyer from entering the farm liable to the seller. Of the three passages just cited, this is the hardest to square with Bartolus's point. All of course relate to the illicit use of force by a sitting tenant, evidently for his own utility, but only the first two also make an incomer who uses force to evict a tenant liable, even when he has legal title.

[37] Above, n. 28.

[38] Bartolus here omits Aquinas's reference to Aristotle, *Politics*, 3.5, 1279b6 and *Ethics*, 8.10, 1160b8. Our translation deviates only slightly from that of R. W. Dyson, ed., *Aquinas: Political Writings* (Cambridge 2002), pp. 250–1.

[39] Verse 6.

9

were moved by a holy and just purpose.[40] However, because the aforesaid names denote division and schism, I think it is not right for an honest man to assume either of them, except for some weighty reason, by analogy with *Dig.* 36.1.65(63).8.[41]

IV

With regard to the fourth question – that is, how to prove that someone is of these sympathies – I say that there are three things to be proved.

First, that there are parties in the city.

Second, that they are called by such names.[42]

Third, that a certain person adheres to the party which is called by a certain name.

On these grounds it is concluded that he is of that sympathy. Let us examine them.

First, I have said that one must prove that there are parties in the city. On which point it must be noted that when there are two parties in a city, of which each has a share in rule, as in the city of Todi,[43] then the proof is easy. When there are two parties, of which one rules the city, and the other stands deposed but formerly ruled, then similarly the proof is easy: namely who was ruling shortly before, and who rules now. Sometimes a single city has been ruled from the distant past under one name, and then it is difficult to prove that someone is of a party other than that under whose name the city is ruled, as I shall immediately explain.

Secondly, I have said that one must prove that a certain party is called by a certain name; and that is easy.

Thirdly, I have said that it must be proved that a certain man adheres to that party. This can be proved in the city of Todi with the greatest ease, for there they are called to public office under that name and are not admitted otherwise.[44] So it is clear to what sympathy they belong, because they have performed a deed which cannot be performed without

[40] Quaglioni, *Politica e diritto*, p. 99, suggests that this sentence was originally a marginal gloss, not by Bartolus, which found its way into the text.
[41] *Dig.* 36.1.65(63).8. By the modern paragraph division of the *Digest*† Bartolus means §10 (*Si vero nominis*): there is no harm in taking the name of a respectable man if the praetor insists on this so that legacies may be conveyed to their intended recipients.
[42] Bartolus's formulation here is in the singular – *tali nomine* – but he must mean both Guelfs and Ghibellines.
[43] Above, p. 3.
[44] See Introduction, p. xix.

recourse to the right and name of that sympathy, as in *Dig.* 29.2.20.4.[45] Or it is sufficiently proved because he said so explicitly – namely that he belongs to that sympathy; for no one is considered to say what he has not turned over in his mind, as in *Dig.* 33.10.7.2,[46] or because he favoured that party in counsels and in arms and in other actions. Understand also that this applies to voluntary actions. For what if one party were outside the city, and the other which ruled the city committed troops against them? Certainly those who went would not, on this account, be said to belong to the same sympathy as the insiders, for they went on the orders of those who ruled the city, whom they necessarily had to obey. Hence, when the matter is in doubt, they are assumed to have acted more out of necessity than will, as in *Dig.* 29.2.6.4.[47] However, if nothing of the kind can be proved, it suffices if it can be proved of their ancestors, for a son is presumed to belong to the same sympathy as his father, as in *Cod.* 9.8.5.1;[48] *Dig.* 21.1.31.21.[49]

I return to what I have said about a city which has been ruled from ancient times under one name, and which does not have exiles by reason of faction, or if it has them, then not under the name at issue. For example, the city of Pisa[50] has been ruled from ancient times under the name of the Ghibellines, and although it has exiles, yet both insiders and outsiders go by this name. To explain: suppose that in Pisa there is a statute that no Guelf may be admitted to any office.[51] I say that this statute ought to be understood to apply to any person belonging to that sympathy within the city of Pisa and with respect to that city. For in doubt, statutes must be

---

[45] *Dig.* 29.2.20.4: someone is deemed to be acting as heir 'whenever he accepts what he could not accept if he did not hold the name and legal position of heir'.

[46] *Dig.* 33.10.7.2 (concerning a legacy of furniture) relates the opinion that nobody says what he does not intend.

[47] *Dig.* 29.2.6.4 is about a man who, mistakenly believing himself to be subject to the paternal power of another, accepted an inheritance on the instructions of his putative father. The text argues that under these circumstances he has not acquired the inheritance for himself or his 'father'. Bartolus returns to a later paragraph in *Dig.* 29.2.6 in *On the Tyrant* in order to support a similar point: below, p. 46.

[48] *Cod.* 9.8.5.1, on the *Lex Iulia maiestatis*,† notes that the sons of those convicted of treason are feared to have inherited the criminality of their fathers.

[49] *Dig.* 21.1.31.21: slaves of certain nationalities are reputed good, those from 'a notorious people' are considered bad.

[50] Bartolus acted as assessor at Pisa, before teaching at the university 1339–43.

[51] Bartolus may be thinking of ch. 160 of *Breve del popolo e delle compagne del comune di Pisa*, the 1330 vernacular version of the statutes of 1313: *Statuti inediti della Città di Pisa*, ed. F. Bonaini, 3 vols. (Florence 1854–7), vol. II, p. 631.

understood with respect to what is done relating to the territory[52] of the power enacting the statute, as in *Dig.* 2.1.20;[53] 42.5.12.1;[54] *Sext.* 1.2.2.[55] And therefore, because there is no such party within that city, it does not appear that someone can bear a sympathy towards something which does not exist, as in *Dig.* 45.1.56.8;[56] 46.1.16;[57] 50.17.178;[58] 45.3.26.[59]

Wherefore I say that if in the same province there were some city of Guelf sympathy intending to make an attempt on the government [*status†*] of the city of Pisa, and some citizen adhered to that city, giving assistance, counsel, and favour against the government of the city of Pisa, then he would truly be a Guelf, by analogy with *Dig.* 48.4.4.[60] For truly he commits [treason] within that city and against it.[61] But if you were to suppose a Pisan to be rector in the city of Perugia,[62] the government of which is Guelf, yet which is not hostile but friendly to the city of Pisa, then, although such a person is a Guelf in Perugia, he is nevertheless not on that account said to be a Guelf in Pisa, nor does he come within the terms of the statute. With respect to different situations someone may belong to different sympathies, as I have said, by analogy with *Dig.* 26.8.15.[63]

Furthermore, I say that if it were proved that someone was born of a Guelf line in the ancient sense, dating from the time of the conflict between the church and Emperor Frederick, nevertheless he is not on

---

[52] We incline to the variant signalled by Quaglioni, *Politica e diritto*, p. 142, line 223.

[53] *Dig.* 2.1.20: one may disobey an officer who administers justice beyond the limits of his territory.

[54] *Dig.* 42.5.12.1 limits the authorization issued by a judge to seize and sell property to the locality administered by that judge.

[55] *Sext.* 1.2.2, *Ut animarum*, a decretal of Boniface VIII (1294–1303), concludes: 'For it is not without fault to obey a judge outside his territory.'

[56] *Dig.* 45.1.56.8 gives an example of an obligation lapsing when its object, in this case a slave, dies before the obligation is fulfilled.

[57] *Dig.* 46.1.16: 'No one can incur obligation as a surety to one to whom the principal promisor is not under an obligation.'

[58] *Dig.* 50.17.178: 'When the principal case does not stand, for the most part, those which follow do not have any standing either.'

[59] *Dig.* 45.3.26 begins: 'There cannot be a usufruct without a person entitled.'

[60] *Dig.* 48.4.4 lists the misdemeanours for which a Roman citizen will be guilty of treason under the *Lex Iulia maiestatis.*†

[61] English requires a substantive here; our choice of 'treason' is justified by Bartolus's immediately preceding legal citation.

[62] In 1230 it became a legal requirement that the *podestà*† be a foreigner: S. R. Blanshei, *Perugia, 1260–1340: Conflict and Change in a Medieval Italian Urban Society*, Transactions of the American Philosophical Society, n.s. 66, pt. 2 (Philadelphia, PA 1976), p. 54.

[63] *Dig.* 26.8.15, allows for the same tutor† to be both the defendant and the plaintiff. Cf. above, n. 20.

this account said to be a Guelf now, in the sense of which the statute speaks, as I have said above. Nor do I consider reputation or common opinion about someone sufficient proof. For by law someone is believed to be of the same sympathy as his country: it is one of the precepts of the law of nations 'that we obey our parents and our country', as in *Dig.* 1.1.2.[64] Therefore we should not come to the opposite conclusion solely on the basis of reputation or suspicion.

Because of the difficulty of proof in these cases, in some cities all who are said to belong to a certain sympathy are written down in a particular book, so that this may be shown by consulting this book; but this is odious and contrary to equity.

Yet how to prove that one city, or *castrum*,[†] or any sort of community belongs to a certain sympathy is a doubtful matter. In order to clarify it, suppose that there is a statute in the city of Perugia to the effect that any citizen who mounts a cavalry or infantry attack against any other Guelf territory should be punished by a certain penalty.[65] It happens that a certain nobleman was prosecuted for this offence. The prosecution had to prove that the territory was Guelf, the defence that it was Ghibelline.[66] And so the mode of proof was in doubt; and I do not consider reputation or what was common surmise to be sufficient proof, as I have said. So it is the mode of proof which is in doubt.

I answer that I understand a territory to be of the same sympathy as those who rule it, as in *Dig.* 35.1.97;[67] 34.5.20(21).[68] With regard to those who rule cities, there are various modes [of proof]. For some express this when they take up office as rectors of those cities, that is, that they will exercise office for the sake of the standing [*status*[†]] and honour of such and such a party. And whenever the aforesaid conditions are contained in the statutes of these cities, then the proof of these things is clear. Whenever there are cities in which the officials are mixed, with so many Guelfs and so many Ghibellines, and yet there are more officials who are of one

---

[64] *Dig.* 1.1.2 lists the duty to obey one's *patria*, the duty to obey one's parents, and religious duty to God as obligations created by the *ius gentium*[†] or law of nations.

[65] *Statuti di Perugia dell'anno MCCCXLII*, ed. G. degli Azzi, 2 vols. (Rome 1913–16), Bk. 3, ch. 129, vol. II, pp. 143–4.

[66] We have been unable to identify this episode.

[67] *Dig.* 35.1.97: a town (*municipium*)[†] is understood to take an oath (in order to obtain a legacy) when those who conduct its affairs do so.

[68] *Dig.* 34.5.20(21) rules that a legacy made to an illicit collegiate body will be invalid unless made to the members individually, who would accordingly receive it not corporately but as individuals.

sympathy, then the city falls to that party of whose sympathy there are more officials; and the greater number should rule, as in *Dig.* 50.1.19;[69] 2.14.9;[70] 41.1.27.2.[71] But if there are equal numbers in rule, as in Todi, then we must say that it is neither Guelf nor Ghibelline, but a third species, namely common, as in *Dig.* 41.1.27.2. There are some cities and *castra*† which are ruled straightforwardly, without the name of any faction; then it should be established whether there are factions in the city or province, and to which party the said territory has adhered or shown favour, as I have said above concerning a private person. But if this cannot be ascertained, then no assumption should be made about either one sympathy or the other, although it may be possible to do so. And in practice there are many men and many lands which adhere to neither of the aforesaid sympathies, which is at all events most obvious in cities beyond the Alps.

V

As regards the fifth question, namely how to prove that someone has changed sympathy – and I am talking about someone who is known to have belonged to a particular sympathy, for that which did not exist cannot be removed or changed, as in *Dig.* 28.3.5;[72] 35.1.96[73] – I say that these factions, as I have stated, are certain sympathies, just as possession consists in a certain sympathy, and an intention to possess. And it is written 'by the ancients ... that no one can himself change the grounds of his possession', except by the intervention of some external cause, as in *Dig.* 41.2.3.19;[74] 41.2.19.1;[75] 41.3.33.1,[76] and similar passages. So in

---

[69] *Dig.* 50.1.19: 'What the majority of the senate decides is treated as the decision of the entire body.'

[70] *Dig.* 2.14.9 counts several persons as one person if they sue by or are liable under the same legal remedy.

[71] *Dig.* 41.1.27.2 awards ownership of an object welded together from materials belonging to two people to the one whose portion predominates.

[72] *Dig.* 28.3.5 argues that the birth of a posthumous child does not invalidate the institution of an heir in a will if the latter has already been nullified by the failure to meet a condition stipulated in it.

[73] *Dig.* 35.1.96: if a usufruct in a slave is granted by will to someone on condition that if he loses that usufruct, the slave will be freed, the slave is not freed if the grantee dies before the testator.

[74] *Dig.* 41.2.3.19 cites this principle as an opinion of earlier jurists.

[75] *Dig.* 41.2.19.1 cites the same principle.

[76] *Dig.* 41.3.33.1 subjects this principle to a caveat but otherwise endorses it.

this case no one can change his faction [*partialitas*†] and sympathy [*affec-tio*†] without the intervention of some external cause. And that a cause must supervene for a change of sympathy or will is proved naturally. For since the object of the will is a good, either actual or apparent, accordingly someone adheres to one party because it seems to him good. And so when he changes his will, it is necessary that there should be something on account of which he abandons that will and adheres to the other [party]. That is why legislators were moved to say that no one can change the grounds of his possession unless an external cause supervenes. The causes of change which we commonly see are: supervening enmity toward some other individual more powerful than oneself within the same sympathy; or if an inheritance or other great gain has fallen to someone which he cannot conveniently have unless he leaves one party and adheres to the other; or if a new marriage tie joins him to the opposing party, as in *Dig.* 3.3.8–10;[77] 3.3.22.[78] If, therefore, these events happened to occur at the same time as desertion from a party, they afford proof of a change in sympathy, according to the said laws.

What, however, if someone simply stated that he had changed his will and wished to adhere to the other party, and is willing to swear to this effect; is he to be believed? I say that we must inspect the character of persons, as *Dig.* 49.16.5.6[79] shows. What is said in D. 48.1–2,[80] concerning a gentile who has recently come to the faith, applies.

---

[77] The three passages at *Dig.* 3.3.8–10 excuse a procurator† from accepting trial after he has been appointed if a personal enmity has since arisen between him and his principal, or if he has risen in rank, or if he has since received an inheritance.

[78] *Dig.* 3.3.22 allows a principal to change his procurator if the latter has since become a relative by marriage or the heir of the other party.

[79] *Dig.* 49.16.5.6: the word of a soldier claiming to have escaped the enemy after being captured should carry weight and supports his case for reinstatement if he had been a reliable soldier prior to his capture.

[80] *Decretum*, D. 48 cc. 1–2 (from the Council of Nicaea of 325 and a letter of Pope Gregory the Great written in 599) stress the importance of earlier habits and reputation of members of the clergy.

On the Government of a City

Since this is the final part of the Tiber, and thus within the city of Rome –
which is the capital of the world – let us therefore examine certain aspects
of the manner of governing a city; and this investigation is twofold.

First, the manner of governing in relation to laws, either written
or unwritten, as in *Inst.* 1.2.3.[1] This I am not pursuing, because it has
already been treated in different places in different ways.[2]

Secondly, the manner of governing in relation to the persons of the
governors: and certain aspects of this require examination.

First, let us look at how many ways there are of governing a city;
secondly, let us determine which is the better way and, third, which is
the worse. Let us consider some everyday questions concerning these
matters.

I

First – that is, how many ways there are of governing a city – three good
ways of governing may be gathered from our laws and, opposed to them,
three bad ways. These ways Aristotle describes more clearly in *Politics*,
bk. 3, where he gives them their names.[3] But we shall both mention those
names, and also introduce names more in keeping with the present time.

---

[1] *Inst.* 1.2.3 divides the law of Rome into written and unwritten law.
[2] Bartolus appears to be alluding to discussions of government by written law, and
government by custom, such as at *Dig.* 1.1.6, where civil law is said to be partly written,
partly unwritten.
[3] Aristotle, *Politics*, 3.7, 1279a23–b11; Giles of Rome, *De regimine principum*, 3.2.2 (Rome
1607, repr. Aalen 1967), pp. 453–5.

After the expulsion of the kings, there were in the city of Rome three modes of governing. The first was by the people, as in *Dig.* 1.2.2.3–9.[4] And Aristotle calls this regime '*politia*' or 'political'. We, however, call it 'a government by the people', and we do so when such a regime is good and when the common good of all men, each according to his standing, is considered first and foremost by those who rule. But if that multitude of rulers seeks its own advantage, and the oppression of the rich or of another group, then it is a bad form of government, and Aristotle calls it by the Greek name 'democracy'. We, however, call it a perverted people. And concerning these two modes of governing we have *Dig.* 50.4.3.15,[5] where the form of government is said to be good when honours and responsibilities are equally divided according to due degree; and bad when they are divided unequally, because some men are overburdened and others let off lightly. And on account of this the commonwealth [*res publica*†] is destroyed, as is evident there.[6]

The second mode of governing in the city of Rome was by senators; thus by a few rich, good, and prudent men, as in *Dig.* 1.2.2.9.[7] In that case if those few strive for the common good, the rule is good, and is called 'aristocracy' by Aristotle, which is the same thing as rule by the good. But in the city, it was called the government of the senators, and in Venice it is called the government of the grandees [*maiores*]. Yet the more common name is what I said before, that is, rule or government by the good. But if those few do not strive for the common good, but are only some rich and more powerful men oppressing the others and bent on their own gain, then the regime is bad and is called 'oligarchy' by Aristotle, which is the same thing as the rule of the rich or the government of the bad: which name is common enough, whence we have *Dig.* 1.18.6.2.[8]

---

[4] *Dig.* 1.2.2 describes the changes in Rome's constitution over the centuries. The paragraphs Bartolus cites here cover the period between the expulsion of Rome's first kings and the devolution of governmental power to the senate.

[5] *Dig.* 50.4.3.15 enjoins provincial governors to distribute civic burdens and offices fairly.

[6] The danger in *Dig.* 50.4.3.15 is that cities might otherwise be abandoned.

[7] *Dig.* 1.2.2.9 does not mention the qualities of the senators, merely the reasons why the senate came to exercise authority: it was hard for the *plebs*, and even harder for the entire citizenry, to assemble once the population had grown.

[8] *Dig.* 1.18.6.2 does not contain the actual term 'oligarchy', but Bartolus evidently identifies with the vices of oligarchy the ills this passage seeks to avert – the text urges provincial governors to prevent 'more influential people' from mistreating 'those of lower station'.

17

The third mode of governing is by one man, concerning which there is *Dig.* 1.2.2.11.[9] And according to Aristotle this is called kingship [*regnum*]. But if he is a universal lord, we call it empire, as in the same passage;[10] if he is a particular lord, we sometimes call it a kingdom [*regnum*], sometimes a duchy, a margraviate, or a county, as in *Feud.* 2.54(55).4.[11] We call kingship by the common name of natural lordship, and we do so when the said lord aims at the common and a good end. If, however, he aims at a bad end and his own advantage, then according to Aristotle it is called tyranny, for indeed it is so termed according to laws and tradition, as in *Cod.* 1.2.16;[12] 1.2.6 and the note there;[13] *Dig.* 42.4.7.4.[14]

So we have six ways of governing, three good and three bad, each one called by its own name. Nevertheless, every bad form of governing can be called by the common term tyranny: that is, tyranny of the people, tyranny of the few, and tyranny of one.

Moreover, there is a seventh type of governing, the worst, which now exists in the city of Rome.[15] For in Rome there are many tyrants who are so strong in different localities, that one cannot prevail against another. Indeed, the common government of the whole city is so enfeebled, that it cannot overcome any of these tyrants, nor [prevail] against any follower of these tyrants, except to the extent that they allow. This form of governing Aristotle did not posit, and rightly: for it is a monstrosity. For what if someone should see a single body having one common head that is

---

[9] *Dig.* 1.2.2.11 describes such an important moment in the history of the Roman constitution that it is worth quoting in full:

> Most recently, just as there was seen to have been a transition toward fewer ways of establishing law, a transition effected by stages under the dictation of circumstances, it has come about that the commonwealth has had to be entrusted to one man (for the senate had been unable latterly to govern all the provinces honestly). An emperor [*princeps*†], therefore, having been appointed, to him was given the right that what he had decided be deemed to be law.

[10] *Imperium.*† The word does not appear in *Dig.* 1.2.2.11.
[11] *Feud.* 2.54(55).4 – we correct Quaglioni's reference – prohibits the division of a duchy, margraviate, or county.
[12] Below, *On the Tyrant*, n. 59.
[13] Below, *On the Tyrant*, n. 15.
[14] *Dig.* 42.4.7.4 lists 'the cruelty of a tyrant' among several legitimate reasons for going into hiding.
[15] Cola di Rienzo's tribunician regime of 1347 had purported to solve the anarchy in the city, but exacerbated the problem. The chaos which ensued defies a brief summary, but is accurately characterized by Bartolus: F. Gregorovius, *History of the City of Rome in the Middle Ages*, trans. A. Hamilton, 8 vols. in 13 (London 1894–1902), vol. VI, pt. 1, pp. 231–376, pt. 2, pp. 377–89.

feeble, and many other common heads which are stronger than the one, and which are mutually hostile? Clearly this would be a monster, and so this form of governing is called monstrous. For this has come about by divine sufferance, in order to show that all worldly glory is unstable. Thus the city of Rome, which is the capital of manners and the capital of polities [*politiae*], ends up as such a monstrosity in respect of its government: to express it more accurately, it is neither a government, nor does it take the form of a government, by analogy with *Dig.* 1.5.14;[16] *Extra* 1.31.14.[17]

II

Secondly, we should see which is the better manner of governing. This inquiry is necessary for jurists, since when universal lords are negotiating the reform of a city, they either consult jurists or entrust the matter to them, or, when these jurists themselves are acting as assessors, any complaint about the government of a city is put before them. So we must investigate what the better manner of governing is. Aristotle treats this subject in *Politics*, iii;[18] but it is more clearly examined by Giles of Rome, of the order of Augustinian Hermits, in his book *De regimine principum*, who was a great philosopher and a master of theology.[19] So I shall present his opinion and follow his reasoning; but I shall not use his words or those of Aristotle, for jurists, to whom I address myself, would not know them. But I shall use their reasoning and I shall prove it by the laws; afterwards I shall describe my own views.

So Giles says that there are three good ways of governing, which are discussed above.[20] The first way of governing is that of the multitude or by the people, and this is good if it aims at the right end. The second way of governing is better: the government of the few. And the third way is the best: namely monarchy, or the governance of a single king. This last point – namely that a regime of one is the best type of rule – he proves by four reasons, from which two other points may be concluded.

---

[16] *Dig.* 1.5.14 excludes those born with monstrous deformities from the category of children.
[17] The canon *Quoniam in plerisque*, promulgated by Innocent III at the Fourth Lateran Council (1215), prohibits 'one and the same city from having two different bishops, as one body with two heads, as if a monster'.
[18] Aristotle, *Politics*, 3.13, 1283a23–1284b34.
[19] Giles of Rome, *De regimine principum*, 3.2.3–4, pp. 456–60.
[20] Giles of Rome, *De regimine principum*, 3.2.3, pp. 456–8.

First as follows: peace and the unity of the citizens ought to be the final aim of the ruler, as in *Dig.* 1.18.13.*pr.*;[21] *Auth.* 3.4.2.[22] But this peace and unity can be better achieved and preserved if there is rule by one rather than by many: therefore it is better to be ruled by one. The proof is as follows: under the rule of many there cannot be peace except insofar as those many are one in will. And this is obvious, because if they quarrel, their action is impeded by conflict, as in *Dig.* 27.10.7.3; 8.3.28, and other similar passages.[23] And on this basis the argument goes: 'A thing belongs better to that thing because of which it belongs',[24] as in the Authentic *Multo magis* after *Cod.* 1.2.14; *Dig.* 12.2.24.[25] But the rule of many is good on account of unity; far better still, therefore, is the government of unity itself which is exercised by one.

Secondly, this is proven because the city itself and commonwealth is rendered more powerful; the reason being that the more virtue is unified, the stronger it is, rather than being dispersed among many, as in *Auth.* 6.13.1.[26] If, therefore, all civil capacity [*civilis potentia*] is concentrated in one, it will be more effective; and by means of that the ruler [*princeps*†], on account of the greater power, will be able to govern better.

Thirdly, an art or skill is better the more it imitates nature, as in *Dig.* 1.7.15 and 16.[27] But the whole city is one person and one artificial,

---

[21] *Dig.* 1.18.13.*pr.*: a provincial governor should ensure his province is peaceful and orderly.

[22] *Nov.* 17.2 orders provincial governors to 'take care to prevent all tumults among the people and keep complete peace in the cities'.

[23] *Dig.* 27.10.7.3 mentions a case of disagreement between two curators, *Dig.* 8.3.28 a disagreement between two co-owners.

[24] Aristotle, *Posterior Analytics*, 1.2, 72a30, cited by Giles of Rome, *De regimine principum*, 3.2.3, p. 456, whom Bartolus paraphrases here. The principle set out by Aristotle is as follows: 'For that which causes an attribute to apply to a subject always possesses that attribute in a still greater degree' (in the translation of H. Tredennick, *Aristotle: Posterior Analytics: Topica* (Cambridge, MA 1960)).

[25] By implication of its position after the Authentic *Sicut alienatio*, the Authentic *Multo magis* prohibits alienation of monasteries 'even more' than of the property belonging to them; Giles of Rome also employs the phrase *multo magis*. Digest 12.2.24 argues that a father will be 'even more' able to profit from an oath sworn by his son. The phrase 'A thing belongs better' etc. is Bartolus's only comment on this Authentic in his own commentary on the Code: *In primam Codicis partem commentaria* (Turin 1574), fo. 20vb.

[26] *Nov.* 85.1 restricts the right to manufacture and sell weapons to specific persons.

[27] The end of *Dig.* 1.7.15 limits adoption of certain people by others, *Dig.* 1.7.16 explaining that adoption 'may take place as between those persons for whom the natural relationship could in principle hold good'.

imaginary man, as in *Dig.* 5.1.76;[28] 46.1.22.[29] But in a natural man we see one head and many members: so if a city were to be ruled thus it would be ruled best, because this imitates nature more closely. To the same effect see *Extra* 1.31.14;[30] and this seems to be clinched by C. 7 q. 1 c. 41,[31] where bees and dumb creatures, who lack reason, constitute a single king over themselves.[32]

Fourthly, Giles says that this is established through experience, since he says that he sees 'provinces not living under one king to be in penury, not enjoying peace, and to be troubled by dissensions and wars. But those which live in the opposite condition know no war, rejoice in peace, and flourish in plenty.'[33] From which he concludes that the rule of the people[34] or of the multitude is good, if it aims at a single end; but the rule of a few is better, because it has greater unity. But monarchy, or the rule of a single king, is the best, because there unity is found most perfectly.

But against these reasons Giles himself advances various arguments,[35] which he draws from the writings of Aristotle, and he endeavours to answer these. I shall test them by reference to the laws. In order to prove this, he first points out that there are three requirements for any good ruler.

First, perfect rational discernment, for him to know the just from the unjust, and to distinguish the licit from the illicit, as in *Dig.* 1.1.1.1.[36]

Second, he ought to have right intention.

Third, he ought to have perfect steadfastness.

---

[28] *Dig.* 5.1.76: the replacement of some or all the judges in a case does not make it into a new case; the same, *mutatis mutandis*, goes for a legion of soldiers, and, most significantly for Bartolus here, a people remains the same now as a hundred years ago even though nobody is alive from that time.

[29] *Dig.* 46.1.22 states that 'an inheritance functions in place of a person, like a *municipium*,† a *decuria*† or a partnership'.

[30] For *Extra* 1.31.14, see above, n. 17.

[31] *Decretum*, C. 7 q. 1 c. 41 is an excerpt from a letter attributed to Pope Gregory the Great (in reality by Jerome), beginning: 'Among the bees there is one ruler; cranes follow one in elegant order; there is one emperor, one judge in a province.'

[32] Bees are also discussed by Giles of Rome, *De regimine principum*, 3.2.3, p. 457.

[33] Giles of Rome, *De regimine principum*, 3.2.3, p. 458, reproduced almost *verbatim* by Bartolus here.

[34] Bartolus employs Giles of Rome's term *regimen populi* here, not *regimen ad populum*, which is Bartolus's usual formulation: Giles of Rome, *De regimine principum*, 3.2.3, p. 457.

[35] Giles of Rome, *De regimine principum*, 3.2.4, pp. 458–60, following Aristotle, *Politics*, 3.11, 1281a40, 1281b16; 3.15, 1286a30–2; 5.1, 1302a9–15; 5.9, 1309a34–9.

[36] *Dig.* 1.1.1.1 says of jurists (not rulers) that they discriminate 'between fair and unfair' and distinguish the licit from the illicit.

These are proved from the definition of justice, where it is said to be the constant and perpetual will to render to each his right, as in *Dig.* 1.1.10.[37] From these three requirements, three arguments arise against what has already been said.

First: that the more there are, the more they see, and they have a clearer rational discernment than one man, as in *Cod.* 6.22.8;[38] so in this respect it is better to be ruled by many.

Second: that the intention of the ruler is right when he considers the public good more than his own, as in *Cod.* 6.51.1.14.[39] But if the multitude has dominion, even if it aims at its own good, it will thereby fall less short of the common good than if one man were to rule and aim at his own advantage: so it is better to be ruled by many.

Thirdly, the ruler ought to have perfect steadfastness, so that he is not corrupted by anger or greed, because justice ought to be constant and everlasting, as in *Dig.* 1.1.10, cited above. But it is more difficult for a multitude to grow angry and be corrupted than for one man, as in *Cod.* 6.22.8,[40] cited above, and by analogy with *Cod.* 4.20.9.[41] So it is better to be ruled by many.

Answering which, Giles says that one king or prince ought to have with him many counsellors and men of the worthier sort: and therefore he will see just like the many, nor can he lightly be corrupted unless the whole council is corrupted. But if this king should follow his own judgment, then he is not a king but a tyrant: and so it is not good for such a man to have dominion. So says Giles.[42]

I do not think that these statements should be understood straightforwardly; and for this reason, speaking as a lawyer, I would say in explanation of the above, first, that not all rule by one man is called the rule of a king. For sometimes there is one man who rules, and yet he is a judge,

---

[37] *Dig.* 1.1.10, continuing: 'The basic principles of law [*ius*] are: to live honourably, not to harm any other person, to render to each his own.'

[38] *Cod.* 6.22.8 prescribes the participation of multiple witnesses ('so many eyes ... so many senses ... so many hands') in the recording of a blind person's will, so as to preclude fraud.

[39] Here Justinian, in renouncing his imperial privilege of claiming the property in lapsed wills, explains that 'what benefits everyone in common is preferable to the interest of Our Privy Purse'.

[40] Above, n. 38.

[41] *Cod.* 4.20.9 lays down that no judge is to accept the testimony of a sole witness.

[42] Giles of Rome, *De regimine principum*, 3.2.4, p. 460. Both Giles and, following him, Bartolus refer to the corruption of the whole *consilium*, translated immediately above as 'counsel'; the second instance, however, clearly alludes to a group of individual advisors and is therefore rendered as 'council' here.

as are provincial governors and proconsuls – as in the titles on the office of a governor[43] and on the offices of proconsul and legate[44] – and as are the *podestà*† and rectors of cities as in *Cod.* 7.44.3, and the note there;[45] *Cod.* 1.55 on defenders† of cities; and throughout *Auth.* 3.2.[46] For theirs is to judge according to the laws. They do not hold the rank [*status*†] of kings, but one appropriate to ministers; nor do regalian rights belong to them but to the cities they rule, or to another superior, or to the fisc, as in *Cod.* 1.54.5; 3.26.1; *Dig.* 49.14.1.[47] And God ruled the people of Israel through judges of this sort for a very long time, as we learn throughout the book of Judges. But sometimes one man rules a city or province, who makes law as he pleases, and everything belongs to him, and this is called the rule of a king.

Let us now see what the right of this king is, so that we may learn whether it is good to be ruled by kings. Concerning this the Lord speaks thus through the prophet Samuel, 1 *Kings* 8:[48] 'This will be the right of the king who shall hold sway over you. He will take your sons and place them in his chariots; and he will make them his horsemen and make them run before his chariots. And he will appoint some as his tribunes and centurions; others as cultivators of his fields and reapers of crops; others again will be makers of arms and of his chariots. He will make your daughters his perfumers, cooks, and bakers. Moreover, he will take your fields and your vineyards and best olive groves and give them to his slaves. He will take a tithe of your crops and the fruit of your vineyards in order to give it to his eunuchs and his household. And he will take away your best slaves, both male and female, and your asses, and put them to his own use. He will take a tithe of your flocks, and you shall be his slaves', etc. Behold the word of God. According to this, to be ruled by kings seems to be worst of all: because they inflict so many ills on their subjects and – what is worse – they reduce them to servitude, which is compared to death, as in *Dig.* 50.17.209.[49]

---

[43] *Dig.* 1.18.
[44] *Dig.* 1.16, *Cod.* 1.35.
[45] In his gloss *proferant*, Accursius relates what the text says about judges to the *podestà*.
[46] *Nov.* 15 regulates defenders of cities (*defensores civitatum*).
[47] *Cod.* 1.54.5 and *Cod.* 3.26.1 make it clear that fines and confiscated property are passed by the relevant judge either to the treasury or other public organs; *Dig.* 49.14.1 covers denunciations to the fisc.
[48] 1 *Kings* 8, 11–17.
[49] *Dig.* 50.17.209: 'We compare slavery closely with death.'

But these words are explained by the holy doctors:[50] not all these things should be considered lawful for a king, but only those which pertain to the public good. The king will do those things presented above as grievous when he has begun to be a tyrant, which happens easily enough; and because this was going to happen to them, he prophesied in this fashion. So when he says 'This will be the right of the king who shall hold sway over you', these words should be understood as if he were saying: this is not lawful for every king, but he who will hold sway over you shall usurp this right for himself. For the Lord was displeased that they had sought a king, as is said in the same chapter.[51] And this seems to be true from what we read in *Deuteronomy* 17,[52] where what a good and true king ought to do is plainly shown. For the Lord says of the future king: 'When he has been constituted, he will not multiply his horses, nor will he, by augmenting his cavalry, lead the people back into Egypt, especially when the Lord has ordered you by no means whatsoever to return along that same road. He shall not have many wives who will distract his mind, nor an immense weight of silver and gold. But after he has sat on the throne of his kingdom, he shall write down for himself in a book a copy of this law, receiving the exemplar from the priests of the tribe of Levi, and he shall keep it with him and read it all the days of his life, in order that he should learn to fear the Lord his God and to keep His words and ceremonies, which are commanded in the law. Nor shall he raise his heart in pride over his brothers, nor deviate either to the right or the left, in order that he and his sons should reign long over Israel.'

These are the words of God, so let us investigate them further. For He says: 'When he has been constituted.' This implies that someone has to be constituted king by another person, not assume the kingdom himself on his own authority: for then he would not be a king, but a tyrant, as will be said below.

---

[50] From the examples cited by Quaglioni, *Politica e diritto*, p. 158, n. 54, see especially Nicholas of Lyra's *Postilla* to 1 Kings 8 for the distinction between the rightful powers of a king who governs for the common good and the unlawful acts of a king who has become a tyrant: *Biblia sacra cum glossis, interlineari et ordinaria, Nicolai Lyrani postilla et moralitatibus* […], 7 vols. (Lyons 1545), vol. II, fo. 71ra–b; Aquinas employs the same criterion: *Summa theologiae* Ia IIae, q. 105, art. 1 ad 5; further P. Buc, 'Book of Kings: Nicholas of Lyra's Mirror for Princes', in P. Krey and L. Smith, eds., *Nicholas of Lyra: The Senses of Scripture* (Leyden 2000), pp. 83–109, esp. 86–8.

[51] 1 *Kings* 8, 6–8.

[52] Verses 16–20.

24

Then He says: 'He will not multiply his horses', as if to say, let him shun pomp and vainglory, hence he will not multiply his horses. For that is to multiply in excess of what it would be expedient for him to have.

'Nor will he lead the people back into Egypt', etc.: these words may be understood literally, as they stand, that a king of the Jews ought never to seek to occupy the land of Egypt. But they may also be understood allegorically, as if He said: let the king not lead the people back into servitude, with servitude being signified by Egypt, where the people was held in captivity. So with these words He forbids that the people should be weighed down by personal burdens which are, as it were, a species of servitude.

'He will not have many wives': above He forbade vainglory, here He forbids the king wantonness. For this severs the mind of a king from true judgment not only regarding men, but also God, as happened with Solomon, who became an idolator, as in 3 *Kings* 11.[53]

'Nor an immense weight of silver and gold': here He prohibits avarice. For just as there is spending in excess for the sake of pomp, and on this account the people is burdened, so for the sake of avarice too much is extorted from the people.

'After he has sat on the throne of his kingdom, he shall write down for himself in a book a copy of this law' [*Deuteronomium*]: above He forbade that certain things be done, here He commands that certain things be done.

'A copy of this law': according to Isidore, 'Deuteronomy' is to be interpreted as 'the second law', that is, the prefigurement of the evangelical law.[54] Therefore the king ought to be faithful and Catholic, and this the law commands: Authentic *Statuimus* after *Cod.* 1.4.19.[55]

'Receiving the exemplar from the priests of the tribe of Levi': in these priests Holy Mother Church is figured, from whom every king ought to receive the exemplar of Christian law.

'Nor shall he raise his heart in pride': here He reverts to forbidding another thing, that is, pride of the heart, which is the root of all evils.

---

[53] 3 *Kings* 11, 1–5.
[54] Isidore of Seville, *Etymologiarum sive originum, libri xx*, ed. W. M. Lindsay, 2 vols. (Oxford 1911), 6.2.7, vol. II, p. 218.
[55] The Authentic *Statuimus* is one of eleven excerpts, inserted into Justinian's *Code*† by the glossators† of Bologna, from the constitution promulgated by Frederick II and Pope Honorius III at Frederick's imperial coronation in 1220. It demands an oath from all holders of public office that they will extirpate heretics in their jurisdiction.

'Over his brothers': it appears, therefore, that those who are subject to a king are not slaves, but brothers. And so what was said in the preceding authority is understood not of a true king, but of a tyrant.

'Nor deviate either to the right or the left': as if to say: judgment should be right, not corrupted by love or hate;[56] which is as if to say, he should be just. So a good king should be faithful, Christian, and just, not pompous, not an oppressor of his subjects, not wanton, not greedy nor proud.

On the other hand, there are other things which a king should do, which are set out in C. 23 q. 5 cc. 23, 40.[57] But the things which are set out there should be understood in accordance with what has already been said. Although it is laid down there what the king should do and what manner of man he should be in himself, yet it is not set out what a king may exact from his subjects and whence he should take the expenses which befit the royal majesty. But we have this expressly set out in *Feud.* 2.56.1,[58] where it is said that all tributes, tariffs, and public dues, which are individually named, belong to the king; and it also belongs to the king to impose taxes in case of necessity, as is stated there. Moreover, it is also confirmed by the law of the *Digest*† that kings have all power, as in *Dig.* 1.2.2.14.[59]

Having seen what the right of a king is, let us return to the question of whether it is advantageous to a city or people to be ruled by a king. I say that if we consider a king insofar as he is good according to the said criteria, the best rule is the rule of a king, for the reasons given. And this is how I understand what Aristotle and Giles say about this. But if we consider what can come about, because a king himself – or his descendants – sometimes turns into a tyrant, then I say that we ought to consider what can come about when that with which we are concerned tends naturally and probably in this direction, as in *Dig.* 19.2.9.1; 39.2.13.2.[60] Otherwise this ought not to be considered, because '[to await] the chance of

---

[56] We prefer the variant reading noted by Quaglioni, *Politica e diritto*, p. 160, line 270.

[57] These passages in Jerome's Commentary on *Jeremiah* 22, 3 and the spurious *Libellus de duodecim gradibus abusionum*, misattributed by Gratian (and others), to Cyprian, together constitute a significant list of royal duties.

[58] *Feud.* 2.56.1: a twelfth-century list of regalian rights in the kingdom of Lombardy.

[59] *Dig.* 1.2.2.14: 'It is indubitable that from the foundation of the city [*civitas*], the kings had entire power in all that now pertains to magistrates.'

[60] *Dig.* 19.2.9.1: a lessee who should have foreseen a possible outcome is liable for costs because he did not; *Dig.* 39.2.13.2 similarly penalizes a house-owner who should have taken certain precautions against the foreseeable collapse of a neighbouring house. The principle Bartolus cites from *Dig.* 45.1.83.5 invalidates a stipulation to deliver a freeman when he becomes a slave.

adverse fortune [falling on a freeman is neither civil nor natural]', as in *Dig.* 45.1.83.5.

Given this, I make a threefold division of cities or peoples. For a large city or people [*gens*] of the first magnitude is one thing; a larger city or people of the second magnitude is another; and the largest city or people of the third magnitude is yet another.

If we are talking about a large nation or people of the first magnitude, then I say that it is not advantageous for it to be ruled by a king. First, this is proved by the text, because when the city of Rome was of the first magnitude, it expelled the kings, because they had turned to tyranny, as in *Dig.* 1.2.2.3; 1.2.2.1.[61] Secondly, it is proved by reason: it is in the nature of kings to be magnificent in spending on a grand scale, as in *Auth.* 7.4[62] on immense gifts, and by Aristotle in the *Ethics*.[63] But the royal revenues of a single large people of the first magnitude would not suffice to cover royal expenses, for which reason he would need to extort from his subjects, and would become a tyrant. So the condition [*status*†] of such a king tends as a matter of course towards tyranny; and therefore it is not a good form of government, if we consider what may come about as a matter of course. This is the reason why it displeased God that the people sought a king, as in 1 *Kings* 8.[64] Nor is it advantageous for such a people to be ruled by a few; for instance, the rich men of the city. For in these cities the rich happen to be few in number. This will turn out in one of two ways.

The first is that the multitude of the people would resent the rule of those few, however well they ruled, as happened in the city of Siena. For a certain order [*ordo*] of rich men ruled well and prudently for almost eighty years; yet because the multitude of the people was resentful, they had always to stand firm with a large military force. And that order was deposed on the arrival of the lord Charles IV, the most illustrious emperor

---

[61] *Dig.* 1.2.2.3 and 1.2.2.1 read, respectively, 'Then, when the kings were expelled under a Tribunician enactment ...'; and 'The fact is that at the outset of our city [*civitas*], the citizen body decided to conduct its affairs without fixed statute law or determinate legal rights; everything was governed by the kings under their own hand.'

[62] *Nov.* 92 is concerned with immoderate gifts by fathers to sons.

[63] Aristotle, *Ethics*, 4.2, 1122b30–5. Quaglioni, *Politica e diritto*, p. 20 n. 13, plausibly suggests Ptolemy of Lucca's continuation of Aquinas's *De regimine principum* as Bartolus's direct source; see *De regno sive de regimine principum ad regem Cypri*, 2.7, in Thomas Aquinas, *Opuscula omnia necnon opera minora*, ed. R. P. Johannes Perrier (Paris 1949), vol. I, pp. 280–3.

[64] 1 *Kings* 8, 6–8.

of the Romans, who now rules.[65] This prince's action proves that such a manner of ruling is not good in such cities.

Alternatively, there can be another inconvenient result, because those few can divide amongst themselves, as happens naturally: as a consequence rumours, sedition, conflagrations, and civil strife break out in cities, as we have often seen in the city of Pisa. So it is most advantageous to a people of the first magnitude to be ruled by the multitude, which is called a government by the people, as in *Dig.* 1.2.2.3–9.[66] And it is evident that this form of government is good, because in that period the city of Rome expanded greatly, as is clear from *Dig.* 1.2.2.16;[67] 1.2.2.18;[68] 1.2.2.19–20.[69] This is also evident from the authority of the books of Kings, quoted above, for it seems to be more the rule of God than of men.[70] We also experience this in the city of Perugia, which is ruled in this manner in peace and unity. It grows and flourishes. The rulers do not guard themselves from anyone, as they take turns in office, but are themselves guarded by all; and it has often been seen that certain matters decided by the counsel of common men seemed, to the wise and prudent, to have been badly handled; yet the outcome showed that they were dealt with most prudently. This is because this regime is more of God than of men: the said most illustrious emperor strongly commended this manner of ruling, when I was in his presence.[71] So we call this form of government

[65] W. M. Bowsky, *A Medieval Italian Commune: Siena under the Nine, 1287–1355* (Berkeley, CA 1981), esp. pp. 299–307; the review by J. N. Najemy is relevant to Bartolus's diagnosis: *Speculum*, 58 (1983): 1029–33. Charles IV's arrival in Siena on 23 March 1355 precipitated the fall of the Nine. He proceeded immediately to Rome, where he was crowned emperor on Easter Sunday, 5 April.
[66] *Dig.* 1.2.2.3–9 describes the law and magistracies of Rome between the expulsion of the kings and the transfer of the government to the senate.
[67] *Dig.* 1.1.2.16: 'Then, after the ejection of the kings, it was established that there be two consuls in whom a statute laid down that the supreme authority should be vested.'
[68] *Dig.* 1.2.2.18: 'Then, with a growth in population ... it was decided to establish a magistrate with greater power. Accordingly, dictators were put in office from whom there was no right of appeal.'
[69] Continuing: 'the magistrates in question being, however, considered statutory officers'.
[70] 1 *Kings* 8, 11–17.
[71] Charles IV arrived at Pisa on 6 May 1355. Bartolus was a member of Perugia's embassy to the emperor there. Charles made him a privy counsellor, and granted him the privileges of legitimating students of Perugia University and of awarding legal majority to minors, but probably did not, contrary to what has long been thought, grant him a coat of arms: C. N. S. Woolf, *Bartolus of Sassoferrato: His Position in the History of Medieval Political Thought* (Cambridge 1913), p. 3 n. 6; O. Cavallar, S. Degenring, and J. Kirshner, eds., *A Grammar of Signs: Bartolo da Sassoferrato's Tract on Insignia and Coats of Arms* (Berkeley, CA 1994), pp. 8–26; A. Bartoli Langelli and M. A. Panzanelli Fratoni, 'L'ambasceria a

rule for the people or rule of the multitude, as has been said. But this form of government is so called because jurisdiction rests with the people or multitude, not because the whole multitude rules all together at one and the same time. Rather, the people entrusts government to some men for a period, by turns and by rotation, as in the previously cited *Dig.* 1.1.2.16;⁷² and *Auth.* 3.2.1.⁷³ When I say the multitude, I understand the meanest sort to be excepted, as in *Cod.* 12.1.6.⁷⁴ Again, certain magnates who are so powerful that they would oppress the others may also be excluded from this form of government, as in *Dig.* 1.18.6.2;⁷⁵ and we see this in practice. But in these cities, if honours and obligations are distributed according to due degree, then the form of government is good; if [they are distributed] inequitably, then it is a bad form of government and reform is the responsibility of the superior, as in *Dig.* 50.4.3.15.⁷⁶

Secondly, we must investigate the larger nation or people, which is thus of the second magnitude. It is not advantageous for them to be ruled by one king, for the reasons given above; nor is it advantageous for them to be ruled by the multitude, for it would be extremely difficult and dangerous to assemble such a multitude. But it is advantageous for them to be ruled by a few, that is, by the rich and good men of that city. This is explicitly proved by *Dig.* 1.2.2.9,⁷⁷ where with the growth of the city of Rome the senators were created and were vested with all power. The city of Venice is ruled in this way, and so is the city of Florence: for I number these amongst the larger cities. In these cities the suspicions mentioned above are absent. For although they are said to be ruled by a few, I say that these are few with respect to the multitude of the city, but many with respect to another city. Accordingly, because they are many, the multitude does not disdain to be ruled by them. Again, because they are many, they cannot easily divide between themselves, and indeed many remain in the middle, who underpin the stability [*status*†] of the city. And the gloss to

Carlo IV di Lussemburgo', in *Bartolo da Sassoferrato nel VII centenario della nascita: Diritto, politica, società: Atti del L convegno storico internazionale. Todi – Perugia, 13–16 ottobre 2013* (Spoleto 2014), pp. 271–332.

⁷² Above, n. 67. The passage does not state explicitly that the rule of the consuls was by rotation.

⁷³ *Nov.* 15.1 regulates the rota of service of *defensores*† in the cities.

⁷⁴ *Cod.* 12.1.6 excludes from office (*dignitas*) a variety of people 'in vile or abject pursuits and employments, or who occupy base or dishonourable positions'.

⁷⁵ *Dig.* 1.18.6.2 notes that the oath sworn by provincial governors included an undertaking to protect the humble from the powerful.

⁷⁶ Above, p. 17.

⁷⁷ Above, p. 17.

Auth 3.2.1 describes this manner of ruling by a few, when a city has grown to the second magnitude.[78] All of this is true, unless it appears otherwise concerning the ancient manner of governing a city: for it can happen that one nation or people are so used to a particular manner of governing that it has virtually become an aspect of the nature of things for them, and they would not know how to live otherwise. Then the ancient type of government must be preserved, as in *Dig.* 50.4.1.1; 50.4.3.15; 50.4.14.3.[79]

Thirdly, we must investigate the largest nation or people, of the third magnitude. Strictly speaking, this cannot exist in a single city by itself. But if it were a city with dominion over many other cities and provinces, then it would be good for this people to be ruled by one. This is proved by *Dig.* 1.2.2.11,[80] where, after Roman sway [*imperium*†] had vastly expanded and many provinces had been captured, it devolved upon one, that is, the emperor [*princeps*†]. This is also proved by all the reasons presented above by Brother Giles;[81] here the reasons presented to the contrary cease to apply. For in such a multitude there are, of necessity, many good men, from whom a king should take counsel and so place himself on the path of justice. Thus we commonly see in practice that a nation or people is ruled better to the extent that it is ruled under a greater or more powerful king. For this we have the authority of Holy Scripture, *Deuteronomy* 17,[82] where the Lord speaks thus: 'When you have entered the land which the Lord your God shall give you, and when you have possessed it and inhabited it, and have said: "I shall constitute a king over myself, like the other nations have roundabout", then you will constitute him whom the Lord your God has chosen from the number of your brothers. You will not be able to make king a man of another nation, who is not your brother.' These are the words of the Lord.

---

[78] *Nov.* 15.1, as above, n. 73. Accursius's gloss *circulum* explains that the manner of choosing *defensores*† in the cities of Justinian's age is no longer observed in modern cities: 'Today however this is not the case, since it is difficult to assemble all the good men of the city; rather, certain people are elected whose decision all the others observe.' He adds the detail that in Bologna the number of such electors has been reduced to eight.

[79] None of these passages from the title 'On *munera* and Offices', concerned with *municipia*,† justifies such a precise appeal to traditional practice. *Digest* 50.4.1.1 merely defines patrimonial burdens, *Dig.* 50.4.3.15 sets the original establishment of such burdens as the standard to follow in distributing them now, and *Dig.* 50.4.14.3 recommends consideration of the character, place of birth, and wealth of a candidate for such burdens.

[80] Above, p. 18.

[81] Above, pp. 19–20.

[82] Verses 14–15.

When He says 'When you have entered' and 'possessed' and 'inhabited' etc., He implies that it is not a small people which will have a king, but a large one, which is of great standing [*in magno statu*] and enjoys dominion over many, as has been said above.

When He says 'Whom the Lord your God has chosen', it should be understood that every king is either elected directly by God or by electors in the sight of God. For the heart of the electors 'is in the hand of God, and He will direct it where He wishes',[83] as is said of the king in *Cod.* 1.1.8.3.[84] And from this, note that rule by election is more divine than rule by succession:[85] for this reason succession is denounced utterly in ecclesiastical affairs, as in *Extra* 1.17.7;[86] 1.17.11.[87] Accordingly, the election of the emperor who is universal king is done by the election of the prelates and princes; it does not proceed by succession, as in *Extra* 1.6.34;[88] and *Sext.* 2.14.2.[89] For 'God has constituted this rule [*imperium*†] from heaven', as in *Auth.* 1.1.*pr.*;[90] *Auth.* 6.2.1.[91] Yet particular kings exist more by human constitution, as in *Dig.* 1.1.5;[92] and for this reason, it is permitted that these cases proceed by succession. And this is how to understand what Giles says in *De regimine principum*,[93] where he concludes that it is better for a kingdom to descend by succession: this should be taken to refer to a particular kingdom, which can be conveyed like our other goods and rights; but not to the universal one, because that would be contrary to divine authority and the canons.

---

[83] *Proverbs* 21, 1.
[84] A letter by Pope John II to Emperor Justinian in 534, citing *Proverbs* 21, 1: 'The heart of the king is in the hand of God.'
[85] Giles of Rome, *De regimine principum*, 3.2.5, pp. 461–5, asserts the contrary.
[86] *Extra* 1.17.1, the canon *Ut filii* from the Council of Poitiers (1085), prohibits the sons of priests 'and others born of fornication' from being promoted to holy orders, from becoming monks or canons regular, and expressly from being given high ecclesiastical office.
[87] *Extra* 1.17.11 is the decretal *Ad exstirpandas* sent by Pope Alexander III between 1159 and 1181, admonishing the archbishop of Canterbury to expel sons of priests from the churches they held.
[88] *Extra* 1.6.34 is the decretal *Venerabilem*, sent by Innocent III in 1202, explaining to German nobles the papal role in the election of the king of the Romans (i.e. Germany), afterwards to be crowned emperor, again by the pope. Partial translation in B. Tierney, *The Crisis of Church and State 1050–1300* (Englewood Cliffs, NJ 1964), pp. 133–4.
[89] Above, p. 4.
[90] *Nov.* 6.*pr.*
[91] *Nov.* 73.1.
[92] *Dig.* 1.1.5 associates the foundation of kingdoms (*regna condita*) with the law of nations or *ius gentium*.†
[93] Giles of Rome, *De regimine principum*, 3.2.5, pp. 461–5.

When He says 'From the number of your brothers', note that it is dangerous to have a king from another nation. But you will say: how then was the Roman empire transferred by the church to the Germans, that is, the Teutons, as in *Extra* 1.6.34?[94] I answer: all Christians are called our brothers, and so this does not go against the said authority. But there can be no transfer to a Saracen, a pagan, or an infidel, and for this reason there follows: 'You will not be able to have a king of another nation.' And because of this the examination of him who is to be crowned emperor is necessary.[95] Or you can explain these words according to Augustine, where the gloss says 'you will not be able': 'that is, you must not'.[96] For a kingdom is not faithfully preserved by a king of another nation. And for this reason the Roman empire progressively waned before our eyes, after it was separated from the Italians. Yet this has not happened without the secret judgment of God.

I do not speak, however, about small peoples, because they either stand beneath this or that city, as in *Dig.* 50.1.30,[97] or they are leagued with another city or king by some treaty, so that they venerate the majesty of another, as in *Dig* 49.15.7.1.[98] We see this in the cities and *castra*† which are under the protection of this city of Perugia. Just as a frail, small human body cannot rule itself without the help of a tutor† and curator, so these small peoples cannot in any way rule themselves unless they are subjected to another or adhere to another.

So much for the three good types of ruling.

---

[94] Above, n. 88. In *Venerabilem* Innocent III propounds the theory of *translatio imperii*, the claim that the papacy has been responsible through history for transferring the locus of empire from one people to another.

[95] Innocent III also argued in *Venerabilem* that the pope has the authority to examine and if necessary reject a candidate who might be an excommunicate, a tyrant, a fool, heretic, or pagan.

[96] The Interlinear Gloss to *Deuteronomy* 17, 14 reads, as Bartolus accurately quotes, 'That is, you must not.' Augustine is quoted in the *Glossa ordinaria* (gloss *Cum ingressus fueris*): 'Nevertheless He commanded that no foreigner be made king, but a brother born from the same people, not from another. When it says "you will not be able" it should be understood to mean "you must not"': *Biblia sacra cum glossis, interlineari et ordinaria, Nicolai Lyrani postilla et moralitatibus, ad loc.*

[97] *Dig.* 50.1.30: 'Whoever is born in a village is regarded as a member of the *patria* to which the village in question belongs.'

[98] *Dig.* 49.15.7.1 defines a free people as one subject to no other people's power (*potestas*) but also, against the strong implication of Bartolus's comment here, explains that a people bound in an unequal treaty to another such that it must 'amicably preserve the majesty [*maiestas*]' of another people is still free. For Bartolus's commentary on *Dig.* 49.15.7 and related texts, see Appendix III.

III

I now ask which is the worst of the bad modes of governing. On this subject all the philosophers say that tyranny is the worst rule for it constitutes the most extreme degree of malice. Giles states in *De regimine principum* that, as has been said, a form of government is described as good because its chief aim is the common good.[99] But endeavour for the common good is abandoned completely by a tyrant which is why tyranny is the worst rule. Hence if many have dominion, because they are rich or are considered good, or if a multitude has dominion, although those who rule aim at their own rather than the common good, and thus it is rule of the bad or of a perverted people, yet the endeavour for the common good is not abandoned to the same extent. Because, being composed of many, it is not entirely oblivious to the nature of the common good. But if the tyrant is one man, he wholly abandons the common good.

Moreover, just as virtue united for the good is better, so united for the worse it is worse. Therefore a tyrant is the worst. And this is so obvious that no demonstration is necessary.

What has been said above – that the government of many bad men is not as bad as the government of a single tyrant – should be understood when those many aim at a single object and cannot do so except together. It is otherwise if someone were to exercise tyranny on his own account and no one were to have any regard for anyone else, as I have said above concerning the monstrous form of government which now exists in Rome.[100] For if there is a single, corrupt humour which predominates in the whole body, that is bad; but if all the humours were corrupted, and struggled against one another, that would be the worst thing. Woe, therefore, to the city with many tyrants who do not aim at a single end.

Again, it should be noted that a government of many bad men or of a perverted people does not last for long, but is easily drawn into tyranny. We have seen this often enough in practice. Yet this is by divine permission, for it is written: 'Who makes a hypocrite rule on account of the sins of the people', *Job* 34.[101] And because today all Italy is full of tyrants, let us investigate those matters concerning the tyrant which are relevant to jurists.

---

[99] Giles of Rome, *De regimine principum*, 3.2.2, p. 454.
[100] See above, p. 18.
[101] Verse 30.

On the Tyrant

I have worked for some time now, in many treatises, on investigations of the sweetest subjects, which have totally suffused body, heart, and soul with their pleasant flavour. I am so replete, therefore, with the taste of flowing honey, that I have not dared to broach bitter, distressing, and troublesome subjects, especially when I see tyrannical perfidy extending its sway. Yet trusting in the merciful protection of Him Who 'makes the tongues of infants eloquent'[1] – indeed, Who causes lightning to flash in the open spaces in the presence of the gentiles[2] – I dare, with the support of God's arm, to take up so hard and dreadful a subject as that of tyrannical depravity, not in order that I should derive any joy and comfort from it, but in order that all should be capable themselves of ridding themselves utterly of the bond and knot of this dreadful evil, namely tyrannical servitude. From which bitter and extreme mastery may God liberate us, and keep us in His own holy, good, and perfect tranquillity, and make us rejoice together in the sweetness of liberty. Wherefore I, Bartolus of Sassoferrato, a citizen of Perugia, the least doctor of the laws,[3]

---

[1] *Wisdom* 10, 21.
[2] *Exodus* 40, 33; *Psalms* 76, 19; *Psalms* 143, 6.
[3] In October 1348, the University of Perugia successfully petitioned the Council of the *priori*† of the guilds of Perugia to grant citizenship to Bartolus: O. Cavallar and J. Kirshner, *Jurists and Jurisprudence in Medieval Italy: Texts and Contexts* (Toronto 2020), pp. 524–6. In the petition, he was characterized as 'the most distinguished doctor of the laws'. Elsewhere Bartolus deemed the status of doctor superior to any other dignity: F. Treggiari, '"Doctoratus est dignitas": La lezione di Bartolo', in V. Crescenzi and G. Rossi, eds., *Bartolo da Sassoferrato nella cultura europea tra medioevo e rinascimento* (Sassoferrato 2015), pp. 221–38, at 233–8.

before proceeding further with the present treatise on the tyrant, shall briefly pose several questions, which we shall come to unpick afterwards in due course.

First, I inquire whence the term tyrant is derived.

Secondly, I inquire in what manner a tyrant is defined.

Thirdly, I inquire whether there is said to be a tyrant in a single neighbourhood.

Fourthly, I inquire whether there can be a tyrant in a single household.

Fifthly, I inquire of the tyrant of a city how many species of such a tyrant there are.

Sixthly, I inquire who is said to be a manifest tyrant by defect of title in a city.

Seventhly, I inquire whether the acts of such manifest tyrants or things done during their time are valid.[4]

Eighthly, I inquire who is said to be a manifest tyrant by conduct.

Ninthly, I inquire: if some duke, marquis, count, or baron, who has just title, proves to be a tyrant by conduct, what ought the superior to do?

Tenthly, I inquire: what shall we say concerning those things which the supreme pontiff, the emperor, and the legates appear to have done?

Eleventhly, I inquire whether acts done by the aforesaid tyrants who truly have just title are valid.

Twelfthly, I inquire about the tacit or concealed tyrant.[5]

I

First, I inquire whence the term tyrant is derived.

I answer: from the Greek *tyro*, which in Latin is translated as *strong* or *restriction*,[6] whence 'strong kings were called tyrants. Later it came about that the worst, unprincipled kings were called tyrants, who exercised their wanton lust for power and cruellest domination over their peoples'.[7]

---

[4] That is, those things done by others.
[5] D. Quaglioni, 'Intorno al testo del *Tractatus de tyrannia* di Bartolo da Sassoferrato', *Il pensiero politico*, 10 (1977): 268–84, at 270–4, points out that this paragraph is present in only one manuscript of the tract; its authenticity, while possible, is open to question.
[6] Latin: *fortis* and *angustia* respectively.
[7] The quotation is from Isidore of Seville, *Etymologiarum sive originum, libri xx*, ed. W. M. Lindsay, 2 vols. (Oxford 1911), 9.3.19–20, vol. II, p. 365.

According to Huguccio: 'from *tyro*, that is restriction; because he restricts and tortures his subjects'.[8] And that *tyrus* is interpreted as I have said is clear from the interpretations of the Bible, where it is explained thus: '*Tyrus* is rendered *restriction*, or *tribulation*, or *fortitude*,'[9] all of which to evil effect befit a tyrant.

And all this will be useful when we inquire about the condition of a tyrant and about the mode of proof.

II

Secondly, I inquire in what manner a tyrant is defined.

I answer: Gregory in book 12 of his *Morals* defines it thus: 'Strictly speaking, someone is called a tyrant who rules unlawfully in the common *res publica*.†[10] But it should be known that every proud man practises tyranny after his own fashion. For what one person sometimes does in the commonwealth, that is, by the vested capacity of a dignity,[11] another does in a province, another in a city, another in his own household, and another within himself in his own thoughts, by some concealed villainy. The Lord does not consider how much evil someone is able to do, but how much he wants to do. And when there is a lack of external power, he is a tyrant to himself who is dominated by iniquity within; because although he does not oppress his neighbours outwardly, yet inwardly he desires to have the power in order to oppress.'[12] These are the very words of Gregory, which must be taken as law, in D. 15 c. 3.[13] Let us briefly discuss them.

'Strictly speaking … a tyrant' etc.: for just as a king or emperor of the Romans is strictly the true, just, and universal king, so if someone wishes to hold that position unjustly, he is strictly speaking called a tyrant; and

---

[8] Uguccione da Pisa, *Derivationes*, ed. E. Cecchini, G. Arbizzoni, S. Lanciotti, and G. Nonni, 2 vols. (Florence 2004), vol. II, 1225.

[9] Jerome, *Liber interpretationis Hebraicorum nominum*, ed. P. de Lagarde, CCSL, lxxii (Turnhout 1959), p. 97; see Quaglioni, *Politica e diritto*, p. 40 and n. 2.

[10] We retain the Latin here because the preceding adjective 'common' would create tautology where none exists in the original.

[11] By 'dignity' Bartolus means a public office.

[12] Gregory the Great, *Moralia in Iob Libri XI–XXII*, ed. M. Adriaen, CCSL, cxliiiA (Turnhout 1979), 12.38, pp. 654–5.

[13] *Decretum*, D. 15 c. 3, 1 approves the works of all orthodox church fathers for use by the Roman church.

concerning such a tyrant we have *Cod.* 1.2.16;[14] 1.2.6, and what is noted there.[15]

'In the common *res publica*'†:[16] this is understood to mean the commonwealth of the Romans, as in *Dig.* 50.16.16.[17]

'Who rules unlawfully': this comes about because he lacks a title, because he has not been elected, or has been elected unlawfully, or has been elected and rejected, as in *Extra* 1.6.34;[18] or has been elected, crowned, and afterwards condemned by just judgment, as in *Sext.* 2.14.2.[19] And this is said of King Saul in 1 *Kings* 13, where the prophet Samuel speaks thus: 'You have acted foolishly: you have not kept the commandments of the Lord your God, which He gave you. If you had not failed to do so, He would even now have established your kingdom over Israel forever; but in no way shall your kingdom survive any longer. The Lord has sought a man after His own heart, and the Lord has commanded him to be a leader over His people, because you have not observed what your Lord commanded.'[20] It appears, therefore, that a king is deprived of his kingdom on account of sin, and hence he is a tyrant, because he rules unlawfully.

'But it should be known': previously he was speaking of a universal tyrant, here of a particular one, who is not a tyrant in the same strict sense.

'Every proud man': pride is the root of all evils, and this is especially evident in a tyrant. And he proceeds through five species of tyrant, which I shall describe in the appropriate place. One is a general tyrant in the common *res publica* of the Romans; another is the tyrant of a province,

---

[14] *Cod.* 1.2.16 is a constitution by Emperor Zeno nullifying measures taken during the revolt of Basilicus (475–6), when Emperor Zeno was driven out of Constantinople. Bartolus refers to this law repeatedly. For his short commentary on the passage, see *Bartoli a Sassoferrato in primam Codicis partem commentaria* (Turin 1574), fo. 21va–b, and Quaglioni, *Politica e diritto*, pp. 15–16.

[15] *Cod.* 1.2.6 does not mention a tyrant in ordering 'all innovation to cease' and the restoration of 'the ancient practice and the original ecclesiastical canons'. Accursius's gloss to the first words of the law (*Omni innovatione*), by contrast, hypothesizes: 'Since the innovation that the ancient canons were not to apply was perhaps brought about by some tyrant.'

[16] See above, n. 10.

[17] *Dig.* 50.16.16 derives the appellation 'publican' (*publicanus*) for a tax-collector from the fact that 'the designation "public" relates in a number of cases to the Roman people; for cities [*civitates*] are regarded as being in the position of private persons'.

[18] Bartolus has already cited *Extra* 1.6.34 (*Venerabilem*, Innocent III, 1202) to a very different purpose in the *On the Government of a City*: above, pp. 31–2.

[19] See above, p. 4 n. 7

[20] 1 *Kings* 13–14.

who rules unlawfully in his province; another of a city; another of a single household; and another of himself. It remains to be seen whether there may be a tyrant of a single neighbourhood: of this I shall speak below.

'That is, by the vested capacity of a dignity': this can be determined by the preceding or the following.[21]

'Another in a province': in a province someone rules without right just as I said above in the case of the common *res publica.*[†22] And there is another way: if someone has been made governor of a province for a specific term or at the pleasure of the appointer, and at the expiry of that term he has not admitted a successor, he is a tyrant, and falls under the *Lex Iulia maiestatis,*[†] *Dig.* 48.4.2.[23]

'Another in a city': a tyrant in a city will be our chief concern below.

'Another in a household': I shall discuss below how this can be.

'Another practises it within himself, in his own thoughts, by some concealed villainy': the tyranny which consists in thought alone is irrelevant to the jurist, because no one deserves punishment for his thoughts, as in *Dig.* 48.19.18.[24] Yet it should be understood that if someone has made an attempt, or arranged an attempt, even if he has not succeeded, he is to be punished as if he had succeeded, as in *Dig.* 48.4.3 at the end, which is exceptional in this case and certain other crimes.[25] The passage which follows speaks of the punishment which is imposed after examination by the Eternal Judge, and for this reason I do not explain it, but leave it to the theologians. But I do deal with what is useful to us.

'He desires to have the power in order to oppress': it should be particularly noted that a tyrannical act consists principally in the oppression of subjects. For he is called a tyrant 'because he restricts and tortures his subjects', as has been said. Yet tyrannical acts are of many kinds, as we shall see below.

And let this suffice as a commentary on the passage.

---

[21] A textual anomaly identified by Quaglioni is omitted here: *Politica e diritto*, pp. 124, 179, line 95 and n.

[22] Above, n. 10.

[23] *Dig.* 48.4.2 adds to a list of treasonable actions the case of someone 'who has failed to relinquish his province although his successor has arrived'.

[24] *Dig.* 48.19.18: nobody is punished for thinking.

[25] *Dig.* 48.4.3, on the *Lex Iulia maiestatis*, extends punishment for various listed treasonous acts to someone who brings about the perpetration of such crimes.

III

Thirdly, I ask whether there can be said to be a tyrant in a single neighbourhood.

I answer: no, as is clear from the words of Gregory, who did not mention this species of tyranny. This is also proved by reason. The rule of a tyrant is the worst, as has been said, and is diametrically opposed to the rule of a king, which is the best. And since a tyrant is one who rules unlawfully, it is clear that where there is no kingship or princely rule there cannot be a tyrant. Since, therefore, in a province or city there is government by way of a principate, a tyrant can properly be said to arise there. But in a neighbourhood there is usually no king nor any type of government by way of jurisdiction, and therefore no tyrant arises there. For a neighbourhood is not ruled by one man, but by whoever rules the whole city. And although in a neighbourhood there may be certain great and powerful men who oppress the others, yet they are not tyrants, but those more powerful men who are talked of in *Dig.* 4.7.3;[26] 1.18.6.2.[27] Unless you supposed that in a neighbourhood or a certain part of a city someone assumed such pre-eminence that the universal assembly of the city could do nothing there, except to the extent that he himself wished, as the Roman nobles are doing; for then they are rightly said to be a tyrant of that part of the city.

But against this position it could be said that any city is commonly divided into quarters or parishes, and in each part there are some who are called captains or syndics† who preside over the affairs of that part of the city, who are mentioned in *Dig.* 2.14.14.[28] So, since government [*regimen*] exists there, it seems that there can also be a tyrant there.

I reply that such men do not have jurisdiction, although some measure of coercion is sometimes allowed to them in order to levy certain exactions and to denounce offences. For they should be termed servants of those who rule the city, rather than rulers themselves; so they do not rule,

---

[26] *Dig.* 4.7.3. The train of thought begins at the end of *Dig.* 4.7.1: 'Therefore, if he has brought forward a man from another province or a man of greater influence and resources as our adversary, he will be liable', continues through *Dig.* 4.7.2: 'or anyone else who will be a vexatious adversary', and concludes in *Dig.* 4.7.3: 'and we cannot be in an equal position vis-à-vis a person of greater influence and resources'.

[27] *Dig.* 1.18.6.2 enjoins provincial governors to prevent 'more influential people' from mistreating 'those of lower station'.

[28] *Dig.* 2.14.14 merely mentions the manager of a business association (*societas*), not officers of local government.

39

they serve those who rule. Therefore they cannot be called tyrants, but are more powerful on account of their office; and they are able to instil fear, and fall under the constitution *Cod.* 2.19(20).11[29] and *Dig.* 47.13.1.[30]

Furthermore, the misdeeds of these more powerful men in neighbourhoods can be swiftly corrected by those who rule the city; hence the more powerful are not termed tyrants, and hence the blessed Gregory did not mention tyranny in neighbourhoods. For the same reason I say that in the towns, villages, and *castra*† of the *contado*† of any city, in which jurisdiction is not exercised either *de iure* or *de facto*, there cannot be a tyrant, although there may be someone who is more powerful. But if there were a place so strong that someone rebelled against the city and defended himself from it, so that misdeeds there could not, without great difficulty, be corrected by those who ruled the city, then there could be a tyrant there, concerning which we have the passage 'he has held a citadel' in *Dig.* 48.4.3;[31] *Cod.* 11.60(59).2;[32] and he does what is noted at the beginning of *Dig.* 2.8.2,[33] where it is said that whoever is from a well-fortified place or *castrum* is not an ideal candidate for being summonsed.

IV

Fourthly, I ask whether there can be a tyrant in a single household.

It seems not, because there jurisdiction is not exercised. Therefore, etc., as I have said.

On the other hand, there are the words of Gregory related above under the second question.

---

[29] *Cod.* 2.19(20).11 imposes penalties on local officials who intimidate those subject to their jurisdiction into selling them their property, as well as those who abuse the influence of their family and friends to similar ends.

[30] *Dig.* 47.13.1: 'If extortion occurs on the pretended order of the governor, the governor of the province will order the return of what has been obtained and will punish the wrong.'

[31] *Dig.* 48.4.3, the operative phrase being: 'But the *Lex Iulia maiestatis*† makes him liable who injures the public majesty, such as he who surrenders in war or recklessly yields a citadel or camp.'

[32] *Cod.* 11.59(60).2 imposes the death penalty and confiscation on any private person found in possession of lands pertaining to fortresses.

[33] Bartolus gives the substance of Accursius's gloss *fideiussor*, not that of the law.

I answer that a father can be said to have something of a royal right within his own household.[34] For he has jurisdiction over his sons and his slaves, as in *Dig.* 47.2.17;[35] *Cod.* 8.46(47).4.[36] Again, the senior or elder of a household has in some way a certain jurisdiction over his wife, his children, and his slaves; and even an elder brother or a paternal uncle over those in the household who are under twenty-five years of age, as in *Cod.* 9.14.1; 9.15.1.[37] If he rules unlawfully in that household, he is appropriately termed a tyrant. Consequently, if a member of the household were to make any contract or do something similar, out of fear of such a tyrant in the household, it would be rescinded, as if it had been done out of fear of a tyrant, as in *Dig.* 44.5.1.5 and what is noted there.[38] And I have said there how it may be proved that the deed was done out of fear of these tyrants,[39] and this is noted by Innocent at *Extra* 1.40.1.[40] Yet if someone has in his household a brother or the son of a brother who is younger than himself, but older than twenty-five, then the elder does not have this power over the younger, who ought to rule himself by himself, as in *Dig.* 4.4.1.[41] Hence such fear would not be sufficient, so fraud or common fear

---

[34] In what follows, Bartolus is thinking of *patria potestas*, that is, the powers exercised by the head of a Roman family or *paterfamilias*† over wife, children, and slaves.

[35] *Dig.* 47.2.17. Slaves and sons-in-power who commit theft against the head of household are not subject to the action for theft because the head of household, possessing as he does the power to 'ordain' (*statuere*) against them, does not need to take them to court.

[36] *Cod.* 8.46(47).4 begins: 'It seems to be more proper for the disputes which have arisen between you and your children to be settled at home.'

[37] *Cod.* 9.14.1, where it is obvious that in most cases this was indeed within the powers of owners, and *Cod.* 9.15.1, which gives power (*potestas*) to older close relatives as well as mentioning 'authority by a father's right' (*iure patrio auctoritas*), that is, of a *paterfamilias*. Significantly, Bartolus imposes the concept of jurisdiction on all the relationships mentioned in these passages.

[38] *Dig.* 44.5.1.5 lays down that a stipulation with the effect of encumbering liberty cannot be demanded from a freedman (*libertus*); Accursius's gloss allows a freedman a defence if he has promised his patron such a thing out of excessive reverence and love.

[39] For Bartolus's commentary on *Dig.* 44.5.1.5, see his *In primam Digesti Novi partem commentaria* (Turin 1574), fo. 176va: proof that a promise was made out of fear of a superior – here a husband or a bishop in relation to their respective subordinates – would be that there had been preceding threats or blows from such a superior.

[40] *Extra* 1.40.1, *Perlatum est*, a decretal of Alexander III describing a husband acting as a tyrant towards his wife; Innocent IV's commentary (Innocent IV, *Apparatus super quinque libris decretalium* (Frankfurt am Main 1570), fo. 173rb–va) establishes that where duress or fear of death is a likely presumption, the burden of proof passes to the party seeking to deny it.

[41] *Dig.* 4.4.1.2 refers to the consensus among lawyers that a man reaches adulthood at twenty-five and no longer qualifies for the help the praetor extends to those who have yet to reach that age.

41

must be proved if someone wanted to rescind the deeds of such a person. We may also term the abbot of any monastery who rules it unlawfully a tyrant in his own household, either because he is a usurper, as in *Sext.* 3.4.18,[42] or because, although he has a just title, he rules tyrannically, as I shall say below about the tyrant of a city.

V

Fifthly, concerning the tyrant of a city, I ask how many species of him there are.

I answer: from what has been said it is clear that the tyrant of a city is one who rules in a city unlawfully. But just as ruling unlawfully takes many forms, so the species of tyrants are many. For one is an open and manifest tyrant, another a concealed and tacit tyrant. Again, sometimes a manifest tyrant is so by defect of title, sometimes by reason of conduct. Again, in the same way a concealed tyrant is sometimes so on account of title, sometimes on account of defect of title.

So let us examine these further.

VI

Sixthly, I ask who is a manifest tyrant by defect of title in a city.

I answer: he who manifestly rules without just title in a city, as is clear from the aforesaid definition. However, this comes about in many ways. First, if the city or *castrum*† which he usurps does not have the right of electing a rector, but someone bears himself as rector in it, then he is a tyrant, because he rules unlawfully, and he is liable under the *Lex Iulia maiestatis,*† *Dig.* 48.4.3 at the end;[43] again, if at the end of his term of office he remains against the will of him to whom it pertains, as in the same law.

But if you suppose that the city or *castrum* has the right of electing its own rector and that the city has transferred jurisdiction to someone, although under duress; then there may be some doubt, because deeds done out of fear are valid, unless rescinded by the action *Quod metus*

---

[42] *Sext.* 3.4.18, *Eum qui,* a decretal of Boniface VIII, does not mention usurpers precisely, but those who occupy ecclesiastical benefices and offices by violence, or intrude themselves while knowing they have no title.

[43] *Dig.* 48.4.3 makes anyone liable for treason 'who, being a private citizen, knowingly and with malicious intent acts as though holding office or magistracy'.

causa.⁴⁴ Therefore in the meantime he is rector, and it cannot be said that he is a tyrant by defect of title. But the contrary is true, for jurisdiction ought to be transferred voluntarily, and if it is done through fear it is *ipso iure* invalid, as in *Dig.* 5.1.2.*pr.*,⁴⁵ and as is also noted at *Dig.* 4.2.21.3.⁴⁶

Now we must see in what manner violence or fear is inflicted on a people.

I answer: if he raised an army against a city without an order from the superior, as in the said law *Dig.* 48.4.3;⁴⁷ or if, fighting together with a foreign force, he captured the city, as in the *Lex Iulia de vi publica,*† *Dig.* 48.6.3.2.⁴⁸ But if after instigating tumult and sedition together with men of the same city, he has himself elected as lord, then the matter is more doubtful, because the greater part seems to have done this: it seems to be the greater part precisely because it has prevailed. But it must also be said that it can happen in this sort of case that he who is a manifest tyrant by defect of title can also be created through force and fear. What if he occupied the fortifications of some city with a modest force, and with these occupied, a just fear falls on the people? Certainly he is elected through fear, by analogy with *Extra* 2.13.19.⁴⁹ Or what if he prevails with the support of the numerically greater part of the people, but, as commonly happens, they were of the meaner sort, men of base condition? Certainly on this basis it does not seem to have been done by the greater part of the people: for such men ought not to be decurions† or members of the council, as in *Cod.* 12.1.6.⁵⁰ Again, if he has done this

---

⁴⁴ That is, 'On things done out of fear'; see *Cod.* 2.19(20) and *Dig.* 4.2.

⁴⁵ *Dig.* 5.1.2.*pr.* removes jurisdiction over a case from a praetor if a litigant claims the praetor used his powers to coerce him into accepting him as judge.

⁴⁶ *Dig.* 4.2.21.3 nullifies a dowry promised under duress. Accursius's gloss *ullam esse* suggests that the contract is invalidated *ipso iure* by duress.

⁴⁷ *Dig.* 48.4.3, on the *Lex Iulia maiestatis,*† recommends capital punishment for a variety of malefactors, including a person 'who, without the command of the emperor, wages war or raises a levy or prepares an army'.

⁴⁸ *Dig.* 48.6.3.2. Perhaps Bartolus had *Dig.* 48.6.3.*pr.* of the law in mind, which mentions those 'who have entered into a conspiracy to raise a mob or a sedition or who keep either slaves or freemen under arms'. The law also mentions houses in the country.

⁴⁹ *Extra* 2.13.19, the decretal *Pisanis* of Gregory IX. The matter here turns not on any election but on the Pisan possession of certain castles rendering it impossible for the church of Lucca to collect financial dues owed to it from within those castles.

⁵⁰ Also quoted to different effect in the preceding treatise (see above, p. 29 n. 74), *Cod.* 12.1.6 excludes from office (*dignitas*) a variety of people 'in vile or abject pursuits and employments, or who occupy base or dishonorable positions'.

with the inhabitants of the *contado*,[†] as in *Cod.* 11.54(53).1.[51] Or suppose that with a modest, united force of that city, he raised a tumult, when the rest remained dispersed in their homes, for a few united prevail over many who are dispersed: certainly the fear amongst the people was just. Or suppose that at the outset, with a modest force, he expelled or killed one or more of the greater men of the city, on account of which the rest of the people is justly afraid, because it is written: 'I will smite the shepherd, and the sheep of the flock shall be scattered.'[52] That this is a just fear amongst the people is proved by many ancient histories, especially in the book of Judith.[53]

And I say simply that if someone is elected illicitly, having instigated tumult and sedition, then he is a manifest tyrant by defect of title: the explicit case is in C. 1 q. 1 c. 25[54] and C. 14 q. 5 c. 9,[55] where it is said that even if he rules well after the event, he is still a tyrant; which should be understood with the proviso, unless he is excused after the event, as in *Extra* 1.9.10.[56] The truth of this is evident, because if he expels some men from the city without just cause when he celebrates his election, those expelled can be said to have been held in contempt, for they ought to have been recalled, as in *Cod.* 10.32(31).2.[57] So an election carried out while they are held in contempt is invalid, as in *Extra* 1.6.28; 1.6.34; 1.6.36.[58] And thus he is a manifest tyrant by defect of title.

Therefore, the manner of proving that someone is such a tyrant is clear from what has been said.

---

[51] *Cod.* 11.54(53).1 prohibits nobles and others from defrauding the fisc by taking those subject to imperial taxation under their patronage.

[52] *Matthew* 26, 31.

[53] *Judith* 14, 3 and 15, 1–7.

[54] *Decretum*, C. 1 q. 1 c. 25 is an excerpt from a letter written in 446 by Pope Leo the Great (440–61): 'But an appointment which has either been made by sedition or seized by intrigue, even though it offend not in morals or in practice, is nevertheless pernicious from the mere example of its beginning: and it is hard for things to be carried to a good issue which were started with a bad origin.'

[55] *Decretum*, C. 14 q. 5 c. 9 is an excerpt from Augustine's *De bono coniugali*: 'Nor will the perversity of a tyrannical faction be laudable if royal clemency has taken tyrannical subjects in hand.'

[56] *Extra* 1.9.10, *Nisi cum pridem* (Innocent III, 1206), sets out the circumstances in which a bishop may renounce his office.

[57] *Cod.* 10.32(31).2. Bartolus's target is the innocent phrase to the effect that before meeting to nominate new people to their body, decurions[†] 'will be summoned into the council in accordance with the law'.

[58] All three decretals concern election to ecclesiastical office.

44

VII

Seventhly, I ask whether the deeds done by such manifest tyrants by defect of title or in their time are valid.

This question has many ramifications.

First it should be seen whether those things which are done in a jurisdictional capacity are valid. It is certain that acts performed by those tyrants, as if they had jurisdiction, are *ipso iure* null, as in *Cod.* 1.2.16,[59] where the text says 'fundamentally void', and the gloss explains: 'That is, *ipso iure.*'[60] And rightly so, for when it says 'fundamentally', it is as if it were saying that these acts are null from the start, and thus that they have not been valid at any time. The same is true of those things done by officials created by those tyrants, and for the same reason; and this is expressly stated in *Extra* 5.8.1;[61] C. 9 q. 1 c. 5.[62]

But there remains some doubt concerning those things which are done in a city where there is such a tyrant, by other officials whom the city has itself elected on the sufferance of the tyrant. And it seems that they are not valid under the aforesaid *Cod.* 1.2.16,[63] where it is said that what is done in a time of tyranny is *ipso iure* null. For it says so not only of the deeds of the tyrant, but the deeds done during the time of tyranny, and reason persuades that this is the case. For no act is freely done in a city when there is a tyrant, and so it seems to be done by the tyrant himself: in support of this view there is *Extra* 2.26.14,[64] where it is said that during a period of schism no prescription† runs, which implies that during a period of schism no transaction is possible, otherwise prescription would run. But a period of tyranny can be called a period of schism, for a tyrant cuts himself off and separates himself from the communion of the

---

[59] Above, n. 14. The precise phrase (*vacuatis funditus*) Bartolus quotes from the vulgate *Code*† no longer appears in the standard modern edition, but the word which matters to him (*funditus*) does. For discussion, see Quaglioni, *Politica e diritto*, p. 16 n. 3.

[60] Gloss *funditus*.

[61] *Quod a praedecessore*, a canon promulgated by Alexander III at the Third Lateran Council (1179), revoking measures taken by two anti-popes.

[62] *Decretum*, C. 9 q. 1 c. 5 is a canon of Urban II at the Council of Piacenza (1095), quashing ordinations made by 'heresiarchs'.

[63] Above, n. 14. The passage does not say this in so many words; rather, it annuls all innovations in canon law and ecclesiastical organization made during the putative time of tyranny.

[64] *Extra* 2.26.14, *Cum vobis*, is a decretal of Innocent III (1206), establishing substantially what Bartolus says here.

universal empire; and this is obvious, because he falls under the *lex Iulia maiestatis*,† as I have said.

On the contrary: because in that same *Cod.* 1.2.16 it is not said that the acts are null unless they are perpetrated against churches, others therefore seem to remain valid. Furthermore, iniquity would arise: for if the tyranny has lasted for a long time in a city, shall we say that everything proclaimed and done in the court is null? This seems harsh.

I say yes, that where some legal proceedings are taken against rebels or enemies of the tyrant, these are *ipso iure* null. For the rebels or enemies were under no obligation to appear before a judge who was notoriously hostile to them or in a place notoriously suspect to them, as in *Dig.* 36.1.8;[65] 42.4.7.1;[66] 50.7.5(4);[67] and as is expressed in *Clem.* 2.11.2.[68] Yet certain ordinances, sentences, and proceedings are directed against those living inside the city, in which case the matter is more doubtful. But it should be noted that when a free man is held by another under the power of a head of household or of a slave owner, and if while in that condition he knowingly does something or does what he would have done in any case, then the action is valid; and the opposite is true, if in other circumstances he would not have done it, as in *Dig.* 41.1.19;[69] 41.1.54,[70] and the note there; 29.2.6.1.[71] Thus in the case at hand, a free people itself or the officials elected by such a people, currently held under tyrannical power, do something which they would have done in any event, even if they had

---

[65] *Dig.* 36.1.8 states that, before an heir can be compelled to go to a place suspect to him in order to restore the inheritance, 'His age and the law, that is, whether it be lawful for him to go there or not, are also to be considered.'

[66] *Dig.* 42.4.7.1 provides for the praetor to manage the property of 'one who lies fraudulently in hiding, if, in the opinion of a good man, his case is not being defended'.

[67] Presumably section 3 is intended, which begins: 'If someone be charged in a public prosecution, there is no obligation on the accuser to take on an embassy to one who declares himself a friend or relative of the person charged.'

[68] *Clem.* 2.11.2 is the bull *Pastoralis cura*, issued by Pope Clement V in 1313, which sets out the principle mentioned here by Bartolus; further, K. Pennington, *The Prince and the Law, 1200–1600: Sovereignty and Rights in the Western Legal Tradition* (Berkeley, CA 1993), pp. 165–201.

[69] If a free man was under pressure to accept an inheritance by acting as if he were a slave but would have wished to do so anyway, he obtains the inheritance.

[70] *Dig.* 41.1.54.*pr.* makes this point in connection with the acquisition of an inheritance by a free man. Accursius's gloss *sciens* adds nothing significant.

[71] *Dig.* 29.2.6.1 ratifies a claim to bonitary possession by someone in parental power. Bartolus's point is that the father could not be forced to allow this if the claim were to an inheritance under the full civil law, because this would make him liable for debts owed by the estate. Under the laxer rules of praetorian – that is, bonitary – ownership, this was not a danger.

been free in their own power, like the decisions of certain common causes, which any tyrant will allow to proceed under the rules of justice. Then these acts are valid, because they are done voluntarily. There are certain things which would not have been done except on account of the tyrant; and these are invalid because they are not done freely, but out of fear of the tyrant, according to the aforesaid laws. This is what *Cod.* 1.2.16 says. For it is certain that no disposition would have been made with regard to churches by anyone other than legitimate prelates, if there had not been a tyrant; hence deeds of the aforesaid type are said to be fundamentally void. These are carefully weighed according to the condition of the doers, as we say of a minor who does something which a mature, careful person would not have done. I also think that if, during lawsuits, injuries are done by the judges to those whom the tyrant holds under suspicion, then restitution should be made to them on the strength of a blanket ruling, as in *Dig.* 4.6.1.1[72] and the note in 36.1.67(65).2.[73] And I consider that the period for seeking restitution runs from the end of the tyranny, as in other circumstances it does from the end of an absence or of a minority: *Extra* 2.26.14 is relevant here.[74]

The second inquiry with regard to these issues concerns those things which are done in a contractual capacity; and this has many aspects.

For sometimes a city gives or concedes something to the tyrant, and then the contract is *ipso iure* null. For just as a promise made by a captive to the person who has incarcerated him is invalid, so in the same way, a promise or any sort of contract made by a people with that tyrant who holds it captive and in a manner of speaking incarcerated, is invalid. For a tyrant is said to hold a people in servitude, as in *Extra* 3.49.4.[75] We can also say that these contracts are null, by reference to *Cod.* 1.53.1.[76] For if these contracts are annulled in the case of a real judge, then much more

---

[72] *Dig.* 4.6.1.1 contains no such reference to hostile judges but the passage guarantees restitution of rights to so many people under so many circumstances – including duress – that it fits Bartolus's purposes.

[73] *Dig.* 36.1.67(65).2 appears to imply the contrary in insisting that an erroneous or even corrupt judgment by the praetor be put into effect, 'for judgments should be conclusive'. Accursius's gloss at this point adds nothing of substance.

[74] Above, n. 64.

[75] *Extra* 3.49.4 is the canon *Non minus*, promulgated at the Third Lateran Council (1179). Beyond referring to Pharaoh's enslavement of all priests except his own, it contains no such statement, and merely relieves prelates of the necessity of contributing to communal taxes imposed by the lay officers of Italian cities.

[76] *Cod.* 1.53.1 severely limits the capacity of officers such as judges and provincial governors to purchase property or receive it as a gift from those subject to their jurisdiction.

so in the case of a tyrant judging unjustly, by analogy with *Auth.* 4.18.2.1[77] and what is noted at the Authentic *Sacramentum* after *Cod.* 5.35.2.[78]

Sometimes contracts are made between that tyrant and the individual men living under him; and then this contract can be said to be null by reference to *Cod.* 1.53.1.[79] It can also be said that this contract should be annulled, by reference to *Cod.* 2.19(20).11;[80] and especially so if the tyrant has ensured that something is sold to him by coercion, for then he falls under that constitution such that he must return the thing and forfeit the price. Someone can prove coercion if the tyrant did not permit the thing to be cultivated, or if he threatened the possessor unless the possessor sold, or sought other pretexts, or ensured that repeated requests were made of one who had nothing for sale. For the request of a greater person is an order, as in *Dig.* 15.4.1.2, in the gloss on the words 'in the same way as'.[81]

Sometimes such a tyrant makes a contract with foreigners in the name of the city; and then if it subjects or obligates that city to another, it is invalid *ipso iure*, as in *Cod.* 11.54(53).1;[82] *Extra* 5.8.1;[83] *Sext.* 1.6.17.[84] Sometimes he does not subject the city, but contracts in some other way. Then even if this is in favour of the tyrannized city, it still seems that it is invalid, just as we say of the possessor in bad faith of an inheritance, as in *Dig.* 2.14.17.6.[85] Hostiensis concludes the opposite, in his commentary on *Extra* 5.8.1; namely, that it is valid when it is for the utility of the city, just as we say in the case of a minor, by analogy with *Cod.* 2.12(13).14.[86] But if one contract is solemnized partly for and partly against the city, and if

---

[77] See *Nov.* 39.2.1: wantonness shall never be treated better than chastity.
[78] Cf. *Nov.* 94.2. The text excerpted as the Authentic *Sacramentum* deprives a widowed mother who has remarried of her tutelage over her children. Accursius's gloss *contractis nuptiis* argues that this is so even if she does not remarry but behaves licentiously.
[79] Above, n. 76.
[80] Above, n. 29.
[81] *Dig.* 15.4.1.2, where Accursius's gloss *quemadmodum* contains the proverb 'A lord's request is an order.'
[82] Above, n. 51.
[83] Above, n. 61.
[84] *Sext.* 1.6.17 is Nicholas III's decretal *Fundamenta* (1278). It is an effort by the papacy to bring under its control the officer known in the thirteenth century as Senator of Rome, often elected by the Romans but sometimes appointed by external powers such as the kings of Sicily, by nullifying any measures taken by any Senator appointed for longer than one year at a time.
[85] *Dig.* 2.14.17.6: the contract of such a person neither prejudices nor benefits the heir.
[86] *Cod.* 2.12(13).14 gives minors the benefit when they have sustained injury but allows them the profit when they have not.

there are separate clauses, then Hostiensis says likewise, that it is valid in those elements which are in the interests of the city, as in *Dig.* 4.4.29.1.[87] But if the clauses are interdependent, then if the city rejects the contract insofar as it unfavourable, it will not be able to approve it insofar as it is favourable, as in *Dig.* 17.2.23.1; 4.4.41; 4.4.24.4. This is Hostiensis's opinion in his commentary on the said passage.[88] I think this is true enough and in accordance with reason in the case of someone who was not unaware that such a person was a tyrant; for in his case the title 'On the authority of a false tutor'[†89] is of no assistance to him. But if we were to suppose that that same contracting party had been ignorant, then he would be assisted by restitution under that same title, *Dig.* 27.6.1.6.[90] And how it could be possible for someone to be ignorant of a fact as notorious as a man's being a manifest tyrant by defect of title is noted by the gloss to C. 9 q. 1 c. 5.[91]

Sometimes a tyrant does not make a contract, but distrains, receiving himself or through his officials payment of those sums which were due to the commonwealth.[92] Are those who pay quit? On this point it should be understood that sometimes those who are paying are debtors to the city by a contract solemnized with the tyrant himself; then it seems that they are quit, as in *Dig.* 12.6.55.[93] But that law speaks of someone making a contract with a robber promising to him in his [– the robber's –] own

---

[87] *Dig.* 4.4.29.1 allows one clause of a contract to be revoked on behalf of a person under the age of twenty-five without affecting the other parts of the contract. The argument cited from Hostiensis is taken from his commentary on the decretal *Quod a praedecessore* (Alexander III, at the Third Lateran Council, 1179): see Hostiensis, *In primum [-sextum] librum decretalium commentaria*, 4 vols. (Venice 1581); vol. IV, fo. 40vb, on *Extra* 5.8.1. The decretal nullifies ordinations made by the anti-popes Victor IV and Paschal III; Hostiensis's discussion accordingly focuses on contracts made by heretical or schismatic bishops in the name of their church.

[88] The Roman law passages cited here relate to the contract of partnership (*societas*) and two questions arising from the right accorded to minors to apply for restitution (*restitutio in integrum*).

[89] For example, *Dig.* 27.6.1.6: 'This rightly is of no help to one who knows, since he deceives himself', which qualifies the principle set out at the beginning of this passage: 'Those who enter into dealings should not be deceived by the employment of a supposed tutor.†'

[90] *Dig.* 27.6.1.6 notes that restitution will not be made to a plaintiff who knew at the time that he was dealing with a false tutor.

[91] Above, n. 62. The *Glossa ordinaria*† to the *Decretum* by Iohannes Teutonicus (c. 1210, modified by Bartholomeus Brixiensis after 1234) asserts (gloss *Nisi probare*) that 'In those matters performed in public, nobody can claim ignorance.'

[92] Distraint is the legitimate sequestration of property by a public authority, often, as in the case envisaged by Bartolus here, to force debtors to pay what they owe.

[93] *Dig.* 12.6.55: 'If a usurper lets urban land, he will not be liable to return to the payer whatever he gets as rent, but will come under an obligation to the owner.'

49

name; here we are speaking of someone making a contract with a tyrant [acting] in the name of the city. It would appear, however, that a debt can be discharged to him [– that is, the tyrant –] on his own contract, just as it could be to a slave or a son, as in *Dig.* 2.14.27.*pr.*; 15.1.56; 46.3.35.[94] Sometimes a debt is paid which is owed to the city in some way other than by the deed of this same tyrant; and then it appears that the one who pays is not quit, as in the said *Dig.* 12.6.55.[95] The best authority for this is what is noted by Innocent in his commentary on *Extra* 1.6.44, where he seems to be saying that those paying a usurping prelate who has no title are not quit.[96]

However, it seems to me that these opinions are true of someone who pays a robber or a usurping prelate or a tyrant, [but] such a one who is not in a position to bring fear or violent threats to bear on him who is paying because, for instance, the debtor is from another city. If, however, the tyrant can bring fear and force and violent threats to bear on him by reason of the jurisdiction which he exercises, notwithstanding that it is only *de facto* – as, for example, when the debtor is one of his subjects – then by paying the tyrant or the tyrant's official, he is quit, as in *Dig.* 32.27.2; 33.21.3.[97] And this is also proved by reason. For that violent exaction imposed on a debtor is imposed to the injury of the city in whose debt he is: for it is principally the city itself which is tyrannizing here, and therefore it seems to come about through the fault of that city, as in *Dig.* 19.2.25.4; 24.3.66.[98] But when an amount of anything in general

---

[94] *Dig.* 2.14.27.*pr.* relates to a partner in a bank; it is not obvious why this passage caught Bartolus's attention, but it may be because of the partner's capacity to receive the entire payment on his own (cf. 'on his own contract' in the text). *Digest* 15.1.56 allows a slave to take over a debtor's liability to his owner. *Digest* 46.3.35 allows a slave to receive back what he has lent or deposited from his own *peculium*. Accursius's gloss does not relate any of these passages to the themes Bartolus is discussing here.

[95] Above, n. 93. Bartolus is stretching a rather inelastic text here.

[96] Innocent IV, *Apparatus super quinque libris decretalium*, fo. 75ra.

[97] These two passages explore some intricacies of testamentary and trust law. In the first, a payment by a debtor to a beneficiary under the will of the deceased creditor is diverted to the fisc; later, the debtor's heir has no obligation to the beneficiary's heir because the money will be paid by the fisc. Debts to an estate ordered by a judge to be paid to a city as beneficiary of a legacy by the deceased owner of the estate are to be paid on to the heirs if the city fails to fulfil the condition of the legacy, meaning that the original debtors are quit. As throughout this passage, Bartolus is exercising considerable ingenuity in bringing the law to bear on the point at issue.

[98] These passages establish, respectively, that a tenant farmer is liable to the owner if a neighbour cuts down trees due to a quarrel with him, and that a husband who commits fraud or negligence is liable for his wife's dowry.

which is owed perishes through the fault of the creditor, then the debtor is quit by way of an exception, as in *Dig.* 46.3.72.[99] But if the debt were something specific, then there is less room for doubt, because he would be quit *ipso iure*, as in the said law. For this reason, when something specific owed to one person is seized by force, then the best authority is in *Dig.* 18.6.13(12)–14(13), and what is noted there;[100] *Dig.* 13.7.43; 21.2.11; 6.1.15.1.[101] The text draws a similar distinction: namely, whether force is applied by someone having jurisdiction or not, as in *Dig.* 2.11.2.9.[102] But perhaps it may be argued that if a certain tyrant were of such a condition that the payment could be recovered from him without great difficulty, then the paying debtor should not be allowed the exception, as is noted at the end of the said law.[103] It would be otherwise if recovery were not easy, as in *Dig.* 2.10.3.[104] But, as I think, the said distinction applies when someone inflicts violence to the injury of the person on whom it is inflicted; but it is otherwise if violence were done to the injury of his creditor, for the reasons given.[105] Nor, in this connection, do I think that it is necessary for someone to prove that he has been intimidated by a tyrant; for it is sufficient if the tyrant has passed a law or issued a proclamation that someone should pay in this way. For one who paid on account of such a proclamation, had good reason to fear that intimidation would be brought to bear on him; and this is sufficient, as the text says in *Dig.*

---

[99] *Dig.* 46.3.72 allows the would-be payer the defence of bad faith in this case. The next section makes the distinction to which Bartolus refers immediately afterwards.

[100] Bartolus refers to Accursius's gloss *lectos emptos* to *Dig.* 18.6.13(12) which itself refers to *Dig.* 18.6.15(16), where Accursius's gloss fits perfectly the distinction Bartolus is making. The scenario in the first passage is the legitimate destruction by an aedile – that is, by a duly constituted magistrate – of furniture delivered by a vendor to the purchaser which had been left outside on the road through the purchaser's fault. *Digest* 18.6.14(13) allows an action against the magistrate if he acted wrongly.

[101] The first passage merely mentions temporary seizure of a pledge by a centurion of the office of the corn supply; the second appears to contradict Bartolus's point here by insisting that the full purchase price was still owed for land part of which had been sold and assigned to veterans by imperial command; the third allows a defendant sued for the return of property to pay the purchase price if he has been forced to sell it, without making it clear how or why he was forced to sell.

[102] *Dig.* 2.11.2.9 grants a defence to someone who intended to come to a court hearing but 'was kept back by a magistrate and kept back without fraud on his own part'.

[103] The final sentence of *Dig.* 2.11.2.9 denies the defence mentioned in the previous note if a private individual, rather than a magistrate, detained someone from attending a hearing.

[104] *Dig.* 2.10.3 allows legal remedies to those who have sustained losses as a result of others maliciously preventing them, or others, from attending a legal hearing. But neither it nor Accursius's gloss supports the specific point that Bartolus makes here.

[105] Bartolus means the circumstances discussed in *Dig.* 18.16.13(12) and the next law.

27.6.7;[106] which text goes a long way towards excusing those debtors who pay under such circumstances. For there a tutor† was forced to act to the grave detriment of his ward, just as here the debtor was forced to do so to the grave detriment of the city. From this it is clear that collectors and other officials established by these tyrants, who extract money and then spend it on the orders of the tyrant, or hand it over to the tyrant himself, are also quit.

Sometimes such tyrants do not make contracts or distrain, but allow the goods and rights of the city to perish and be prescribed. Then I think that no prescription† runs against the city, as in *Cod.* 7.33.1; *Extra* 2.26.14.[107] I also say that if the tyrant were using any right or jurisdiction pertaining to the city itself, not in such a way that it would be recognized by the city but by another, then insofar as he is concerned he seems to be using the right of another, but insofar as the city is concerned he is not.[108] Rather, by that use the city retains its right, which noteworthy point can be gathered from *Dig.* 43.19.1.11.[109]

VIII

Eighthly, I inquire about the manifest tyrant by conduct, although he has a just title, and although he is less properly called a tyrant, as in C. 14 q. 5 c. 9.[110]

I say that a tyrant by conduct is someone who acts tyrannically, that is, his acts tend not towards the common good but to the particular good of the tyrant. For this is ruling unlawfully. But in order to have an easier mode of proof, let us get down to more specific actions, which have been for the most part presented above, in the first book of this treatise, which

---

[106] *Dig.* 27.6.7. See Bartolus's explanation in the text.
[107] Bartolus means that long and peaceful occupancy of such civic property never matures into full ownership. *Code* 7.33.1, by contrast, means that a municipality† (here called *res publica†*) cannot prescribe ownership under some circumstances, not that it cannot lose its ownership to another by means of prescription. Accursius's gloss *in republica* does, however, allow an alternative reading more favourable to Bartolus's position here. *Extra* 2.26.14 (*Cum vobis*, Innocent III, 1206) lays down that periods of schismatic rule should not be counted as contributing to the hundred-year prescription period protecting the Roman church. See above, pp. 45, 47.
[108] Bartolus means that as far as the tyrant is concerned, he is using the right of the city in his dealings with a third party, but the city would refuse to recognize this.
[109] The passage concerns the maintenance by use of private rights of way.
[110] Above, p. 44.

actions consist in this: that the tyrant oppresses his subjects.[111] They are more clearly enumerated by Aristotle, *Politics*, bk. 5, and by Giles in *De regimine principum*.[112]

First, it is a mark of a tyrant that he eliminates the distinguished and powerful men of the city, lest they should be capable of rising up against him. For we see that tyrants kill their own brothers and relatives, which is a sign of the worst kind of tyranny.[113]

Secondly, they destroy the wise, lest those who are in the know denounce their evil deeds, and incite the people against them.

Thirdly, they extinguish teaching and study. For they not only extinguish learned men,[114] but also act in such a way that [no more] are trained. For they are always afraid of being denounced by learning.

Fourthly, they do not even permit lawful groupings [*sodalitates*] and assemblies [*congregationes*]: for they fear that these might rise against them.

Fifthly, they have many spies throughout the city. For they know that they are doing wrong, and always believe that men are speaking ill of them and plotting against them. And for this reason they lend a ready ear to informers of this sort.

Sixthly, a tyrant strives to keep the city in a state of division, so that any one party, fearing another, will not rise against him.

Seventhly, he makes it his business to impoverish his subjects, so that, being preoccupied with securing the wherewithal to live, they do not consider plotting against him.

Eighthly, he foments wars and makes it his business to send soldiers into foreign parts, so that, being bent on war, they do not scheme against him; and because men are impoverished by wars and turned away from study (which a tyrant desires); and also in order that he should have soldiers for himself, when they are needed.

Ninthly, he forms his bodyguard not from his own citizens, but from foreigners; for he is wary of the citizens.

---

[111] A reference to *quaestio* III of *On Guelfs and Ghibellines*, esp. above, p. 9. This comment confirms that Bartolus conceives of all three political tracts, or 'books', as a single 'treatise': see above, Introduction, pp. xv–xvi.

[112] For Aristotle, see next note. Giles of Rome, *De regimine principum* (Rome 1607, repr. Aalen 1967), 3.2.10, pp. 477–80.

[113] Aristotle, *Politics*, 5.10, 1311a15–20; 5.11, 1313a35–1313b30. For the following list, Bartolus is following Giles of Rome point by point in the passage referred to in the previous note.

[114] *Sapientes*, the term employed by Giles.

Tenthly, when there are parties in the city, he adheres to one and together with it oppresses the other.[115]

Such are the views of these philosophers; let us now examine them.

First, that to eliminate distinguished persons and one's brothers is a tyrannical act. This is true, unless it is done for a just cause, as Romulus did to Remus, in *Dig.* 1.8.11.[116] For who can doubt that if anyone were powerful, quarrelsome and seditious in the city, he should be expelled from it by any just judge, as in *Dig.* 48.19.28.3; 48.19.38.2; 1.12.1.13?[117] Therefore, if it were done for a just cause, it would not be a tyrannical act.

Second, namely, to extinguish the wise [*prudentes*]: [this] should also be understood similarly when it is done without cause, according to the same laws.

Third, that they extinguish teaching and study: this should be understood to apply to studies which are appropriate for that city, as in *Dig.* 27.1.6.2.[118] If, however, he prohibits study for which the city is not fitted, that is not a tyrannical act, as in *Dig.* const. *Omnem*, 7.[119]

Fourth, that they do not even permit lawful assemblies: this is to be taken with the proviso: unless for a reason. For what if an assembly – even a lawful one – has transgressed but once? It can certainly be dissolved by law, as in *Dig.* 49.16.3.9.[120] For I have seen people being assembled under the guise of religion and disturbing the condition of the city. Whether it is a tyrannical act to disturb these groupings must therefore be judged according to the character of the persons.[121]

Fifth, namely, that they have many spies in the city: this can be the act of a just ruler, if it is done for a due purpose, as in *Dig.* 1.12.1.13.[122] For an upright judge has spies in order to correct wrongdoings and other

---

[115] At the corresponding point in Giles's discussion (*De regimine principum*, 2.3.10, p. 480) the tenth mark of the tyrant is said to be the creation of divisions and parties in the kingdom and the subsequent use of them against each other.

[116] *Dig.* 1.8.11 justifies the killing of Remus on the grounds that he sought to leave Rome by climbing over the city wall instead of using a gate.

[117] All the passages concerned establish that seditious and rowdy behaviour may be punished by exile.

[118] This text limits the number of doctors, teachers, and grammarians exempt from public duties in a given city.

[119] In this preliminary constitution, Justinian lays down which cities may possess schools of law.

[120] *Dig.* 49.16.3.9 is about soldiers being demoted for desertion as a group.

[121] That is, the persons involved.

[122] Actually *Dig.* 1.12.1.12, which says that the prefect of the city (*praefectus urbi*) should keep the peace and maintain order; he should, in addition, station guards at various places in order to preserve the peace and 'to keep him informed of what is going on'.

unjust acts in a city. But a tyrant uses spies against those through whom his position may be harmed: for he refers everything to his own utility.

Sixth, that the tyrant aims to keep the city in a state of division: this is a straightforwardly tyrannical act, for harmony amongst the citizens is the principal responsibility of a just judge, as in *Dig.* 1.12.1.12;[123] 1.18.13;[124] *Auth.* 3.4.2,[125] where this is more expressly asserted.

Seventh, that he makes it his business to impoverish his subjects: this is a straightforwardly tyrannical act. For an upright judge ought to receive nothing other than what is due to him, nor should he afflict his subjects with real or personal burdens, as in *Cod.* 9.27.4; 9.27.6;[126] *Auth.* 3.4.9.[127]

Eighth, that he foments wars. To foment internal wars is a straightforwardly tyrannical act. But foreign wars can sometimes be just, whereas an unjust war is a straightforwardly tyrannical act, as in *Feud.* 2.28.*pr.*[128]

Ninth, that he does not form his bodyguard of citizens. This act can be just, for a people can be so ungovernable and so perverted that even a just lord cannot rely on them; this tends to happen particularly in cities which have been recently recovered, even by just lords. For this reason emperors sometimes expelled all the men from a city and replaced them with others, as in *Cod.* 10.1.4; 11.56.1.[129] So too we sometimes see just lords building ramparts and fortifications within the city; these pertain to regalian right, as in *Feud.* 2.56.[130] But with a just lord such measures are occasional, with a tyrant they are standard.

Tenth, adhering to one party and oppressing the other is a straightforwardly tyrannical act, since the ultimate end of civil existence [*civilitas*] is the harmony and peace of the citizens, as I have said.

---

[123] See previous note; there, however, peace means good order at public spectacles.
[124] *Dig.* 1.18.13.*pr.*: the provincial governor is to keep his province peaceful and orderly.
[125] *Nov.* 17.2. orders provincial governors to 'take care to prevent all tumults among the people and keep complete peace in the cities'.
[126] *Cod.* 9.27.4 promises a reward to those who successfully denounce judges for corruption; law 6 in this title also concerns the probity of judges.
[127] *Nov.* 17.9 requires provincial governors to be content with their salaries and not to claim travel expenses or means of transport from their subjects.
[128] *Feud.* 2.28.*pr.* obliges a vassal to serve his lord in war if he knows it to be just or is at least in doubt about it.
[129] *Cod.* 10.1.4 concerns resident foreigners transferred by imperial order to another city. *Code* 11.56.1 prohibits outsiders from possessing land in certain villages and revokes without compensation any contract in violation of this.
[130] *Feud.* 2.56, which Bartolus had already cited in *On the Government of a City*, above, p. 26, includes 'palaces in accustomed cities' among regalian rights, but not fortifications.

All these things are, therefore, signs proving the existence of tyranny, but chiefly these two: namely, keeping the city in a state of division and impoverishing the subjects while afflicting them in their persons and property. This is proved beyond doubt in the headings referred to above.

And from all this it is clear how it may be proved that such a man is a tyrant.

IX

Ninthly, I inquire: if some duke, marquis, count, or baron who has just title is proved to be a tyrant by conduct, what ought the superior to do?

I answer: he ought to depose him, since lords who act in this way hold their people in servitude. And it pertains to the superior to rescue a people from servitude, as in *Cod.* 1.27.1.[131] In the same way it is the duty of the superior to depose tyrants, as in the same title, where it is said: 'We have cast down the mightiest tyrants.'[132]

But under what law do tyrants fall, and by which law do they come to be deposed?

I answer: concerning the tyrant who seizes control without just title, it is certain that he is bound by the *Lex Iulia maiestatis.*†[133] But concerning the tyrant who has a just title but appears to be a tyrant by conduct, I say that because he oppresses his subjects physically, he falls under the *Lex Iulia de vi publica.*†[134] Also, because he keeps the city in a state of division and thus does not allow judgments to be made as they should, he falls under the same law.[135] Again, by imposing new taxes and new duties he falls under the same law, in the final law of that title,[136] the penalty for which is deportation, as in *Inst.* 4.18.8.[137] Thus he forfeits all rights under the civil law, as in *Dig.* 48.19.17,[138] and thus as a person subject to infamy,

---

[131] *Cod.* 1.27.1 mentions that Africa has been restored to liberty by Justinian's reconquest of the province.

[132] *Cod.* 1.27.2.

[133] Bartolus is probably thinking of *Dig.* 48.4.3, which he had already cited in a similar context (above, p. 42): a private person who knowingly and maliciously acts as a public power commits treason.

[134] *Dig.* 48.6. No passage uses precisely the vocabulary of oppression, but physical, armed violence against one's fellow citizens is mentioned several times throughout the title.

[135] *Dig.* 48.6.10 begins by punishing 'Anyone who does something with malicious intent to hinder the safe exercise of justice or to hinder judges.'

[136] *Dig.* 48.6.12: 'Those who impose new taxes are liable under the *Lex Iulia de vi privata.*†'

[137] *Inst.* 4.18.8 in fact decrees deportation only for the use of *armed* force; for non-armed force the penalty is confiscation of one-third of one's wealth.

[138] *Dig.* 48.19.17 refers to convicts who have no rights under the civil law, and who, being without citizenship (*civitas*), are stateless.

he loses his dignity and jurisdiction, as is explicitly stated in the *Lex Iulia de vi privata*† at *Dig.* 48.7.1.[139] Again, for this reason he falls under the *Lex Iulia de ambitu*† at *Dig.* 48.14.1 and also under *Cod.* 4.62.4.[140] He may also be subject to capital punishment, as in *Cod.* 10.20.1.[141]

In addition, I say that if those living in this tyrannical fashion 'conspire in whatever way, either publicly or secretly' against the emperor or his officials, then *ipso iure* they are rebels against the empire and lose their dignity, according to the new law of Emperor Henry.[142]

X

Tenthly, I inquire: what shall we say about those things which we have seen done by the supreme pontiff, the emperor, and the legates? For they have constituted as their own vicars† – namely, of the apostolic see or of the empire – certain men whom they well knew to be tyrants, in lands which those men held through tyranny. Clement VI did this in the city of Bologna with Lord Taddeo Pepoli and his sons, Lord Giacomo and Lord Giovanni.[143] Charles our emperor did the same with the tyrants of Lombardy, as did Lord Giles, cardinal bishop of Sabina and legate of the apostolic see, with many tyrants in the March of Ancona.[144]

I answer: it must be presumed that such great lords do not act in this way without considerable cause. The cause can be twofold. First, on account

---

[139] *Dig.* 48.7.1: those convicted under this law lose all public office and honour.
[140] *Dig.* 48.14.1 states (sec. 3) that 'he who introduces a new tax is by *senatus consultum*†' punished with a fine and infamy. *Code* 4.62.4 punishes contractors who make excessive demands with exile.
[141] *Cod.* 10.20.1.1 decrees that collectors convicted of making excessive exactions incur capital punishment if they persist and are caught.
[142] Bartolus refers here to the constitution *Quoniam nuper est*, issued by Emperor Henry VII in 1313: MGH, *Constitutiones et acta publica imperatorum et regum*, ed. J. Schwalm, iv, pt. 2 (Hanover 1909–11), nos. 931–2, pp. 966–8. It was frequently included in manuscripts – and thus in printed editions – of the Roman law under the rubric *Qui sint rebelles* ('Who rebels are'). The words quoted here are a contraction of the original formulation. Bartolus wrote a famous commentary on this text: *Bartoli a Sassoferrato Consilia, quaestiones et tractatus* (Basle 1588), pp. 285–91; further D. Quaglioni, '"Rebellare idem est quam resistere": Obédience et résistance dans les gloses de Bartole à la constitution "Quoniam nuper" d'Henri VII (1355)', in J.-C. Zancarini, ed., *Le Droit de résistance, XIIe–XXe siècle* (Paris 1999), pp. 35–46.
[143] It was in fact Pope Benedict XII who appointed Taddeo Pepoli papal vicar in 1340. Clement VI (elected 1342) did the same for two sons of Taddeo, Giacomo and Giovanni.
[144] Gil Albornoz became cardinal-bishop of Santa Sabina only in December 1356. This reading is standard, and is therefore almost certain to be original. It suggests that Bartolus was working on this tract at the very end of his life – he died in July 1357.

of some great and difficult matters, which they are obliged to expedite: for just as a responsible sailor will jettison the cheaper cargo in order to save the more valuable, as in *Dig.* 14.2.8;[145] and just as a responsible *paterfamilias*† ought to prefer that the more expensive items should be saved, as is noted in *Dig.* 13.6.5.4;[146] so a just lord sometimes puts up with a tyrant and makes him a vicar,† in order that he can first redress more difficult matters. The second reason may be his love and affection for those who are under the tyrant. For we see physicians acting in accordance with nature, when an illness cannot be cured without great danger to the person; then they strive to support nature, lest the illness advance any further, and as a result nature comes to her own aid. An upright emperor sometimes acts in the same way, seeing that, on occasion, a single tyrant cannot be deposed without the wholesale slaughter of those who are under the tyrant. For their good he makes that tyrant a vicar, so that on this basis the tyrant should be less fearful and should oppress the people less. Meanwhile an occasion may arise on account of which, at the prompting of justice, and without any harm to the people, the tyrant may be deposed.

On account of a recently conferred title, however, these tyrants do not cease to be tyrants if they continue to commit tyrannical acts of this sort. For these misdeeds do not come within the remit of the commission made to them, as in *Dig.* 12.6.6;[147] 42.8.12.[148]

XI

Eleventhly, I inquire whether the deeds of tyrants who have a just title are valid.

I say that either the tyrant has proceeded against his exiles and rebels, in which case the proceedings are invalid, because they were not obliged to appear before a judge who was notoriously hostile to them, as I have

---

[145] *Dig.* 14.2.8 makes a specific point about the ownership of jettisoned cargo without commenting on the sailor's prudence.

[146] Accursius argues at *Dig.* 13.6.5.4, gloss *salvas facere*, that a person who salvages his own property from a natural disaster and abandons something he has borrowed is not liable when what he has borrowed is of negligible value. Neither the law nor this gloss mentions the *paterfamilias*.

[147] *Dig.* 12.6.6.2 states that a procurator† who exceeds the terms of his commission can be sued for the recovery of money paid him which was not owed his principal.

[148] *Dig.* 42.8.12 states that powers of administration granted to a son in power by the head of household (*paterfamilias*) do not extend to alienations from the son's *peculium* in fraud of creditors. The *peculium* was a piece of private property given to sons, wives, and slaves for them to administer by themselves.

stated above;[149] but those proceedings which he has taken against those within the city are valid for as long as he is tolerated in that dignity, as in *Dig.* 1.14.3;[150] *Cod.* 7.45.2;[151] 6.23.1;[152] *Extra.* 1.3.13, and Innocent's commentary on it;[153] *Extra.* 2.27.24.[154] And this applies for as long as he is tolerated.

But what if proceedings have already been instigated against such a tyrant: are his deeds valid while proceedings are pending and before sentence is pronounced?

I answer: sometimes the proceedings are such that a declaratory sentence is passed, as when the tyrant has committed some misdeed on account of which he is *ipso iure* deprived of jurisdiction, or declared a slave or infamous; in that case deeds done after the instigation of proceedings are invalid, as in *Cod.* 6.23.1 where it is stated 'nor has anyone up to this point raised any doubt as to their condition'; and *Dig.* 40.9.15.[155] But if the proceedings are such that he would be deprived by sentence, then in the meantime his deeds are valid, because meanwhile he retains his dignity, as in *Dig.* 49.14.46.6;[156] and expressly at 50.1.17.12;[157] and what is noted at *Cod.* 10.60(58).1.[158] In the same way, if someone were to make a contract with this tyrant or discharge an obligation to him, then it would be valid, as is noted by Innocent in his commentary on *Extra*

[149] Above, p. 46.
[150] *Dig.* 1.14.3 ratifies the acts of a praetor subsequently discovered to have been a slave.
[151] *Cod.* 7.45.2 confirms the validity of an arbitration if the arbiter, later enslaved, was a free man at the time.
[152] *Cod.* 6.23.1 blocks a challenge to the validity of a will on the grounds that the witnesses were slaves because 'the witnesses were present with the consent of all the children, nor has anyone up to this point raised any doubt as to their condition'.
[153] *Extra* 1.3.13, the decretal *Sciscitatus* by Clement III, rules that some addressees of papal letters, such as slaves or those punished by infamy, are prohibited by law from executing those letters by their legal status. Innocent IV, *Apparatus super quinque libris decretalium*, fo. 12rb: objections to the legal capacity of a judge with ordinary jurisdiction are invalid for as long as he is tolerated in office.
[154] *Extra* 2.27.24, the decretal *Ad probandum* issued by Alexander III, actually nullifies a sentence on the grounds that one of the judges was excommunicated at the time of the hearing.
[155] *Dig.* 40.9.15 revokes a manumission carried out by an owner who knew a charge of treason against him was justified.
[156] *Dig.* 49.14.46.6 rules that 'A person subject to a charge can administer his own property, and his debtor may properly pay him in good faith.'
[157] *Dig.* 50.1.17.12 does indeed establish that those answering capital charges maintain their current dignities but can receive no fresh ones.
[158] Where Accursius's gloss *novos* refers to *Dig.* 50.1.17.12 to affirm the same principle.

1.6.44,[159] subject to the caveat that the tyrant did not make a contract which subjugated the city, as I shall explain below.[160]

And on this basis I say that if someone is in [a position of] notable power[161] and has just title, although he be a tyrant by conduct, he is nevertheless granted a special dispensation, as in *Clem.* 3.15.1, for as long as he is tolerated in that dignity.[162] But the opposite would be true if his title were defective, as is noted there.

And I say further, that after such a man with such a title had become a tyrant by conduct, and if he were to secure the concession of any wider jurisdiction to himself by the people, then this would be invalid, on the assumption that the people were acting out of fear, as I said in the preceding discussion.

Furthermore, every contract he made concerning that city, which subjected or bound it, would be invalid: for he is not in the position of a lord when he deprives the city of its liberty, as in *Dig.* 41.4.7.3;[163] and there is an explicit case in *Extra* 2.24.33; *Sext.* 1.6.17.7.[164]

XII

Twelfthly, I inquire about a tacit or concealed tyrant; that is, one who under some veil rules unlawfully in a city. However, this veil comes about in two ways: first, through a title which he causes to be granted to himself; second, through a title which he does not suffer to be granted to himself.

---

[159] Above, p. 50 and n. 96. Bartolus seems to be thinking of Innocent IV's comment (*Apparatus super quinque libris decretalium*, fo. 75rb *in fin.*) to the effect that the deeds of a prelate are valid if he has been duly confirmed by his superior, even if he be a simoniac, for as long as he is tolerated in office.

[160] See the end of this *quaestio*.

[161] The phrase *notabilis potentatus* occurs in *Sext.* 1.6.17, which Bartolus cites below, and is therefore preferable to Quaglioni's *nobili potentatu*: *Politica e diritto*, p. 207, line 640.

[162] *Clem.* 3.15.1 appears to grant no such dispensation. Rather, it allows the offspring of kings and rulers (*principes*) to be baptized in private houses despite the general prohibition of the practice.

[163] *Dig.* 41.4.7.3: a tutor[†] is not regarded as the owner when he is swindling his ward, only when he is managing the ward's affairs honestly.

[164] The passages cited contain anything but explicit instances of the principle Bartolus is trying to establish here. Honorius III's decretal *Intellecto* (1225; *Extra* 2.24.33) revokes alienations made by the king of Hungary to the prejudice of his realm. For *Sext.* 1.6.17, see above, n. 84. The latter does refer to the liberty of the Roman church, and once to the protection of the people of Rome from 'the incursions of oppressors'; it forbids the election of a Senator of Rome for longer than one year.

Concerning the first veil, through the title which he causes to be granted to himself, it should be understood that, as I have said above, a tyrant is, properly speaking, the opposite of a king.[165] But it is characteristic of royal power that it is perpetual and that it enjoys total jurisdiction, as is clear from the texts [*capitula*] referred to above.[166] From these two characteristics, the two tyrannical veils have been devised.

First, that someone causes jurisdiction to be granted to himself for a fixed period, and at the expiry of that period to be reconfirmed, so that his rule appears to be more that of a judge than of a tyrant. But on this point I say that if someone causes this jurisdiction to be granted to him in his own city, his title is null: for no one can have such jurisdiction, as in *Cod.* 1.51.10.[167] This is not the case in the city of Rome, where someone can be a praetor, as in *Cod.* 1.39.2,[168] and a senator for one year only and no longer, as established in *Sext.* 1.6.17.[169] It also does not apply in the case of defenders† of cities, as in *Auth.* 3.2.1;[170] yet these officials do not have *merum et mixtum imperium*,† but only simple jurisdiction. And so the same must be said of one who assumes no title, as I have said above concerning a tyrant by defect of title.

But if you were to suppose a city to have jurisdiction, either by privilege or custom, such that the power of the people making the grant could not be called into doubt, and thus that a title granted in this way in the first place would be valid, then it must be established whether he is a tyrant because he has caused himself to be reconfirmed. This seems to be the case under the common law, because such reconfirmation is not valid: indeed, it contravenes the *Lex Iulia de ambitu*,† in *Cod.* 9.26.1.[171]

But if you were to suppose that the power of the people was such that it could dispense from this law, then it must be established whether he has so entrenched himself during his first period of rule that the people

---

[165] Above, *On the Government of a City*, p. 26.

[166] Bartolus seems to be referring to *On the Government of a City*, where he notes on the basis of *Dig.* 1.2.2.14 that 'kings have all power' and, further, that 'particular kingdoms' descend by succession on the basis of *Dig.* 1.1.5 and Giles of Rome, *De regimine principum*, 3.2.5, pp. 461–5. In his commentary on *Dig.* 2.2.1 he includes kings in the category of magistrates possessing perpetual jurisdiction: *Bartoli a Sassoferrato in primam Digesti Veteris partem commentaria* (Turin 1574), fo. 53ra.

[167] *Cod.* 1.51.10 punishes certain provincial judicial advisors who remain in office for longer than four months.

[168] *Cod.* 1.39.2 orders three praetors to be appointed each year in the city of Rome.

[169] Above, n. 84.

[170] *Nov.* 15.2 appoints defenders of cities to represent the provincial governor.

[171] *Cod.* 9.26.1 punishes various office-holders who seek reappointment.

have of necessity to elect him for a subsequent period. In that case he is truly a tyrant, elected through fear, and thus a tyrant by defect of title. If, however, he were to be freely elected, but a tyrant by conduct, then you can say the same as we said before.

The second veil is when certain tyrants cause themselves to be given some title which involves almost no jurisdiction, as when they cause themselves to be made Standard Bearers or *gonfalonieri*,[172] or they arrange for the custody of the city to be committed to them, or they have themselves made captains of the mercenaries or of the men-at-arms. For on this basis they state that they are not tyrants, because a tyrant must have all jurisdiction, just like a king. For no one can be said to rule without any, or with only a limited, jurisdiction. Certainly, he is not a tyrant on the basis of this title. But when, on the basis of it, he attains such power that he arranges the offices of the city as he wishes, and the officials obey him as lord, then I say that if he commits tyrannical acts or causes them to be committed, he is truly a tyrant. For he rules in the city when the organs of government obey him; and he rules unlawfully, because he performs tyrannical acts, and thus he is a tyrant.

But how will it be possible to prove this, when a concealed tyrant of this sort does not act for himself, and rarely enters the palace, but the organs of government obey his written orders and his agents?

I answer: the proof is difficult, since when these things are done, witnesses may not be called. With this in mind, a decretal established in a particular case that someone's power should be proved by oath, in *Sext.* 1.3.11.[173] But I do not think that this applies generally. For there the oath-taker only obtains a judge by this procedure, but this does not create any other prejudice against him against whom the oath is taken; and therefore I think that this must be proved in some other way. For it should be understood that although certain acts cannot be directly proved of themselves, yet they are still capable of proof, as I said in my book on alluvial

---

[172] The office of Standard Bearer of Justice was an innovation of the thirteenth century, particularly in those Italian cities where the *popolo* organized itself against the magnates. In Perugia, for instance, this official is first attested in 1305: S. R. Blanshei, *Perugia, 1260–1340: Conflict and Change in a Medieval Italian Urban Society*, Transactions of the American Philosophical Society, n.s. 66, pt. 2 (Philadelphia, PA 1976), p. 55.

[173] *Sext.* 1.3.11, the decretal *Statutum* of Boniface VIII allowing a plaintiff who is too scared to enter the city or diocese where he ought by law to plead his case or who, with good reason, fears the power of his adversary, to have the hearing convened elsewhere, so long as he promises on oath to the judge concerned that this is the truth.

deposit.[174] Although alluvial deposit cannot be seen as it rises, yet from its having been formed it follows of necessity that the river has deposited it. Again, although the conception of a son cannot be seen, it is taken as full proof that he is born in the house of a woman cohabiting with a man, as in *Dig.* 1.6.6.[175] For since proof is to convince a judge, these facts go far enough towards convincing the judge. So it is in the present case, if someone has proved that the city is in a state of division (for perhaps one party has been expelled), that evil deeds are committed there and irregularities go unpunished, that the citizens are greatly burdened, and similar things which are included among the tyrannical acts we have discussed above. Furthermore, if such a man who has that title is the most powerful man in the city, and if it is a matter of public report that he has caused the aforesaid things to be done, then I think that tyranny is sufficiently proven. For these acts cannot proceed from anyone other than this most powerful man; together with the aforesaid public report, this is enough to convince the judge. This agrees with what we said about one who rules justly: that it suffices that he is held and reputed to do so, as in *Dig.* 1.14.3.[176] By the same reasoning, it says a lot if someone is held and reputed to be a tyrant.

But are the deeds performed during such a period of tyranny valid?

I say the same as I said above about a manifest tyrant who causes these deeds to be done by the officials elected by the city.[177]

And all this is true when the greater part of the people is oppressed, burdened, and discontented. For if some were kept away from the city, or others were mistreated within the city, and were not called to public honours, but in other respects the city were well ruled and the common utility were fostered, then such a man with this sort of title or a similar eminence would not be a tyrant in the straightforward sense of the word, because the common utility is fostered under such a government, and this is diametrically opposed to tyranny. But in respect of those things which were done against outsiders and the enemies of such an eminent man, then although he rules the commonwealth well, I think the same should be said as if they were done by a tyrant. For there is nothing to prevent someone being termed a tyrant with respect to particular persons, but

---

[174] Above, Translators' Note, p. xxxix; cf. *On Guelfs and Ghibellines*, p. 13.
[175] *Dig.* 1.6.6 argues that if a husband has been absent for ten years, a one-year-old child found on his return is not his son.
[176] Above, n. 150.
[177] Above, pp. 45–6.

a just judge with respect to the community, as in *Cod.* 5.7.1.[178] For this reason it should be understood that just as one seldom comes across an entirely healthy man, who suffers from no bodily defect, so one rarely comes across any government which attends entirely to the public good and in which there is no hint of tyranny. It would be more divine than human if those who rule had absolutely no regard to their own advantage, but only for the common utility. We call it a good government, rather than a tyrannical one, when the common and public utility prevails over the personal interest of the ruler; but a tyrannical one, when more attention is paid to personal utility. This is said by Giles in *De regimine principum*, 3.2.11,[179] and particular notice should be taken of this, when we consider how to prove whether someone is a tyrant.

There is a third veil, when someone does not allow any title to be granted to him in the city, but organizes its organs of government in such a way that everything proceeds according to his will. I say that it can be proved that they are tyrants in the way described immediately above, namely, that tyrannical deeds are done in the city; that he is the most powerful man with the greatest following; and that, according to public report, he causes such deeds to be done. It is inevitable that many things necessarily happen during a period of tyranny, on account of which the evil mind of the tyrant cannot remain hidden and an easy mode of proof will become apparent.

Indeed, with regard to those things which are done in a period of such tyranny, I reiterate what I said immediately above.

And whether there can be a tyrant in a neighbourhood or a certain part of a city or in the *contado*,† I have said above.[180]

---

[178] *Cod.* 5.7.1 punishes local judges who abuse their office in order to force women in their jurisdiction to marry them. Neither this text nor its gloss supports Bartolus's comment here.

[179] Giles of Rome, *De regimine principum*, 3.2.11, pp. 480–1.

[180] Above, pp. 39–40.

Appendix I

The Preface to Bartolus's *Tiberiadis*[1]

In the name of the Father, the Son, and the Holy Spirit, Amen.

The Tiberiad is the region located next to the river Tiber. The Tiber, moreover, is a notable river in Italian parts. For it passes through the Roman city which is the head and mistress of all cities. It joins the sea in the territory of the same city. It is navigable there, and retains its name as far as the sea. The Tiber, moreover, takes its name from Tiberius, the Roman emperor, from whom we have some promulgated laws, and this river is mentioned several times by this name in our laws. For this river flows round that laudable mountain where the happy city of Perugia is situated, and, passing for a long distance through its territory, has plains, hills, and further populous places around it, graced with numerous and beautiful buildings, fertile [and] very pleasing to the eye, for they look like pleasure gardens.

And so, when I was free from lecturing, and for relaxation was nearing a certain *villa* close to Perugia and lying above the Tiber, I took to contemplating the bends of the Tiber, alluvial deposits, islands created in the river, and changes in the riverbed. And I began to think a little about what the law was concerning the many questions which had arisen in practice, and others which I myself would devise from contemplating the river;

---

[1] See Introduction, pp. xiii–xiv. The translation is based on the text in O. Cavallar, ed., 'River of Law: Bartolus's *Tiberiadis* (*De alluvione*)', in J. A. Marino and T. Kuehn, eds., *A Renaissance of Conflicts: Visions and Revisions of Law and Society in Italy and Spain* (Toronto 2004), pp. 30–129, at 84–5.

without, however, intending to go further, lest I forestalled the relaxation for the sake of which I had come.

And that night, when I was asleep, with daybreak imminent, I dreamed that a certain man came to me, with a peaceful countenance, and said: 'Write down what you have begun to think about, and, because it is necessary to study it visually, illustrate it with diagrams. Here I have brought you a pen with which to write, compasses with which you can measure and draw circular figures, and a ruler for you to draw lines and create diagrams.'

To which I said: 'Heaven forbid that I should illustrate what pertains to the laws with diagrams. For if I were to do that, far more people would laugh at me than praise me.'

Then, looking at me with a perturbed expression, he said: 'Bartolus, I know what modicum of talent you have from God. Are you, then, afraid of being mocked for a good act? The lives of Christ and all the saints contradict that; in performing good deeds, they paid no heed to insults, derision, and blows. But you also have a modicum of moral goodness. For this fear, by which you are drawn away from the good, is opposed to that moral virtue which is called courage. It is in your power to do good, but you have no power to decide what others say.'

To which I said, ashamed, 'I agree with you. But I spoke thus at the prompting of my first impulse.'

He said, 'So start secure in your mind, for the Lord will be with you in accomplishing this work, and will reveal many things to you which are unknown to you.'

And so, arising, and having placed my trust in Him who had promised He would be with me in the prosecution of it, I have started this work. I called the whole thing *Tiberiad*, so that in it not only the Tiber itself would be discussed, but also many things which occur in the region of the Tiber – thinking it appropriate that, just as the laws have proceeded to everybody from the city of Rome, so what is said about the Roman river Tiber applies to all rivers. And I have divided it into three books: in the first I shall treat alluvial deposit; in the second, the island created in a river; in the third, the riverbed. And then in two days I composed and explained the diagrams of the first book. On the third day I began the diagrams of the second book, and since certain questions had occurred to me and I was thinking hard about them, a certain Brother Guido of Perugia visited me, with no intention of staying; a great theologian, a polymath in all things, who had been and was my teacher in geometry.

But then it rained so heavily that he was forced to spend the night and stay the course of a whole day with me. Then I said: 'I truly know that God is with the completion of this work.' I compared everything mentioned above with him, and finished designing the diagrams of the second book with him, and experienced many spiritual joys from [our] spiritual exchanges together. But what I was going to say in the third book I stored in my mind, and have returned to Perugia with all this and have revised it, and composed a small book in the form below. And I have deposited it in your university in the year of the Lord 1355.

Appendix II

Legislative Autonomy and the Universality of the Roman Empire[1]

Bartolus articulated his principal ideas about political life as a teacher, in his lectures on Roman law for university students. The texts in this appendix are excerpts from two of his most important commentaries. The first is Bartolus's most famous single lecture, an extended commentary (called a *repetitio*) on *Digest*[†] 1.1.9, the law *Omnes populi*, which he delivered in Perugia on November 3rd, 1343.[2] Bartolus here sets out the relationship between the civil law of particular peoples or cities, natural law, and *ius gentium*.[†] He then explains why certain peoples are able to pass their own statutes without authorization by the emperor, and differentiates such peoples from those which cannot. The second is his commentary on one of the two constitutions issued by Emperor Henry VII at Pisa in April 1313. It contains the fullest expression of Bartolus's commitment to the universality and divine mission of the Roman empire and was written sometime after 1355, in the last years of his life.

Digest 1.1.9: *All peoples* [populi] *who are governed by laws and customs use in part their own law, in part the law common to all men. For what each people has established as law for itself is particular to that city and called the civil law, as being the particular law of that city. But what natural reason has*

---

[1] See Introduction, pp. xxix–xxx.
[2] M. Bellomo, *I fatti e il diritto: Tra le certezze e i dubbi dei giuristi medievali (secoli XIII–XIV)*, Collana i Libri di Erice 27 (Rome 2000), p. 484 n. 49.

established among all men is equally observed by all mankind, and is called the law of nations [ius gentium†], *as the law which all nations employ.*[3]

It is permitted to every people which has jurisdiction to enact its own law, which is called civil law. But that which is observed in equal measure by every nation is called the law of nations [*ius gentium*]. This is what the text says. [The first part] draws a twofold distinction, as far as the words '*For what each people ...*'. The second part begins where it gives an example of the first element of the distinction, as far as the words '*But what ...*'. The third [part] begins where it gives an example of the second element and lasts until the end of the law. Put the principal statement of the law as follows. It was said above that the laws which the Roman people uses are of various kinds.[4] Therefore I ask, is the law which each people uses civil law? I answer [as above]: 'It is permitted to every people ...' etc. Pick out the points of special note for yourself.

The first objection is that the relative pronoun 'which' or 'who', when it is added to a certain general quantity without a copulative particle, restricts the category, as in *Dig.* 32.46.[5] But here it says 'All peoples who are governed by laws ...' etc., and thus it implies that there are some who are not ruled by laws or customs, which is untrue, since all use the law of nations, as here at the end. Solution: the gloss says that this is said on account of wild men who do not use customs or laws, or reason, as in *Inst.* 1.2.1.[6] This is not correct, because such wild men do not constitute a people, therefore this law which says '*All peoples ...*' cannot be referring to them. Others say that this is said on account of peoples formed recently who have no fixed law as in *Dig.* 1.2.2.1,[7] and there is a note there by Iacobus de Arena.[8] But this opinion does not seem correct to us

---

[3] *Bartoli a Sassoferrato in primam Digesti Veteris partem commentaria* (Turin 1574), fo. 9ra–vb. Exceptionally, we here give the entire source text for ease of reference in reading the lengthy extracts from Bartolus's commentary on it.

[4] *Dig.* 1.1.6.1 explains that the Romans use written as well as unwritten laws.

[5] In a legacy, the phrase '*and* what has been acquired' augments, whereas the omission of 'and' restricts, what is granted.

[6] *Inst.* 1.2.1 repeats *verbatim* the first words of this passage from the *Digest†* which Bartolus is explaining here. Accursius's gloss *legibus et moribus* accounts for the apparent implication of the text – that there are some peoples who are not ruled by laws and customs – by reference to *homines sylvestres* or 'wild people' who are not regulated by such norms.

[7] *Dig.* 1.2.2 gives a history of Roman magistracies and legislative organs from archaic times to the second century AD. The paragraph cited here recalls how in the beginning the Romans did not live by defined laws or legal rights and left the management of all matters to their kings.

[8] See Iacobus de Arena, *Commentarii in universum ius civile* (Lyons 1541, repr. *Opera iuridica rariora*, xvi, ed. D. Maffei, E. Cortese, and G. Rossi (Bologna 1971)), fo. 63va. Iacobus

either because such peoples do use laws and customs, although not fixed ones. You should say therefore that this relative article is not used in a restrictive sense but declaratively in this way: *'All peoples who'* – namely, all of them. The reason is that the quality identified by the relative article applies to each member of the category. There is a similar case at *Cod.* 1.1.1 and *Cod.* 6.49.6.[9] So either the quality which is mentioned supplementarily by the relative pronoun applies to each member of the category, and it is used declaratively as here and similar passages, or it does not apply to each member of the category, and then either the relative article is used without a copulative particle and is used restrictively, or it is used with a copulative and in that case it is used augmentatively: *Dig.* 32.46.[10]

The second objection is that it seems that only the emperor may make law, as in *Cod.* 1.14.12.5.[11] Here, however, it says *'All peoples, who use laws'* etc. and therefore erroneously, since it implies that any people can legislate. Solution: some say that this law has been corrected by that one, which is wrong because a correction of law should be avoided where possible, as in *Cod.* 3.30.*un.*[12] Or the gloss says that here it is talking about the law of nations, there [*Cod.* 1.14.12.5] about each people's own law.[13] What the gloss means is that the former is called the law of nations. Further, specific civil law can be made by a people, as here, but only the emperor can make common civil law, as in the contrary passage. Or say that only the emperor makes law, and no other single person, as is noted at the contrary passage,[14] but the people can certainly make law, as here and *Cod.* 1.14.12.4.[15]

discusses the same gloss by Accursius, observing that newly created peoples – *populi* – have no definite law or custom. Iacobus's final reference there makes no sense as it stands and presumably was originally to *Dig.* 1.2.2.1.

[9] *Cod.* 1.1.1 begins 'We desire that all peoples who are governed by the moderation of our clemency'; the final section of *Cod.* 6.49.6 imposes a restrictive interpretation of a relative pronoun earlier in the text.

[10] As above, n. 5.

[11] Justinian here refers to the emperor as 'he who alone is permitted to legislate'.

[12] The text does not contain a statement of this principle as such, but, in Bartolus's view, an example of it.

[13] See gloss *Suo proprio* to *Dig.* 1.1.9:

But how can a people's own law, or the law established by nations, apply since only the emperor can make laws, as in *Cod.* 1.14.5, which contradicts this? Answer: this has been corrected by that one, according to some; or say rather that here it is talking about the law of nations which applies between all nations almost by nature itself, and that law of nations which is specific to a particular people and is not general, so there is no contradiction.

[14] See the beginning of Accursius's gloss *solus imperator* at *Cod.* 1.14.12.5: 'Meaning no other person alone. Hence the Roman people can even today make law.'

[15] Bartolus means that *Cod.* 1.14.12 is actually in agreement with what *Dig.* 1.1.9 says, once this distinction between the single emperor and the corporate Roman people has been applied.

The third objection is that this text appears to contradict itself, because it says *'But what natural reason ...'* etc.; afterwards it says that this is called the law of nations, whereas it ought to be called natural law because natural reason introduces it. Solution: I admit that the law of nations can be called natural law, according to its true signification as is noted above, *Dig.* 1.1.1.; *Inst.* 2.1.11.[16] Or solve it [by saying] that it can be called natural law, as you say, but more properly it is called the law of nations. For when the word 'natural' is used in relation to reason it is understood to refer to the law of nations, for it is not common to all animals lacking reason, but only to peoples [*gentes*], and this is what it means here. Also, sometimes the word 'natural' is used in relation to man, and the same applies, because it is understood to mean the law of all peoples [*gentes*], as above, *Dig.* 1.1.3: 'nature has established among us a relationship of sorts ...'.[17]

The contradictions dealt with, since this law treats of the particular law which a city itself establishes for itself, that is, statutes, let us therefore treat the subject of statutes by way of principal and accessory questions. In the first place I ask who can make statutes; second, how; third, on what matters; fourth, whom does a statute bind once made; fifth, from what moment it binds; sixth, whether statutes may be interpreted; seventh, how statutes should be applied in a legal judgment.[18]

Therefore, I ask first who can make statutes, and first whether every people can make statutes on its own and without the authority of a superior? And it appears that the authority of a superior is required, as in *Cod.* 10.65.5.[19] *Auth.* 3.2.1.1 is relevant.[20] However, Gulielmus de Cuneo treats this here, but less than satisfactorily, so say as follows.[21] Either you are

---

[16] Bartolus's first reference is to the gloss *Quod natura* at *Dig.* 1.1.1.3, where Accursius notes that one signification of natural law is the *ius gentium*† (law of nations) and refers to *Inst.* 2.1.11 where 'the law of nature ... can be described as the law of all peoples'.

[17] *Dig.* 1.1.3 states that the right of self-defence emanates from the *ius gentium* and explains that nature has established a relationship of sorts between human beings.

[18] This list is translated in full here because it communicates the breadth of fourteenth-century jurisprudence on the statutory legislation of the Italian cities; only the first principal question, and elements of the second, are translated in what follows.

[19] *Cod.* 10.65.5, on public embassies, rules that a verdict on a matter brought to the praetorian prefect of Illyricum by his provincials should be affirmed in a public place by the established authority.

[20] See *Nov.* 15.1, where elections to the office of defender† of cities are to be confirmed by a prefect.

[21] *Lectura super Digestum Vetus*, in Oxford, Bodleian Library, MS. Bodley Can. Misc. 472, fos. 1ra–77vb, at 2vb. Gulielmus de Cuneo argues that peoples who elect their own judges, who are then confirmed by the emperor, may pass statutes without the explicit permission of a superior.

asking about a people which has no jurisdiction, such as villages and *castra*† which are simply subject to some city or lord, or about a people which has all jurisdiction granted by the emperor or has prescribed it,²² as in *Auth.* 3.3.*pr.* at the end of the long gloss.²³ Or you are asking about a people with limited jurisdiction, such as jurisdiction over civil cases only or petty criminal cases, such as numerous *castra* in the March [of Ancona]. In the first case, either such a people wishes to make a statute relating to the decision of legal cases, or to the administration of the property of the people itself. In the first case, either the authority of the superior of that people has been given, and it [i.e. the statute] is valid, as in *Cod.* 6.23.31.2, where the custom of country folk is to be upheld because the emperor, or the people to which those rustics were subject, has approved it.²⁴ *Extra* 1.2.8 and 9 are relevant.²⁵ This is what the said law, *Cod.* 6.23.31.2, says. Or the authority of the superior has not been given, and it is invalid, because [the people] lacks jurisdiction and making statutes is jurisdiction in its generic signification as is clear from the definition, *Dig.* 2.1.1.²⁶ And when something is withheld, everything is withheld which leads to it: *Dig.* 23.1.16.²⁷ But if you are asking about those matters which pertain to the administration of their own goods, such as spending common funds, statutes can be made unless they favour individuals: *Dig.* 50.9.1 and 4.²⁸ In the second case, where a people has all jurisdiction, it can

---

²² See *praescriptio*.†
²³ See gloss *iurisdictione*, where Accursius argues that when jurisdiction is granted to lower magistrates such as defenders† of cities, other powers included in the general categories of *merum* and *mixtum imperium*† are not covered by the grant. However, he concludes with reference to the practice of the cities of his day in Italy: 'But the contrary is observed, be it by custom, be it because this is sometimes granted to certain cities by emperors, such as by Frederick to the Lombards' – a reference to the Peace of Constance.† Bartolus was prompted to mention prescription here by Accursius's reference to custom.
²⁴ *Cod.* 6.23.31.2 makes certain allowances for the inexpert testamentary practices of illiterate country people, and so exemplifies the imperial approval which Bartolus mentions here; however, the text mentions no other authority, such as Bartolus's city, to which such people are subject.
²⁵ Innocent III's decretals *Cum accessisent* (1207) and *Cum Martinus Ferrariensis* (1198). The first orders a papal judge-delegate to confirm a statute passed by the canons of a cathedral and confirmed by the pope, unless the canons have meanwhile contravened that statute by their own practice. The second allows cathedral canons, under certain circumstances, to accept more among their number than the limit laid down in their own statute.
²⁶ The definition of jurisdiction Bartolus has in mind appears in Accursius's gloss to *Dig.* 2.1.1, not the text itself. Accursius parsed jurisdiction as 'The power introduced by public law with the obligation of speaking the law and establishing equity.'
²⁷ *Dig.* 23.1.16 argues that if a marriage between certain persons is prohibited, so is betrothal.
²⁸ Both texts regulate the decrees made by an *ordo*, that is, any honourable and legally defined rank or group. The two examples given here relate to doctors, who are permitted to restrict

make a statute without waiting for the superior's authority, as here and *Inst.* 1.2.1–2,[29] and *Dig.* 42.5.37.[30] And that in this case there is no need to wait for the superior's authority is clear from the example of custom, which is introduced by the tacit consent of the people and is equiparated with statute, in which it is established that the authority of a superior is not required, *Dig.* 1.3.32.1.[31] And that the general nature of this law should be taken to refer to a people with jurisdiction is clear from the text of *Inst.* 1.2.2, where it explains with reference to the people of Rome and the Athenians. For by this law and similar laws a free licence to make statutes seems to be granted, and so the authority of a superior is not required, although provincial governors in the lands of the church have it otherwise. In the third case, when they have limited jurisdiction, they can make statutes in those matters over which they have administration or jurisdiction, not in others without the authority of a superior, as emerges from what has been said.

Secondly, I ask whether collegiate bodies can make statutes.[32] It appears that legal and approved collegiate bodies can make statutes on those matters over which they have jurisdiction, and they can makes statutes with respect to those things which pertain to the members of the collegiate body themselves, as in *Cod.* 3.13.7 and what is noted expressly there by the gloss,[33] and *Cod.* 4.18.2.2.[34]

---

entry into their profession, and decurions,† whose decrees will be struck down if they favour individuals.

[29] The first repeats *Dig.* 1.1.9; the second explains that civil law takes its name from the *civitas* which promulgates it, mentioning Athens as an example.

[30] *Dig.* 42.5.37 refers to a statute of Antioch; nothing is said there about superior authority.

[31] *Dig.* 1.3.32.1:

Ancient custom is deservedly observed as if it were law, and this is the law which is said to be established by use. For since the laws themselves bind us for no other reason than that they have been accepted by the judgment of the people, then with good reason those things which the people has approved without any writing shall also bind all. For what difference does it make whether the people has declared its will by voting or by actions and deeds themselves? Accordingly, it is absolutely correct that it has been accepted that laws may be abrogated not only by the vote of the legislature, but also by the tacit consent of everyone expressed through desuetude.

[32] Bartolus was almost certainly thinking of guilds, which would be an equally valid translation of *collegia* here.

[33] *Cod.* 3.13.7 upholds the jurisdiction of judges who are set over a particular profession against the claims to exceptional status made by persons in imperial service. See the introductory gloss *Per iniquum*, which applies this norm to the jurisdiction of the consuls of the money-changers in thirteenth-century Bologna.

[34] The text does mention and supports a custom – not a statute – to the effect that whatever money-changers have promised unconditionally should remain in force.

Thirdly, I ask whether a part of a city, say a quarter, can make statutes. It seems so, as if it were a sort of approved collegiate body: *Dig.*
30.32.1[35] and *Cod.* 11.66.6 where it talks about fortresses and so on.[36] In
favour of this there appears to be an explicit case at *Dig.* 1.2.2.8.[37] But
since jurisdiction does not reside in a particular part of a city, but in the
whole people or council which represents the people, as is said below
and noted further on at *Dig.* 2.1.6,[38] I say to this that they cannot pass
statutes about the decision of legal cases without the confirmation of
the whole people, but they can pass statutes relating to the manner of
expediting the business which is incumbent on that part or quarter, as
was said above. *Digest* 1.2.2.8 does not conflict with this [interpretation],
indeed it supports it, because those plebiscites are valid thanks to subsequent confirmation, as is clear from the passage. And this is how Iacobus
de Belviso understands it.[39]

Fourthly, I ask whether judges can pass statutes. And it seems that they
can, at *Dig.* 2.2.1, according to the gloss,[40] *Dig.* 1.3.9,[41] *Cod.* 1.26.2,[42] and
it is clear in all the edicts of the praetors, as was said above in the preceding law.[43] On the other hand, it appears that they cannot, at *Cod.* 7.57.6,[44]
Dig. 50.9.2.[45] But you are to distinguish, because either you are asking
about the major judges such as senators, praetors, and the praetorian prefect who are equiparated with the kings who nowadays exist throughout

---

[35] If a legacy is left to a part (*pars*) of a town (*civitas*) for the benefit of the commonwealth (*res publica*†) of that town, the legacy is valid.

[36] The text puts into the same category those who have served a town council, a guild (here: *collegium*), and fortresses (*burgi*); Bartolus's attention has been caught by the inclusion of an apparently physical locality in this list.

[37] An important text relating how the Roman *plebs*, in discord with the senate, seceded from the city and passed its own plebiscites which, upon the re-establishment of civic concord, were recognized as having legal force.

[38] *Dig.* 2.1.6. No commentary by Bartolus survives on this passage.

[39] No commentary or relevant additional gloss by Iacobus de Belviso survives on either *Dig.* 1.1.9 or *Dig.* 1.2.2.8.

[40] See Accursius's gloss *Qui magistratum*, where any magistrate is said to be able to promulgate a specific law, although not a general one, this latter category being the exclusive monopoly of the emperor.

[41] *Dig.* 1.3.9: 'There is no doubt that the senate can enact law.'

[42] *Cod.* 1.26.2 gives conditional authority to rulings given by the praetorian prefect.

[43] That is, *Dig.* 1.1.8, which describes the *ius honorarium* – that is, praetorian law – as the living voice of the civil law.

[44] A petition posted by a provincial governor does not have the authority of an adjudicated matter.

[45] Decrees passed by an insufficient number of decurions† are invalid.

the world, as the doctors are wont to say at length at *Dig.* 1.11.*un.*,[46] and these can pass statutes and constitutions, as in *Dig.* 1.1.8[47] and the said law *Cod.* 7.57.6. The same can be said of a legate of the apostolic see, as in *Extra* 1.30.10.[48] Or you are asking about the others who are not of such dignity, and then they hold either a perpetual dignity or for life, such as counts [and] margraves in their lands, and bishops in their dioceses, and then they can pass statutes, as in *Extra* 1.33.2,[49] and *Sext.* 1.2.2.[50] This is what the text means [in the constitution] after *Feud.* 2.58 where it says 'statutes'; which 'cities, consuls or any other person' I understand to refer to the aforesaid lords with perpetual, not temporary, jurisdiction.[51] The reason is that, just as the emperor, who is the lord of everything, makes universal law, so those who are lords of a part make statutes relating to a part. Or you are asking about judges with temporary jurisdiction, such as *podestà*† and rectors of the lands generally,[52] and then they either wish to pass statutes or constitutions having convened the council and nobles of the city, and they can, as in the aforementioned *Dig.* 2.2.1, and the gloss there agrees,[53] and at *Dig.* 50.9.1 and 2.[54] And this is how the text after

---

[46] This title, consisting of a single text, describes the origins and changing fortunes of the office of praetorian prefect. 'Equiparated' means that there is a precise legal equivalence.

[47] Above, n. 43.

[48] Gregory IX's decretal *Nemini dubium* (1227–34) gives legatine statutes perpetual force in the relevant province even after the legate's departure from that province.

[49] *Si quis venerit*, an excerpt from a letter of Gregory the Great (601), expelling from the church anyone who contravenes a bishop's decree.

[50] The decretal *Ut animarum* of Boniface VIII (1298) limits the binding effects of a bishop's statute to his own diocese.

[51] Frederick II's constitution *Ad decus*, promulgated at his imperial coronation in 1220, was by Bartolus's time routinely copied at the end of the *Libri feudorum*† and cited as part of that collection; sections of it had also been added at the relevant points to *Cod.* 1.3, a title on the privileges of the clergy. The standard modern edition of the *Libri feudorum* (K. Lehmann, *Consuetudines feudorum, editio altera*, ed. K. A. Eckhard (Aalen 1971)) omits it; see MGH, *Constitutiones et acta publica imperatorum et regum*, ed. L. Weiland, ii (Hanover 1896), no. 85, pp. 107–9, at 107. See further, *The Libri feudorum (The 'Books of Fiefs'): An Annotated English Translation of the Vulgata Recension with Latin Text*, ed. and trans. A. Stella (Leyden 2023), pp. 25, 39.The passage Bartolus quotes, not quite accurately, nullifies 'all statutes and customs which cities or places, *podestà*, consuls or any other person shall attempt to promulgate or uphold against the liberty of the church and ecclesiastical persons'.

[52] Bartolus means, as the next clause makes clear, subordinate civic officials of the Italian cities.

[53] Presumably another reference to Accursius's gloss *Qui magistratum* at *Dig.* 2.2.1, which contains no such observation about convocation of the council and nobles.

[54] *Dig.* 50.9.1 reserves the decision of how many doctors there should be to the *ordo* (presumably of decurions†) and landholders of each locality, not to the provincial governor;

Feud. 2.58 should be understood. Or he wishes to do it alone, and he cannot, as in *Cod.* 7.57.6.[55] But he can certainly pass an ordinance or law valid for his entire period in office regarding what is required by circumstances, to the effect that nobody is to export grain from the city, that nobody may bear arms, or that nobody is to serve as a retainer or stipendiary, or to go out at night and suchlike, as in *Dig.* 1.12.3,[56] *Cod.* 11.2.4,[57] and *Dig.* 2.2.1 is also relevant.[58] From these passages it is clear that the provincial governors sent by the church are not able to pass statutes or constitutions without the counsel of the men of the province, because they do not belong to the major judges since they are in the category of *Clarissimi* [judges] as is noted at *Dig.* 1.11.*rub.*[59] Also, they have temporary jurisdiction, whereas those whom I have termed major judges are *Illustres* or *Spectabiles*, as is noted at the rubric of *Dig.* 1.11 and *Dig.* 1.18.[60] But the opposite is observed by custom or by special concession of the pope.[61]

I ask as the second principal question how statutes are made.[62] And indeed, if major judges or lords do it, it is sensible that they do this with the advice of experts, as in *Cod.* 1.14.8.[63] But if they wish they can do it on their own impulse and publicize it to their subjects, as in *Cod.* 1.14.3;[64] yet if statutes are passed by the people, the procedure is that the whole people shall be convened, or the men who belong to the council of the people

the second text rules that decrees made when the proper number of decurions is not present are invalid.

[55] Above, n. 44. The presumably unintended change from plural to singular is in the original.

[56] *Dig.* 1.12.3, on the duties of the urban prefect, seems to be cited here to support Bartolus's point that such orders are only valid for as long as the judge is in office, but no longer. It lays down that the urban prefect has no official power once he has left the city's boundary. The match is not obvious.

[57] *Cod.* 11.2.4 describes a specific, complicated situation in which the praetorian prefect had the authority to issue orders to a guild (*coetus*) of shipowners.

[58] Above, n. 40.

[59] The gloss to the rubric of *Dig.* 1.11 only notes that the praetorian prefect is a so-called *Illustris*.

[60] For *Dig.* 1.11, see preceding note. *Dig.* 1.18 covers the duties of provincial governors. The gloss to the rubric notes that they are *Clarissimi*, whereas the grander magistrates treated in the preceding section were *Spectabiles*.

[61] The above is from the first and the longest four of eight subquestions in this first principal question. They are the most relevant to the matters dealt with in Bartolus's three political tracts.

[62] Ed. cit., fo. 10ra–va.

[63] *Cod.* 1.14.8 establishes that any new general provision should be considered by the nobles of the imperial palace, then the senate together with the judges.

[64] This constitution mentions the publication of edicts as a sufficient condition of their general validity.

which represents the people, as is noted at the rubric of *Cod.* 8.52(53),[65] and this calling together is to be done on the authority of the *podestà*† or another magistrate with solemnity; that is, by sounding a trumpet or ringing the bell or by the voice of a herald, as in the third gloss to *Cod.* 10.32.2[66] and *Dig.* 50.17.160.1,[67] and it is noted there that they are summoned to the court [*curia*] or to another public or accustomed place, as in the said *Cod.* 10.32.2 and *Cod.* 10.65.5.[68] When they are thus ordered and brought together it should be seen whether they are two-thirds of the people or council, which is required: *Cod.* 10.32.45,[69] and it is noted below at *Dig.* 3.4.3.[70] Nor does it suffice that they are summoned unless two-thirds are present, as in *Cod.* 10.34.3, where it is said that the decree is not to be recited from a written tablet, which is to say that it is not enough for them to be summoned by the sound of the *tabella* unless they come.[71] And this is how Odofredus understands it there,[72] although the gloss gives a different explanation, as is noted at the said *Dig.* 50.17.160.1.[73] When they are

---

[65] The relevant part of Accursius's gloss reads: 'Or say that, although two instances constitute a custom, this is true if it has pleased the people or council, which represents the people [*quod eius vicem repraesentat*], that the same should be done in future.' There is a slight difference between Accursius's formulation and that of his teacher, Azo, according to whom the approval of the people or governor – 'si populo vel praesidi placuerit' – was necessary. See E. Cortese, *La norma giuridica: Spunti teorici nel diritto comune classico*, 2 vols. (Milan 1962–4), vol. II, pp. 144–6.

[66] Actually, the fourth gloss (*Solenniter*), explaining the requirement that decurions† be summoned with solemnity 'at the sound of a trumpet or bell'.

[67] A so-called rule of law (*regula iuris*) according to which 'Anything publicly done by the majority is ascribed to everyone.' Accursius's gloss *refertur* begins: 'If the people is publicly summoned, namely by a trumpet or bell, or by the voice of a herald, even though not everyone comes, all appear to do what those who have come do.'

[68] See above, n. 19.

[69] Once again, the order of decurions in the towns and cities of the late empire is providing the model for Italian civic institutions; *Cod.* 10.32.45 establishes that 'two-thirds of the order [of decurions], when present in the city, provides the equivalent of the whole council'.

[70] Another passage requiring the consent of two-thirds or more of the decurions, this time before a legal action can be initiated in their name.

[71] The passage from the *Code*† is clear enough in requiring a verdict from a judge to confirm the sale of decurions' property, not just the decurions' own decree on a written tablet. It is not clear how this could have a *sound*, however, and some confusion seems to have prevailed over the meaning of *tabella*; the gloss to this passage notes an ambiguity and associates the word with *tabellio*, that is, a notary, and infers that the passage prohibits the use of a delegate to make the decision known.

[72] Odofredus de Denariis's comments on *Cod.* 10.34.3 contain nothing of relevance (Odofredus, *Super tribus libris codicis* (Lyons 1550), fos. 41vb–42ra, in Odofredus, *Lectura super codice*, reprinted in facsimile in *Opera iuridica rariora*, vi, ed. D. Maffei, E. Cortese, and G. Rossi, 2 vols. (Bologna 1969), vol. II).

[73] Above, n. 67.

thus brought together a proposal should be made by one [of them] in one or other of two ways. For it can be made generally: 'What does it please you to enact on such a matter?' and they will be advisors on such a proposal, and this method can be gathered from *Dig.* 16.1.2.1.[74] The other method is that a specific and defined proposal is made and it is asked whether the people approves that such should be a law or statute, and this method can be gathered from *Inst.* 1.2.4,[75] and *Inst.* 4.3.15.[76] What pleases the majority will stand as law, as in *Dig.* 50.1.19,[77] and *Dig.* 50.17.160.1[78] and *Dig.* 3.4.3[79] and the said *Cod.* 10.32.45.[80] However, there are some who distinguish here: either a statute is passed which goes beyond the law, and the consent of the majority suffices, as in the aforesaid laws, or it is passed against the law, and then it is necessary that no one dissents, as in *Auth.* 3.2.ep.,[81] and Cinus notes the same thing at *Cod.* 8.52(53).2.[82] But this is not correct, because the section of *Auth.* 3.2 is a special case, whereas what has been said is the common law, but sometimes a different procedure is set by statute.

I ask secondly: I have said above that all are to be summoned, but what if one part has expelled the other part from the city?[83] Distinguish: either some are absent voluntarily from the city, then the whole power remains with those present, as can be argued on the basis of *Dig.* 26.5.19 and *Cod.* 10.32.45.[84] But if they have been expelled, then either the right to enact statutes belonged to the expelled or it did not. If the latter is the case, for example because they did not belong to the council, then the absence of

---

[74] Here the motion by the two consuls leading to the issue of the *senatus consultum*† *Velleianum* is quoted.

[75] *Inst.*1.2.4 defines a law (*lex*) as 'what the Roman people used to establish on the motion of a senatorial magistrate, for instance a consul'.

[76] *Inst.* 4.3.5 reveals that the precise wording of the *Lex Aquilia* was proposed to the Roman people, which then deliberated on it.

[77] *Dig.* 50.1.19, on inhabitants of *municipia*,† establishes that what the majority of the local senate decides shall be taken to have been enacted by all.

[78] Above, n. 67.

[79] Above, n. 70.

[80] Above, n. 69.

[81] *Nov.* 15, epilogue: a defender† of cities who serves beyond his two-year stint must be re-elected by all the voters.

[82] Cinus makes this distinction in an addition to his commentary on the *Code*†: *Cyni Pistoriensis in Codicem [...] commentaria* (Frankfurt am Main 1578), fo. 525ra.

[83] See above, *On Guelfs and Ghibellines*, p. 8.

[84] For the second citation, see above, n. 69; the first allows decurions† to appoint tutors† in the absence of those who would normally do so, so long as the majority agree; Bartolus's point thus goes considerably beyond his textual authorities.

the others who have been expelled is no obstacle when those who have remained in the city can enact statutes, as in *Dig.* 1.2.2.8, where it is said that there is no doubt that the power to legislate remained with those who stayed.[85] Or the power to legislate did belong to the expelled, just as to those who remain, because they belonged to the council, and then they were either expelled with just cause, and afterwards the power to legislate remains with those who have stayed, because, since they do not obey their city, they lose all the rights deriving from their own city, as in *Dig.* 4.5.5,[86] and thus they lose the power to make statutes, which is why the power remains with those who are present. Or they have been expelled without just cause, perhaps out of envy, and then, although the statutes passed by those who remain perhaps apply to them, by *Dig.* 8.3.11,[87] they cannot apply in prejudice of those who have been expelled, 'lest through his maliciousness' etc., *Dig.* 47.2.12.[88]

Thirdly, I have said that all are to be summoned to the same place. I ask, what if all members of the people give their consent separately in their own homes, and this is confirmed by a publicly accredited document: is this valid? It seems so, as we say in the case of custom, *Dig.* 1.3.32[89]

---

[85] On this particular section of *Dig.* 1.2.2, see above, n. 37. The passage does not contain the express statement which Bartolus extracts from it.

[86] *Dig.* 4.5.5 explains among other things that those who revolt lose their citizenship. In our passage, 'all the rights deriving from their own city' translates the phrase 'omnia iura propria civitatis suae', that is: all the rights they enjoy thanks to being citizens of their own city. In the singular, *ius proprium* is the phrase employed by Gaius in *Dig.* 1.1.9 to describe the law of a single city; the plural *iura propria* means the rights which derive from that particular law. All the cities Bartolus is concerned with belonged in his opinion to the Roman empire, meaning that persons banished from them still enjoyed another stratum of rights as Roman citizens.

[87] There is such a stretch between what *Dig.* 8.3.11 says and what Bartolus wants from it that his precise reasoning for citing it is unclear. The text concerns the grant of a servitude – the closest parallel in English law is an easement – by several but not all the co-owners of a piece of land. Technically, the servitude is not created until all have granted it, but the more liberal interpretation is that those who have cannot prevent the recipient from using his right.

[88] The phrase quoted is not in the *Digest*† passage, which merely declares that an action for theft is not available to a possessor in bad faith, and comes instead from *Cod.* 5.14.11.4, which holds a husband to the same standard of due diligence regarding his wife's property as his own.

[89] Above, pp. xxxiii n. 27, and Glossary, *consuetudo*. For a custom to be proven to exist, at least two instances of it had to be identified over a certain period, usually no shorter than ten years. Since custom also arose from the tacit consent of the people, Bartolus naturally thinks of it as an example of a type of norm which is consented to discretely, or disjunctively, rather than explicitly in a gathering. It was a cliché in medieval jurisprudence that statute and custom proceeded *pari passu*.

and *Dig.* 8.4.18,[90] and *Dig.* 39.3.10.[91] I believe the contrary, for two reasons. The first is that in those matters pertaining to several people in a corporate capacity [*ut universos*] the consent of all is required at the same time as in the aforementioned *Cod.* 10.32.2,[92] [and] more explicitly *Extra* 1.6.55.[93] The second reason is that in those things in which the consent of the greater part prejudices the lesser part, even if [the matter] pertains to several people as single persons,[94] their agreement is required all at once as in *Dig.* 2.14.7.19.[95] So [the text] here agrees with the foregoing: it is requisite that it be done together. Nor is what is said about custom an objection, because a plurality of acts and the passage of time takes the place of such a gathering. Nor are the aforementioned *Dig.* 8.4.18 and *Dig.* 39.3.10 an obstacle because they are talking about what is common to several as single persons, nor does the agreement of one party prejudice the other. Fourthly, I have described what is done in practice.[96] I ask how the will of the people is to be explored? And it seems that express verbal agreement is needed, as in *Dig.* 1.3.32,[97] since this is the difference between statutes and custom, because the one arises from express agreement, the other from tacit agreement. But I believe one should say that spoken words are required on the part of the consul asking the question or making the proposal, whereas from the side of the people responding a verbal response is not required, but signs indicating consent suffice, according to what was put forward in the proposal, whether by standing up or sitting down, whether by [casting] white beans or black, arguing from *Dig.* 44.7.2.[98] And in support of this I particularly

---

[90] *Dig.* 8.4.18 allows several co-owners to impose a servitude on their estate 'even if they do not all make the grant at one and the same time'.

[91] The consent of all owners of a site from which water is channelled must be obtained.

[92] The text – on which see above, n. 66 – mentions the decurions† being summoned into the council.

[93] Gregory IX's decretal *In Genesi* (1227–34) insists that an ecclesiastical election is only canonical if the electors vote together rather than apart.

[94] That is, 'ut singuli', rather than belonging to or affecting several persons in their corporate capacity, or 'ut universi'.

[95] A passage on the obligation of co-creditors under an agreement, in which Bartolus interprets the phrase 'si convenerint in unum …' to mean that they must have reached that agreement when gathered together.

[96] The text is not clear at this point.

[97] Cf. above, p. 79, and Glossary, *consuetudo*.

[98] *Dig.* 44.7.2 discusses obligations arising from consent in which 'no special quality of words or of writing is required …'.

cite *Dig.* 36.1.67.3, where it says 'or when asked they can answer or indicate by a nod'.[99] This is also how the final gloss to *Dig.* 1.2.1 should be understood, and *Dig.* 1.3.32,[100] and this is what is observed by custom. In fifth place I ask whether the creation of statute can be committed to particular persons and it seems not, because just as a testator cannot commit it to others to form his will,[101] as in *Dig.* 28.5.32 and 71(70),[102] because a will is a particular law, as in *Auth.* 4.1,[103] and as is noted at *Cod.* 7.26.2.[104] Moreover, this [power to make statute] has been committed specially and cannot therefore be delegated, as in *Dig.* 1.21.1.[105] On the contrary, that it could [be delegated]: *Dig.* 1.2.2.9.[106] You are to say that either judges or lords who have the authority to do this wish to delegate it, and they cannot, because this has been granted to them specially, as major judges, as in *Dig.* 1.21.1, or the people wishes to confer it, and it can, as in *Dig.* 1.2.2.3 and 9, and the reason for the difference is clear. Or say that the reason is that he to whom it is conferred by the people appears to be an ordinary judge and not a delegate, because the people can confer ordinary jurisdiction as in *Dig.* 2.1.6, but other judges do not give ordinary jurisdiction, however this cannot be delegated, therefore ... etc.[107]

---

[99] The passage discusses how a mute heir might express willingness to accept an inheritance. Bartolus's quotation is more or less accurate.

[100] *Dig.* 1.2.1 and Accursius's gloss *evidentiorem* are not about signs of consent, but the importance of providing a preface to a proposal, and of understanding the beginning of a case. On *Dig.* 1.3.32, see above, n. 89.

[101] That is, he cannot get others to make up his mind for him and express that decision.

[102] Both passages are about last wills and testaments, and attribute absolute primacy to the wishes of the testator.

[103] *Nov.* 22.2 states an ancient maxim of Roman law to the effect that 'As each has made a bequest concerning his own property, let that be law [*ius*].'

[104] *Cod.* 7.26.2 nullifies a sale of slaves by tutors† in contravention of the wishes of the deceased. Bartolus might have Accursius's gloss *non potuerunt* in mind, where what is against the will of the deceased is said to be against the law.

[105] *Dig.* 1.21.1 prohibits the delegation of powers which have been specially granted by law, the senate, or by imperial constitution.

[106] On *Dig.* 1.2.2 see above, n. 7. This paragraph attributes the senate's eventual powers to issue *senatus consulta*† to the difficulties in assembling the entire plebeian class, let alone the whole people, of Rome for the purpose of passing laws. Bartolus then refers to an earlier paragraph describing how, after the expulsion of the kings from Rome, tribunes – by implication, not the whole people – issued a law.

[107] Bartolus seems to be thinking of Accursius's gloss *Nec ipsa lex* to *Dig.* 2.1.6, which lists custom among the sources of ordinary jurisdiction, because custom was uncontroversially created by the people. Neither Accursius nor the *Digest*† passage itself attributes the power to confer ordinary jurisdiction to the people as explicitly as Bartolus suggests here.

Commentary on the Constitution *Ad reprimendum* of Emperor Henry VII[108]

Of the whole world.[109] Contra: because the greater part of the world does not obey the emperor. Solution: That is *de facto*, but by law it is otherwise. We have something similar concerning *Daniel*, chapter 2, where it says as follows of Nebuchadnezzar, who was at that time universal emperor:[110] 'You are the king of kings, and the God of heaven has given you the kingdom, strength, glory and power [*imperium*†], and wherever the children of men dwell, or the beasts of the field and the birds of the heaven, He has given them into your hand, and has made you ruler over them all', which should be understood according to law, because *de facto* not everyone obeyed him, as we read in the chronicles, as in the gloss to *Daniel*, chapter 2.[111] Again, contra: because he has no jurisdiction in the lands of the church, as in *Clem.* 2.11.2.[112] Solution: the church possesses by gift of the emperor, indeed of the emperor who promulgated the present law, as in *Clem.* 2.9.un.,[113] hence the emperor appears to possess, as in *Cod.* 1.17.1.6.[114] Or: although the property right [*dominium*†] of any particular thing is not his, nevertheless what is said here is true, just as [someone] is said to be the owner of the flock even if one sheep is not his, as in *Dig.*

---

[108] MGH, *Constitutiones et acta publica imperatorum et regum*, ed. J. Schwalm, iv, pt. 2 (Hanover 1909–11), no. 929, pp. 965–6.

[109] *Bartoli a Sassoferrato Consilia, quaestiones, tractatus* (Basle 1588), pp. 261–91, at 262. The opening sentence of the constitution asserts that 'the good order [*regularitas*] of the whole world rests in the tranquillity of the Roman empire'.

[110] *Daniel* 2, 37–8.

[111] Nicholas of Lyra's gloss *Dedit in manu tua* explains: 'Here the part is taken for the whole by synecdoche, because not all the habitable land was subject to him, but the greater part of it': *Biblia sacra cum glossis, interlineari et ordinaria, Nicolai Lyrani postilla et moralitatibus* [...], 7 vols. (Lyons 1545), vol. IV, fo. 298rb.

[112] Clement V's bull *Pastoralis cura* (14 March 1314) challenged Henry VII's summons of Robert, king of Naples, to Pisa on a charge of treason; the pope's principal contention in this regard was that Robert was known to be in the kingdom, a fief held of the papacy, and therefore outside the jurisdiction of the empire at the moment the summons was issued.

[113] Clement V's bull *Romani principes*, promulgated on the same day as *Pastoralis cura*, was the papal rejoinder to Henry VII's contention that he was not bound by an oath of fealty to the papacy.

[114] In the constitution *Deo auctore*, Justinian commands the compilers of the *Digest*† to attribute the same authority to the ancient jurisconsults whose works, excerpted and edited, were to constitute the fabric of the new compilation, 'as if their efforts had derived from imperial constitutions', adding 'We rightly make all their works our own, since all authority imparted them derives from us.'

6.1.2 and 3.[115] And on this basis it is clear that the emperor is rightly called lord of the world, namely: the universal owner, although individuals are the owners of their plots of land.[116] Hence he himself can vindicate the world from those in possession, as in *Cod.* 7.37.3[117] and *Dig.* 14.2.9,[118] nor is there any need for us to say that everything is his as far as protection is concerned and so on, as is noted on the prefatory constitution to the *Digest*,†[119] because on the contrary everything belongs to him if it is considered universally.[120] Or thirdly, sticking by the opinion of Holy Mother Church, first there was the Babylonian empire, secondly there was the empire of the Persians and Medes, thirdly there was the Greek empire, the fourth was the Roman empire. Finally, with Christ's advent, this Roman empire became the empire of Christ, and therefore both swords reside with Christ's vicar,† the spiritual and the temporal. For Christ is the stone cut out without hands, whose kingdom shall never be destroyed, concerning which Daniel prophesied in the aforementioned *Daniel* 2, where all these empires are described explicitly. Say, then, that before

[115] *Dig.* 6.1.2 and 3 explain that one may vindicate a flock without vindicating those animals in it which belong to others, and that replacement animals can on their own constitute the original flock. *Dig.* 6.1.1.3 ('It is sufficient if we own the flock itself, even if particular animals may not belong to us …') would have been a better match here than *Dig.* 6.1.3.

[116] One context is influencing the choice of vocabulary in another here. For Bartolus it is natural to call an owner of a *universitas*,† which here has the same sense as the flock (*grex*) just mentioned, a universal owner; the owners of specific units of property within it become *singuli* in Latin because *universitas* very often meant a corporation consisting of people rather than property, a corporation which was contrasted with the *singuli* or individuals viewed in their non-corporate aspect.

[117] *Cod.* 7.37.3 extends the same protection to those who acquire property from the private patrimony of the emperors as that already accorded those who acquire from the fisc (i.e. the imperial treasury), explaining 'For since all of it is understood to belong to the emperor, what is the difference whether the property alienated is part of his private patrimony or belongs to the fisc?'

[118] Here the emperor Antoninus Pius is quoted as calling himself 'Lord of the earth' (*mundi dominus*).

[119] The constitution *Omnem* prefaces the *Digest* and is not included under any numbered title. In his gloss *sanctionem*, Accursius explains that Justinian's phrase 'The whole body of the law of our *res publica*'† means the law of the whole empire (*totius imperii*) 'which is his, and the things contained in it, by reason of jurisdiction or protection, as here, not by reason of property right'. The distinction between the emperor's *dominium*† in the sense of his jurisdiction over everything, and *dominium* in the sense of ownership of everything, which was denied him, was axiomatic for most medieval jurists and thought to descend from a debate in the presence of Frederick Barbarossa between two of the most influential Bolognese lawyers of the mid twelfth century, Bulgarus and Martinus. Accursius relates this apocryphal meeting in his gloss.

[120] 'Universally' (*universaliter*) is used in the same sense here as immediately above to mean collectively; see above n. 116.

Christ the Roman empire depended on him[121] alone and it was rightly said that the emperor was lord of the world and that everything was his. But after Christ the empire is with Christ and his vicar and is transferred by the pope to the secular emperor, as in *Extra* 1.6.34.[122] Hence if we say that everything belongs to the Roman empire because it is now Christ's empire, it is true if we are referring to the person of Christ, but if we are referring to the person of the secular emperor it is not strictly true that everything belongs to him or is under his jurisdiction, because the lands of the church are not; for the pope reserves them to himself, in whom empire [*imperium*†] principally resides. Therefore, in this constitution, whether he is referring to the empire or to his own person, he has expressed himself carefully. For he does not say that jurisdiction over the whole world is his, but that the good order of the whole world rests in it [or him]. For he has, in a certain way, to regulate the lands of the church, namely by defending them and by devotedly preserving the church as he has sworn in the aforesaid *Clem.* 2.9.*un.*[123] And I say this provisionally and for now; for so I believe the church maintains, so I believe the emperor to mean, and if I misunderstand this or anything else, I am ready to correct myself.

[121] That is, the emperor.
[122] For Innocent III's decretal *Venerabilem* (1202), see above, *On the Government of a City*, n. 88.
[123] See above, n. 113.

Appendix III

The 'City, Emperor unto Itself'

The following texts are excerpts from Bartolus's commentaries on the Roman law. They illustrate the exegetical contexts of his most important ideas about the non-recognition of the emperor by cities, and their numerous applications in the daily business of government.

Dig. 2.1.1[1]

I say thirdly that when jurisdiction coheres with a territory, whether actively or passively,[2] it does so not as an attribute of the territory itself, as Gulielmus de Cuneo says,[3] but in a different way, as appears from the law *Dig.* 2.1.5,[4] where it says that he who has ordinary jurisdiction has it in his own right, that is, by a right residing in his own person, not in the territory itself, and the text in the aforementioned paragraph *Dig.* 50.16.239.8[5] explains this more clearly. Therefore, in order to under-

---

[1] *Bartoli a Sassoferrato in primam Digesti Veteris partem commentaria* (Turin 1574), fo. 47ra–b.
[2] Jurisdiction coheres with a territory passively when there is no magistrate appointed there to activate it.
[3] *Lectura super Digestum Vetus*, Oxford, Bodleian Library, MS. Canon. Misc. 472, fos. 1ra–77vb, a fo. 16rb, where 'Jurisdiction adheres to the territory ...', and fo. 16va, where 'jurisdiction refers principally to the territory'.
[4] *Dig.* 2.1.5: only someone who holds jurisdiction in his own right, rather than by concession from another, may mandate it to someone else.
[5] *Dig.* 50.16.239.8 derives the word *territorium* from the right which a magistrate has of *terrendi*, that is, of 'terrifying' in the sense of driving off or driving out within those confines.

stand this you should know that certain rights are entirely real, being owed by a thing to a thing, such as servitudes, and these are attributes in the proper sense of pieces of land. There are certain rights owed to a person in a thing, such as ownership [*dominium*†], a pledge, and suchlike. So just as ownership coheres with the person of the owner, yet is in the thing, so jurisdiction coheres with the office and the person of him who holds the office, yet is nevertheless in the territory, and thus it is not an attribute of the territory but rather of the person. And this equiparation of jurisdiction with ownership is demonstrated as follows. The emperor [*princeps*†] has all jurisdiction, as above, *Dig.* 1.4.1,[6] and on account of this he is said to be lord of the world, as below, *Dig.* 14.2.9.[7] Just as any judge is said to be *princeps* of the city or territory over which he presides, as in *Dig.* 27.1.15.9,[8] he can rightly be called the lord of that entire territory understood in its universal aspect, as I have said of the emperor on several occasions, and at greatest length with reference to the first constitution of this book.[9] The pleasing and true consequence follows from this that if the emperor or someone else were to grant you a territory universally, he appears to grant you the jurisdiction universally, because just as he who grants a single thing appears to grant the ownership of the single thing, as in *Dig.* 18.1.25,[10] so he who grants a territory universally appears to grant the jurisdiction which is the same as the ownership of any particular thing. It would be different if he were to grant a particular aspect or a particular, single thing, as in *Dig.* 18.1.24.[11] What is noted at *Dig.* 1.4.3 is relevant.[12] I have talked about this at *Cod.* 10.10.2.[13] And it

---

[6] *Dig.* 1.4.1 begins: 'What has pleased the emperor has the force of law, since by the *Lex regia* which was passed concerning his *imperium*† the people conferred to him and on him all its *imperium* and power.'

[7] *Dig.* 14.2.9 quotes the words of Emperor Antoninus Pius: 'I am the lord [*dominus*†] of the earth, but the law is the lord of the sea.'

[8] *Dig.* 27.1.15.9 refers to a magistrate as *princeps* of the city.

[9] See Appendix II, p. 84 for the distinction between the emperor's *dominium* as ownership and as jurisdiction. Bartolus engages with this issue at *Bartoli a Sassoferrato in primam Digesti Veteris partem commentaria*, 2 vols. (Turin 1574), fo. 4ra–b.

[10] *Dig.* 18.1.25.*pr.*: if a sale is made of 'Either this or that property', the purchase applies to whichever of the two the buyer chooses.

[11] *Dig.* 18.1.24: small portions of a piece of land are included in the sale of the larger piece to which they are accessories.

[12] Accursius's gloss *Beneficium* notes that the sale of a house includes its adjacent appurtenances.

[13] *Bartoli a Sassoferrato in Tres libros Codicis commentaria* (Turin 1574), fo. 8ra: a concession of something 'in its complete condition' by the emperor is understood to include everything pertaining to it.

is clear from this that jurisdiction does not cohere with a territory in the proper sense. To that extent it is said to cohere with the territory because it sets a limit to the territory, as in *Dig.* 2.1.20.[14] But you will say: on the contrary, it coheres with the thing, for we see that cities and *castra*† have jurisdiction. I answer: on the contrary, it coheres with their people and their community,[15] as at the end here, and the gloss is speaking of the right to inflict moderate punishment,[16] because they are represented persons which have jurisdiction, and they themselves appoint the *podestà*† and suchlike, hence jurisdiction inheres in persons and pertains to persons. And this is how what is said here should be understood. According to Gulielmus de Cuneo there is a case in point at *Dig.* 1.5.20.[17]

Dig. 3.1.1.10[18]

Note that only the emperor and senate can restore someone's good name,[19] and in the same way the pope and college of cardinals in spiritual matters and temporal matters among those who are subject to the church; otherwise they cannot, as Innocent notes at *Extra* 2.27.23.[20] But I ask whether a people can restore someone's good name by statute? The principal statement of the law here appears to be that it cannot.[21] But this is true of the infamy which is imposed according to the form of some statute which could be removed by another contrary statute, for 'There is nothing so natural, as to dissolve something in the same way as that

---

[14] *Dig.* 2.1.20: a judge passing judgment outside his territory should not be obeyed.

[15] Ed. cit.: 'communitates'. Our reading is sanctioned by Munich, Bayerische Staatsbibliothek, MS. Clm. 5476, fo. 39rb.

[16] *Dig.* 2.1.1. Accursius's gloss *Litigantibus dare* notes that a judge may only delegate those cases which pertain to him by right of his magistracy (rather than by a special commission from a superior authority), and that this is an example of jurisdiction. Bartolus's point seems to be that the gloss gives an example of jurisdiction which is clearly that of a judge, i.e. a person, not a territory.

[17] Oxford, Bodleian Library, MS. Canon. Misc. 472, fo. 7va; *Dig.* 1.5.20: someone who has gone insane retains his rank, dignity, magistracy, and authority, just as he retains his own property.

[18] *Bartoli a Sassoferrato in primam Digesti Veteris partem commentaria*, fo. 98vb.

[19] That is, after a court has condemned them to *infamia*, 'infamy' or evil reputation, which brought with it major legal disadvantages.

[20] Innocent IV, *Apparatus super quinque libris decretalium* (Frankfurt am Main 1570), fo. 350va: the pope can only award restitution of full legal rights – *restitutio in integrum* – to the inhabitants of the Papal State, unless they are clerics. He concludes by noting that other ecclesiastical judges can restore those sentenced to infamy, but only in the Papal State.

[21] The passage on which Bartolus is commenting denies the praetor any independent power to restore to good name, reserving this solely to the emperor and senate.

in which it has been put together.'²² The same is true of other kings and princes [*principes*†] who recognize the emperor as lord. But if it were a king, prince, or people who did not recognize the emperor as lord, then the restitution to good name would be valid among themselves, because such a people is called a free people, as is noted at *Dig.* 49.15.24, and among themselves it is called emperor unto itself, as is clear there.²³

Dig. 4.4.3²⁴

The emperor, not an inferior judge, can award a minor the administration of his own goods. This is what the text says. Note principally from this that administration of their own goods cannot be awarded to minors by the statutes of cities, because the emperor has reserved this to himself, as here and *Cod.* 2.44.2.²⁵ Nevertheless, cities which do not recognize the emperor as lord – and so their people is free, as is noted at *Dig.* 49.15.24²⁶ – could perhaps do this by statute, because the city itself is emperor unto itself.

Dig. 39.2.1²⁷

I ask how what I see comes about: that nowadays all the rulers [*rectores*] of cities and *castra*† throughout Italy exercise the rights pertaining to *merum* and *mixtum imperium*†? I answer: you should know that we have three kinds of corporation [*universitas*†].²⁸ One, which constitutes a province, is large and this possesses *merum* and *mixtum imperium* according to the

---

²² *Dig.* 50.17.35; Bartolus simply repeats the first few words of this rule of law.
²³ See Accursius's gloss *Vel praedones*; of the five different kinds of *populus*† Accursius lists here, the third is constituted by 'free peoples, who are subject neither to us nor anyone else'. There is of course no indication that Accursius thought a free people was an emperor unto itself, and Bartolus does not say so in his commentary on *Dig.* 49.15.24: see below, pp. 102–7.
²⁴ Ed. cit., fo. 133rb.
²⁵ *Cod.* 2.44.2 implies that the privilege of full majority can be awarded only by the emperor.
²⁶ See above, n. 23.
²⁷ *Bartoli a Sassoferrato in primam Digesti Novi partem commentaria* (Turin 1574), fo. 24rb–va.
²⁸ This passage derives from a section of a famous *consilium*, or professional opinion, by Bartolus: *Bartoli a Sassoferrato Consilia, quaestiones, et tractatus* (Basle 1588), *Cons.* i.189, pp. 118–20.

common law, as in *Dig.* 1.18.6.8[29] and *Dig.* 39.2.4[30] and the whole of *Cod.*
1.40.1.[31] The second kind of corporation is less large, which constitutes
a city; and by the common law jurisdictions cohere with this only up
to a certain quantity in less serious criminal matters, but they[32] do not
have much *merum* and *mixtum imperium*† as in *Cod.* 1.55.1[33] and *Auth.*
3.2.3.2, *Auth.* 3.2.6.1 and *Auth.* 3.2.1.1.[34] This does not apply in the case
of certain cities to which this [*imperium*] has been granted by the common law such as the city of Rome, as in *Dig.* 1.12.1.4,[35] and certain other
cities in Lombardy which have it by that constitution of Frederick *On
the Peace of Constance*† which the gloss was referring to at the aforementioned *Auth.* 3.2.1.1, at the end of the long gloss.[36] But other cities have
merum and *mixtum imperium* either by special privilege or by legitimate
custom or perhaps they use it *de facto*. The third kind of corporation is
the smallest such as a *castrum*,† village [*villa*], and suchlike, and these,

[29] *Dig.* 1.18 is a title about the powers of the provincial governor. The paragraph cited here
accords governors 'who rule entire provinces' the right of the sword or *ius gladii* – that is, the
power of life and death – as well as the power to send condemned criminals to the mines.

[30] This passage, in the same title as the present law, makes clear that the praetor or provincial
governor directs municipal magistrates on certain kinds of administrative business (in this
case relating to securities given against apprehended damage to property).

[31] The passage has no obvious relevance and is also very short, whereas Bartolus's phraseology
implies a more substantial passage; he might mean the entire title *Cod.* 1.40, 'On the Office
of Provincial Governor'.

[32] The switch from singular to plural is in the original; Bartolus means the Italian cities
(*civitates*).

[33] *Cod.* 1.55.1 instructs a municipal magistrate to act only upon judicial appeals of minor
importance, and to refer all others to a higher court.

[34] *Nov.* 15, sections 3.2, 6.1, and 1.1. The first two limit respectively the judicial competence
of defenders† of cities to cases worth up to 300 *aurei* and to less serious crimes; the third
makes defenders of cities swear, on their assumption of office, that they will perform
their functions according to law and right, before being confirmed in office by a prefect.
Bartolus usually argues that, according to strict law, cities possess no *merum imperium*:
see below, p. 111 for his comment on *Cod.* 2.3.28. So his qualified rather than categorical
denial here – to the effect that cities do not hold much *imperium* – comes as a surprise. The
parallel passage in *Consilium* i.189 does not include this qualification. However, Bartolus
elsewhere divides both *merum* and *mixtum imperium* into separate strata on a descending
scale and allocates different levels of *imperium* to separate magistrates, which might explain
his formulation here.

[35] *Dig.* 1.12.1.4, in a title on the duties of the prefect of the city of Rome, puts all crimes
committed within the hundredth milestone of the city under the jurisdiction of the prefect.
Note Bartolus's automatic inference here that if the magistrate possesses such jurisdiction,
the corporation which is the city also possesses it.

[36] Accursius's gloss *Iurisdictione* (*Nov.* 15.1.1) notes that although cities do not have *merum*
and *mixtum imperium*, some have been granted it by emperors. He instances Frederick I
and the Lombards.

since indeed they are subject to some city or another large *castrum* have no jurisdiction, but the city to which they are subject has jurisdiction over them: *Dig.* 50.1.30,[37] *Cod.* 5.27.4,[38] *Cod.* 1.3.28.4,[39] *Auth.* 7.1.[40] Sometimes such *castra*[†] are not subject to any city, but are subject to the provincial governor alone; then the magistrates of that municipality have the same jurisdiction as defenders[†] of cities and concerning these we have *Cod.* 1.56 according to one reading, which Azo mentions there in his *Summa*; according to another way of reading it, it refers to the title *On defenders of cities* (*Cod.* 1.55).[41] Therefore, those *castra* which use *merum* and *mixtum imperium*[†] either have this by privilege, or by custom, or they use it *de facto*. Now, therefore, on the point in question: in this law,[42] and *Dig.* 39.2.4,[43] and everywhere, municipal magistrates or rulers of *castra* not subject to cities are called defenders of cities insofar as they have [their authority] in accordance with the common law, although I say the same concerning those cities and *castra* which have *merum* or *mixtum imperium* by privileged title or by custom as what is said here, and below at the beginning of *Dig.* 39.2.4, about the praetor or provincial governor.

Dig. 42.1.45.1[44]

And what is said here: 'without an order from the emperor'[45] I think is the same nowadays in the cities which recognize no superior. For the people of this city and the council can reduce a penalty. I think it is the same in the case of anyone else to whose treasury the penalty imposed pertains,

---

[37] *Dig.* 50.1.30, in a title dedicated to citizenship of *municipia*,[†] establishes that anyone born in a village has as his or her *patria* the *municipium* to which that village belongs.

[38] The passage refers to the home town of a testator as his *patria*; it does not mention any subordinate community.

[39] A village or a rural district (*territorium*) is said in passing to be under the jurisdiction of the local city.

[40] *Nov.* 89.2.2 mentions a landed estate or village paying tax to its local city.

[41] *Cod.* 1.56 is about municipal magistrates, the immediately preceding title is about defenders of cities. In his *Summa codicis*, Azo first relates *Cod.* 1.55 to the magistrates of cities and title 56 to those of smaller settlements such as *villae* and *burga*. However, he then relates and endorses a second interpretation according to which both titles relate to the same magistrates on the grounds that the law also calls cities municipalities. See Azo, *Summa super Codicem, Instituta, Extraordinaria* (Pavia 1506, repr. *Corpus Glossatorum Juris Civilis* ii (Turin 1966)), p. 19.

[42] That is, the law on which Bartolus is commenting, *Dig.* 39.2.1.

[43] See above, n. 30.

[44] Ed. cit., fo. 127va.

[45] The text prohibits the increase or decrease of an award after a judgment of court unless with the emperor's authority.

such as the counts and barons who have regalian rights in some place; but they cannot [impose] the penalty of infamy or any other non-pecuniary penalty: *Dig.* 3.1.1.10.[46]

Dig. 42.1.57[47]

I ask: say that someone below the age of puberty or a minor succeeds to a king or count who passes his jurisdiction on to his heirs: who will exercise [that] jurisdiction? I answer: his guardians [*tutores*†], until his puberty, to whom the universal administration [of his affairs] belongs: *Dig.* 27.10.7.[48] There is an express text in support of this, to the effect that if he is a spendthrift the curator himself will carry out [administration] at *Sext.* 1.8.2,[49] taken in conjunction with *Dig.* 42.4.7.10.[50] But after puberty, the ward administers those things which pertain to simple jurisdiction on his own, as if he were appointed by the emperor, in full knowledge, who has granted the kingdom or county in such a way that it should pass to heirs, as here.[51] But he cannot give away or perform those things pertaining to administration without a curator, by argument from *Dig.* 50.2.6.1,[52] and what I have said above in the second objection.[53] But what if a city wanted to give a ward or infant jurisdiction to exercise through a curator or tutor? I answer that it should first pass a statute, by argument from *Dig.* 43.24.3.4.[54] *Digest* 50.4.11.1 is relevant, where, in case of doubt, a

---

[46] See above, p. 87.

[47] Ed. cit., fo. 129ra.

[48] The curator is responsible for the health, well-being, and property of a lunatic.

[49] *Sext.* 1.8.2: the bull *Grandi non immerito*, issued by Innocent IV at the First Council of Lyons in 1245, effectively removes King Sancho IV of Portugal from the administration of his realm and gives it to the king's brother.

[50] A curator is appointed to represent a lunatic against creditors.

[51] *Dig.* 42.1.57 explains that, should a minor under the age of twenty-five be appointed praetor or consul and give judgment in the exercise of his jurisdiction, this will be valid, 'for the emperor who made him a magistrate endowed him with full authority'. Bartolus thus applies the law relating to magistrates' appointments under the emperors to the affairs of hereditary kingdoms and counties.

[52] Decurions† under the age of twenty-five have no vote.

[53] A law lecture usually began with an explanation of what that day's passage from the *Corpus* meant, before introducing any objections to the interpretation. At the start of his commentary on the law in hand, Bartolus cited *Dig.* 50.2.6.1 as an objection to the point made here by *Dig.* 42.1.57, and resolved the problem by pointing out that the former is about decurions who have no simple jurisdiction, only the power to administer the goods of the city; administration is, however, prohibited to those under the age of twenty-five.

[54] Municipal law can give additional privileges to a curator of the public administration allowing him to do what would otherwise be prohibited.

statute is limited to those who are suitable.[55] For if a city were unable to make a dispensation, there would be no question for that law to address; which without doubt applies in cities which do not recognize a lord in temporal matters, because then the people is free and uses all imperial jurisdiction, as is noted below at *Dig.* 49.15.24.[56]

Dig. 43.6.2[57]

These two laws are against the men of this city because they have their houses on the walls of the city, which is not allowed without the permission of the emperor, as you see here.[58] Nevertheless, they have permission from the people and commune of this city, and they say it is a free people subject to no one, so this people is the emperor in this city, therefore it can give permission.

Dig. 47.22.1.2[59]

Note that somebody may not belong to two collegiate bodies [*collegia*†]; I will explain below how this is to be understood.[60] Secondly, note that what belongs to a corporation belongs to the individuals, which is apparent because each receives his portion.[61] In opposition to this there is *Dig.* 1.8.6.1,[62] *Dig.* 2.4.10.4.[63] Some say: I concede that what belongs to a cor-

---

[55] The passage allows for a municipal law to prefer men of a certain status for civic offices so long as they are suitable.

[56] Once again, neither the gloss nor Bartolus's commentary on *Dig.* 49.15.24 – for which see below, pp. 102–7 – makes these precise points.

[57] Ed. cit., fo. 147va.

[58] *Dig.* 43.6 is about the praetorian interdict protecting sacred places from building and defacement. The second and third laws establish that city walls should not be damaged or used for habitation.

[59] *Bartoli a Sassoferrato in secundam Digesti Novi partem commentaria* (Turin 1574), fo. 148ra.

[60] Bartolus returns to this in his commentary on the fourth law of this title on illicit corporate bodies. His answer is that some corporations are subdivided into smaller corporations; thus a scholar may belong to the university of Perugia as well as to the corporation of students from his home region.

[61] The passage establishes that in leaving one college in favour of another he prefers, the ex-member takes with him whatever he contributed to the common fund.

[62] An important text establishing that what belongs communally to a city (*civitas*) does not belong to separate individuals but to the city corporately.

[63] Manumitted slaves (freedmen or *liberti*) were prohibited from summoning their ex-owners to court. This text establishes that a slave manumitted by a collegiate association or city may summon individual members of such a body to court because he is the freedman of that body which manumitted him, not of the individuals.

poration belongs to the individual members, nor do the contrary passages conflict with this because in each of them [the contrary] has been established on the grounds of the great obstacle which would result were it otherwise.[64] So some people say, as the gloss relates. But this opinion is not correct. For what belongs to a corporation does not belong to its individual members because a corporation is a represented person in itself: *Dig.* 46.1.22.[65] Nor does the present text conflict with this, because I admit that when a corporation is dissolved in relation to all [its members] or just to one, the things which belonged to the corporation become the property of the individuals, as here.

Dig. 47.22.4[66]

Let us therefore see for what reasons collegiate bodies [*collegia*†] are permitted by the common law. To see the matter clearly, you should know that some collegiate associations are permitted by the law of nations, some by the civil law. By the law of nations [there is] the collegiate association called a people of a single city, *castrum*,† or village [*villa*]: *Dig.* 1.1.5, where it says 'buildings were put up, estate boundaries were settled' and so on,[67] and this is the opinion of the gloss at *Dig.* 3.4.1.[68] However, Innocent seems to think at *Extra* 1.31.3 that they do not enjoy

---

[64] Bartolus is summarizing Accursius's gloss *Competit* here. The argument is that such manumitted slaves are only said to be the freedmen of their corporate ex-owners here because otherwise the obstacles to summoning any citizen to court would be too great; this passage should not, therefore, be cited in support of the proposition that whatever is owned by a corporation is not owned by its individual members because there is a special reason in this case for drawing that distinction, which would otherwise be inoperative.

[65] An inheritance, like a *municipium*,† a *decuria*,† or a partnership (*societas*), functions in place of a person.

[66] Ed. cit., fo. 148va.

[67] *Dig.* 1.1.5 employs the phrase *aedificia collocata*. The verb can simply mean to erect, set up, or build, and our translation respects this; however, Bartolus's point is about geographically nucleated communities, so the sense here is that under the law of nations buildings were put up in close proximity to one another.

[68] *Dig.* 3.4.1 is in the title on actions in the name of or against corporate bodies. It establishes that legislation limits the right to form a partnership (*societas*) or collegial association (*collegium*) and that such organizations are only permitted in rare circumstances. Accursius's gloss *Aliorum* does not mention *ius gentium*† as the normative justification for the existence of such associations, although it does number among legal corporations 'the congregation of any city whatsoever, town, or *castrum*'; Accursius then refers to *Inst.* 2.1.11, which states that civil laws only began once cities – *civitates* – had been founded; there is no express linkage with the *ius gentium* here.

the privilege of a city, *castrum*,[†] or town unless it is approved by a superi-or.[69] But I do not think this approval is necessary since it is permitted by the law of nations [*ius gentium*[†]]. Also, it is not prohibited by the civil law, except when that collection of buildings verges on jealous rivalry with a city, as in *Dig.* 50.10.3[70] and *Cod.* 8.10.10.[71] And these things are true in order for it to be called a people, but in order for that collection of buildings to be a city, or *castrum*, or town, the authority of the superiors would be needed. Because in our usage it is not called a city unless it has a bishopric, but it could not have a bishopric without the authority of a superior, although it would be called a *castrum*, territory [*terra*],[72] or community [*communantia*] according to another way of speaking, and it would be a people, or a licit collegiate body [*collegium*[†]]. Innocent admits nevertheless that such a collegiate body of a city, *castrum*, or town would *ipso facto* be approved if the superior wrote to it as a city, *castrum*, or town. This is what he says; nevertheless, as I think, no confirmation is required. Some collegiate bodies are approved by civil law, such as the bodies which are formed for religious purposes, as above in the first law of this title,[73] hence the associations of the *Disciplinati*, the Associations of Mercy,[74] and of those helping the downtrodden and suchlike are approved by the common law. But against this there is *Sext.* 3.17.1,[75] where no collegiate association for religious purposes may be formed without the authority of the pope. Solution: either someone wants to found a collegiate body for religious purposes in such a way that [its members] remain secular persons, such as the associations of *Disciplinati* and the others we have mentioned, and these are allowed according to the common law, as here.

---

[69] Innocent IV, *Apparatus super quinque libris decretalium*, fo. 148ra, insists that the corporation of a city, *castrum*, town, or *borgo* can only be constituted by a superior, such that 'even if there were as many men congregated together as there are in Rome, and they did not have the tacit or express permission of their superior to constitute a corporation, they would not be able to appoint a judge unless they had other rights and a corporate privilege'.

[70] A private citizen may undertake public works without the emperor's permission unless out of jealous rivalry with a city.

[71] The inhabitants of several provinces are allowed to surround their farms and property with a defensive wall.

[72] The word can mean the association of persons living in a particular place.

[73] *Dig.* 47.22.1 permits the formation of collegiate bodies for religious purposes.

[74] Numerous confraternities were founded in the Italian cities of the later middle ages with the objective of providing a version of the religious life for lay people. These two were some of the most successful.

[75] Gregory X's decree *Religionum diversitatem*, published in the Second Council of Lyons in 1274, repeats the prohibition in canon 13 of the Fourth Lateran Council (1215) of new religious orders.

Or, someone wants to found a collegiate body for religious purposes in such a way that [its members] become ecclesiastical persons, and this cannot be done without the authority of the pope, as in the contrary text cited. Further, the common law also allows a collegiate body of doctors[76] and scholars as in the Authentic *Habita* after *Cod.* 4.13.5,[77] *Extra* 1.3.41,[78] *Extra* 1.38.7,[79] and *Extra* 5.5.5.[80] Further, collegiate associations of a large number of people plying the same trade in the same city or place are permitted by the common law, as in this law, such that the gloss to *Dig.* 3.4.1[81] says that all the trades listed below at *Dig.* 50.6.7 have an approved collegiate body.[82] By the common law poor people are also permitted to form a collegiate body together for the maintenance of their subsistence, provided they only meet once a month, as in *Dig.* 47.22.1.[83] All other collegiate associations and all other groups [*sectae*] and all other leagues [*colligationes*] are prohibited. And so all those groups formed in cities which are not formed in order to expedite those matters which they have to expedite together, and those leagues which are formed between cities and between princes, and barons, are invalid. This is Innocent's opinion at *Extra* 5.31.14;[84] and *Dig.* 49.15.7[85] is no objection where it is said that cities form alliances with each other and join together, because this is true when other cities, not allies or free cities, are bound in alliance with the

---

[76] Bartolus means holders of academic doctorates, not physicians.

[77] Frederick Barbarossa's constitution *Habita* of 1155 grants scholars, and in particular professors of canon and Roman law, certain legal protections. It does not mention corporate organizations of either students or teachers. It was one of the modern imperial constitutions incorporated into the *Corpus iuris civilis*.† For the text, see W. Steltzer, 'Zum Scholarenprivileg Friedrich Barbarossas (Authentica "Habita")', *Deutsches Archiv für Erforschung des Mittelalters*, 34 (1978): 123–65, at 165.

[78] Gregory IX's decretal *Ab excommunicato* appears to have nothing to do with the point at issue.

[79] Innocent III's decretal *Quia in causis* (1203) grants the corporation (*universitas*†) of scholars at Paris the right to appoint legal procurators.†

[80] Honorius III's decretal *Super specula* (1219) orders bishops and cathedral chapters to send selected appropriate clergy to be trained in theology faculties.

[81] See above, n. 68.

[82] In the gloss *Aliorum* to *Dig.* 3.4.1 Accursius refers to *Dig.* 50.6.7, a title on the law of immunity from public services, where forty-three different trades, professions, and public offices are mentioned.

[83] The text allows men of the lower orders to meet once a month; they are not explicitly described as indigent.

[84] Innocent IV, *Apparatus super quinque libris decretalium*, fo. 526va: three or more cities or barons cannot form leagues without permission from the *princeps*,† because they have little to do with one another which could justify such an association.

[85] Below, n. 139.

Roman people holding *imperium*.† But a large number of cities or barons under the same king, lord, or prince are not allowed to form such a confederation with each other, for these are prohibited organizations and associations. From all this it can be concluded that the cities of Tuscany which do not recognize a superior in temporal matters can ally together as free cities, but many *castra*† or towns beneath a single city or lord cannot do this, as has been said.

Dig. 48.1.7[86]

I ask, who can dispense from a condemnation to infamy? I answer: the text says only the emperor or senate: *Dig.* 3.1.1.10.[87] We say the same of the pope in the lands of the church, because he can issue a dispensation to those condemned to infamy. The same is true of the college of cardinals during a papal vacancy; it is otherwise in the case of kings and princes. This is Innocent's opinion at the aforementioned *Extra* 2.27.23.[88] I ask whether a single city could impose infamy or relax a condemnation to infamy? It seems not, because a single city cannot pass a statute on these matters, which are not within its jurisdiction: *Dig.* 2.1.20 and it is noted there,[89] and *Dig.* 42.5.12.1.[90] But a case concerning infamy is not in the jurisdiction of a city, since it is reserved to the emperor: *Dig.* 3.1.1.10,[91] so therefore, etc. Solution: I would say that since every city in Italy nowadays – and particularly in Tuscany – recognizes no lord, it has within itself a free people and has in itself *merum imperium*,† and has as much power over its people as the emperor has over everything: *Dig.* 49.15.24, and it is noted there.[92]

---

[86] Ed. cit., fo. 153va–b.

[87] Above, p. 91. Bartolus makes the same main point here as in his commentary on *Dig.* 3.1.1.10, but gives a more detailed explanation.

[88] Above, n. 20.

[89] *Dig.* 2.1.20 states that there is a penalty for obeying a judge who administers justice beyond his territory or who gives judgment in a case exceeding the maximum amount of money allowed for his jurisdiction. Neither the gloss nor the relevant passage in the *Digest*† commentary purporting to be by Bartolus mentions cities at this point.

[90] Authority to take possession given by a judge only relates to a place belonging to the judge's jurisdiction.

[91] Above, p. 87.

[92] Below, p. 103.

Dig. 48.17.1.2[93]

Note here that after the registration [of a wanted person] the accused should be notified, and thus it is an argument that the term of a banishment runs from the day of notification, not from the day the banishment was imposed, just as here the year runs from the day of notification, not from the day of registration. In this matter, however, follow the customs and the statutes of cities. Secondly, note the manner of summonsing a person who is in another's territory: letters are written to the judge in whose territory the defendant is, so that that judge notifies the defendant; and this is a noteworthy text, where it says '... must also send letters, etc.'. This is relevant to the question of whether a judge of this city could summons by messenger or by letters someone living outside his territory. A decretal says not: *Clem.* 2.11.2, where the pope declares invalid the sentence passed by the emperor at Pisa, where he had summonsed by edicts King Robert, who was living in the lands of the church, and thus in another's territory.[94] For the pope says that the pope himself should have been requested by the emperor to summons the king in his own territory, but that the emperor could not issue a summons himself. Cinus disputed this question at Siena,[95] and says that a summons made orally or by edict can be issued concerning someone who is in another's territory: *Cod.* 1.3.32.5, where there appears to be an explicit case;[96] *Cod.* 1.28.2.[97] However, a summons to arrest a person could not be issued, as in *Auth.* 9.9.5, placed after *Cod.* 9.9.15.[98] But concerning that decretal he says that no peaceful answer can be given, but that it should pass with the other errors of the canonists. This is what he says. I, as someone living in the lands of the church, am accustomed to uphold that decretal, and say it

---

[93] Ed. cit., fo. 189rb–va.

[94] For Clement V's decretal *Pastoralis cura*, see above, Appendix II, n. 112.

[95] See G. M. Monti, ed., *Cino da Pistoia, Le 'Quaestiones' e I 'Consilia'* (Milan 1942), pp. 59–74; K. Pennington, *The Prince and the Law, 1200–1600: Sovereignty and Rights in the Western Legal Tradition* (Berkeley, CA 1993), pp. 197–8.

[96] *Cod.* 1.3.32.5 permits the praetorian prefect to summons a priest living outside the capital in one of the provinces.

[97] *Cod.* 1.28.2 generally prohibits the urban prefect from summonsing people from the provinces to his court, but allows certain exceptions.

[98] *Nov.* 134.5 states that the provincial governor will seize those accused of crimes in another province and summonsed by the governor of that province. This paragraph was thought important enough to merit insertion in Justinian's *Code*,† which, unlike the *Novels*,† was the subject of standard lectures.

is legally correct. For you should know that sometimes there are several judges holding separate jurisdictions, nevertheless those jurisdictions depend upon one ruler [*princeps*†], such as the governors of different provinces appointed by the emperor, or by one king; then one can issue a verbal summons in the territory of another; this is what *Cod.* 1.3.32.5 says, with similar passages, as though this were taken to be permitted by the ruler who appointed them. *Dig.* 46.3.100 is also relevant as an argument, and *Dig.* 26.7.47.2.[99] Some have separate and distinct jurisdictions, such that one does not depend upon the other, nor are they under the same lord, such as the pope and emperor. Then one may not issue a summons in the territory of the other. This is what the aforementioned *Clem.* 2.11.2 says. But he should request the judge in whose territory [the accused] is to summons him, as is said here,[100] and this [is true] insofar as we hold the opinion of Dante, as I have discovered it in a book he wrote entitled *Monarchia*, in which book he debated three questions, one of which was whether the empire depends upon the church, and he held that it did not, but on account of this he was nearly condemned for heresy after his death.[101] For the church maintains that the empire depends upon the church, by elegant arguments which I omit, and I say that one judge may issue a summons in the territory of another judge, to whom he is not subject, as in the aforesaid *Cod.* 1.3.32.5. But he cannot issue a summons in the territory of a greater judge, from whom he has his jurisdiction, out of reverence for him, arguing from *Dig.* 39.2.4.9, and from what I have said there.[102] There is nothing more for you to consider here.

[99] *Dig.* 46.3.100 and *Dig.* 26.7.47.2 are concerned with tutors† in different regions of the Roman empire. The first allows provincial tutors to arrange for a debt to be paid to them in Rome, the second explains that tutors of Italian property should inform those responsible for provincial property if they discover that provincials are in debt to their ward.

[100] *Dig.* 48.17.1.2, the passage Bartolus is discussing here, states that provincial governors must send letters to the magistrates of the places where the accused live to inform them that they are to answer charges.

[101] Dante, *Monarchia*, ed. P. Shaw (Cambridge 1995), Bk. 3. Dante was never prosecuted for heresy, alive or posthumously; but in 1329, within a few years of his death, Cardinal Bertrand de Pouget attempted to have *Monarchia* condemned as heretical, and had it ritually burned. In 1554 it was placed on the Index of prohibited books, where it remained until the late nineteenth century; see the summary in A. K. Cassell, *The Monarchia Controversy* (Washington, DC 2004), pp. 34–9.

[102] *Dig.* 39.2.4.9 merely excuses a municipal magistrate for not acting on a plea of anticipated injury if the superior court of the provincial governor is close by. In his commentary on that passage (*Bartoli a Sassoferrato in primam Digesti Novi partem commentaria* (Turin 1574), fo. 28ra), Bartolus distinguishes between an inferior judge with delegated jurisdiction,

Dig. 48.19.4[103]

Note this text [which proves] that a judge cannot give someone who has been expelled or sent into exile permission to return or come back, but only the emperor can do so and nobody else. And you should understand what the text says here: 'for some particular reason', because the will of the emperor is just cause.[104] And I understand it to be the same in those cities in Italy: since they are emperors unto themselves they can give an exile permission to return. I think the same is true of all cities which have permission to make statutes on these major matters, for they can pass laws to the effect that exiles may return; they will then have permission to return by authority of the law, and by the authority of the emperor, who has granted [the city] permission to make laws and statutes, arguing from *Dig.* 43.24.3.4.[105]

Dig. 48.19.16.10[106]

This gloss is cited by the doctors [of law] on the question of whether a corporation committing a crime is punished less harshly.[107] In my judgment this is a most subtle question, for first we need to see if a corporation can commit a crime; secondly, we need to see if it can be punished. And there appears to be a text to the effect that it can commit a crime at *Dig.* 4.2.9.1 with its gloss,[108] and there is a note at *Dig.* 3.4.7,[109] and *Dig.* 50.17.160 and the gloss there.[110] There seems to be a text to the contrary

---

which lapses in the presence of the superior, delegating judge, and one holding ordinary jurisdiction, who should refrain from displaying certain insignia of office in the presence of his superior, but does not lose his jurisdiction.

[103] Ed. cit., fo. 197rb.

[104] *Dig.* 48.19.4 does indeed conclude by prohibiting anyone from giving such permission 'except the emperor, for some particular reason'.

[105] Above, n. 54. The passage mentions officers who have been granted the right to make certain concessions by the emperor. This is in the context of municipal law.

[106] Ed. cit., fo. 200ra–b.

[107] This section of *Dig.* 48.19.16 explains that some crimes are punished more harshly to set an example when lots of people commit them, the example given being highway robbery. Accursius notes in his gloss *Multis* that under some circumstances punishment is milder when a large number of malefactors are involved.

[108] The text, from the title on the interdict for acts performed under duress, makes clear that a crowd of people (*populus†*), an order of decurions† (*curia*), collegiate body, or corporation can exercise illegitimate duress. Accursius's gloss *Collegium* argues that such bodies can commit fraud and duress.

[109] Accursius's gloss *Non debetur* argues that a corporation can commit injury.

[110] See Accursius's gloss *Refertur*, where a corporation can be penally liable.

at *Dig.* 4.3.15.1.[111] Moreover, a corporation is a purely legal entity[112] and has neither a soul nor understanding, therefore it cannot commit a crime: *Dig.* 9.1.1[113] and *Dig.* 48.8.12,[114] and this appears to be what Innocent thinks at *Extra* 5.39.53.[115] Others say that a corporation can commit a crime of neglect – *Cod.* 1.2.10[116] – but not of commission, for the reasons already given. Cinus relates their opinion at *Cod.* 8.4.7.[117] This is incorrect, because I see a corporation committing a crime of commission in the Authentic after *Cod.* 1.3.2[118] and at *Feud.* 2.53[119] and [the constitution] after *Feud.* 2.58.[120]

What shall we say? To understand this question we should see first whether a corporation is anything other than its members. Some say not, as is noted at the aforesaid law *Dig.* 3.4.7.1[121] and *Dig.* 47.22.1.2,[122] and all the philosophers maintain this, and the canonists, who maintain that the whole does not differ in a real sense from its parts. The truth is that if

---

[111] Here an action for fraud is given against the decurions† who committed it, not against the citizens of the municipality.

[112] Latin: *nomen iuris*, literally 'a name of law'. We borrow this translation from Q. Skinner, *From Humanism to Hobbes* (Cambridge 2018), p. 26 and n. 105.

[113] An animal lacking sense cannot commit offensive injury.

[114] An infant or a madman who kills a person is not culpable.

[115] See Innocent IV, *Apparatus super quinque libris decretalium*, fo. 557rb, whose argument here shaped all medieval discussion of corporate criminal liability. Honorius III's decretal *Gravem venerabilis* had excommunicated the counsellors and officers of the commune of Pisa who had passed legislation hostile to the church. Innocent IV noted that this was because the *universitas*† itself could not be punished, on the grounds that it was incapable of committing a crime.

[116] *Cod.* 1.2.10 is only relevant thanks to its location in the title 'Holy Churches, Their Property and Privileges'; it imposes penalties on ship-owners who withdraw their vessels from public services, regardless of any privilege of rank or religion. This would, in Bartolus's terms, constitute a crime of omission – *not* contributing a ship – which could theoretically be perpetrated by a church. Accursius's gloss *Corrigimus* explores the liability of a church as a corporation for the misdemeanours of its representatives.

[117] *Cyni Pistoriensis in Codicem [...] commentaria* (Frankfurt am Main 1578), fo. 483va, where this distinction is attributed to certain, unnamed, lawyers.

[118] *Item nulla*, section 2 of Frederick II's constitution *Ad decus* (see Appendix II, n. 51) orders that 'No community, or public or private person' is to impose taxes and other exactions on ecclesiastical property and persons.

[119] This is a constitution issued in 1158 by Frederick Barbarossa, proclaiming a peace under oath. The relevant section sets a fine of 100 pounds of gold for a city (*civitas*) which violates the peace.

[120] See above, Appendix II, n. 51: section 3 of Frederick II's *Ad decus* threatens with imperial banishment any community which persists in a state of excommunication incurred for crimes against the church.

[121] Accursius's gloss *Non debetur* finishes by citing the opinion that 'A corporation is nothing other than the individual men who are there.'

[122] Above, pp. 92–3.

indeed we are speaking truly, properly, and according to what really exists, then what they say is true, for a corporation of scholars is nothing other than the scholars; but by fiction of law what they say is not true, because the corporation represents one person which is something other than the scholars or the members of the corporation: *Dig.* 46.1.22.[123] Which is apparent, because if all those scholars withdraw and others return, it is nevertheless the same corporation. Again, if all the members of a people die and others take their place, it is the same people: *Dig.* 5.1.76,[124] and so according to a fiction of law a corporation is something other than the persons who constitute the corporation, because it is a kind of represented person. This established in advance, the question is whether a corporation can commit a crime. I answer: strictly speaking it cannot commit a crime because strictly speaking it is not a person, as has been said; nevertheless this is something fictive taken for something true, as we lawyers do take it. If the question is whether a corporation can commit a crime, I say that it can. A corporation can commit a wrong of omission, because the corporation is obliged to do something which, if it is omitted, the corporation omits; even though this comes about through the negligence of those in charge of the corporation, nevertheless the corporation itself is said to be negligent: *Cod.* 1.2.10[125] along with *Dig.* 17.1.8.4.[126] But concerning a wrong which has been committed or which consists in actively being committed, pay attention, for there are certain things which can only be done by the corporation itself, such as passing statutes, granting jurisdiction, imposing taxes, and suchlike; in this case a corporation can commit a delict, as in the aforementioned Authentic after *Cod.* 1.3.2 and the constitution after *Feud.* 2.58.[127] For it cannot be said that any private person does this, but it is done by the corporation itself where that right

---

[123] Above, n. 65.

[124] A people is the same now as it was a hundred years before, even though nobody survives from that time. The context is the substitution of judges appointed to hear a case, which despite that remains the same case.

[125] Above, n. 116. Accursius's gloss *Corrigimus* draws the lesson from this law that a church can be penalized for the actions of its prelate.

[126] Co-tutors are liable to be sued if one of their number fails to perform a task which they have mandated him to perform.

[127] Bartolus refers to section 1 of *Ad decus*, and to section 3, for which see above, n. 120.

is located: *Dig.* 1.1.9[128] and *Cod.* 3.13.7.[129] There are some things which do not relate to those rights located in the corporation, such as committing murder or acts of violence and suchlike, and then the corporation cannot properly be said to do [such things] because they require a real person: *Dig.* 4.3.15.1.[130] But in a loose sense they are said to be committed by the others who rule the city, or by others whom the city has charged [with this task] by operation of statute: *Dig.* 41.2.1.22[131] and the next law,[132] *Dig.* 38.3.1;[133] and this is how I understand *Dig.* 4.2.9.1 with its gloss, and *Dig.* 50.17.160 with its gloss.[134]

Dig. 49.1.1.3[135]

Say there is a city which recognizes no superior, and which elects its own governor [*rector*] and does not have any other officer [set over it]: who will be the judge of appeal? I answer: the people itself or the *ordo*[136] which appoints that officer, because this is the only superior to the people itself, and is emperor unto it, as is noted at *Dig.* 49.15.24.[137]

Dig. 49.15.24[138]

You should know that there are two principal kinds of people [*gens*]: first, the Roman people [*populus*†], secondly foreign peoples, as is demonstrated

---

[128] For Bartolus's commentary on the famous law *Omnes populi*, see above, pp. 69–81.

[129] *Cod.* 3.13.7 merely reinforces the authority of judges over practitioners of particular professions, regardless of their rank.

[130] Above, n. 111.

[131] From the title on acquiring and losing legal possession, this passage explains that citizens of a municipality† can acquire nothing because the consent of all is not possible. Hence, they do not possess the public buildings of the municipality.

[132] *Dig.* 41.2.2 picks up on the final statement of the preceding text to the effect that in the opinion of some, the citizens cannot acquire possession through a slave belonging to their municipality; here, it is said that the rule actually observed is that they can. Bartolus sees this as a parallel of the loose sense of personal agency he is discussing.

[133] The citizens of municipalities are here given the same rights over the property of the municipality's freedmen and freedwomen as those enjoyed by a normal patron (*patronus*: the former owner of a manumitted slave).

[134] See above, nn. 108, 110.

[135] Ed. cit., fo. 207rb.

[136] *Ordo* often refers to an honourable echelon within a Roman city or municipality, particularly the decurions,† in which context it has no natural translation. Helpfully, Bartolus's own commentary on *Dig.* 50.9.1 (a passage which leaves it to the *ordo* and the landholders of each community to decide how many doctors there should be) begins: 'Note that by the common law the *ordo* of a city, that is, the priors† or *antiani*† ...'.

[137] See following text.

[138] Ed. cit., fo. 228ra.

by *Dig.* 49.15.7.[139] On the first point, I ask who is called the Roman people? The gloss says that this is taken to mean the entire Roman empire:
Dig. 50.1.33.[140] But you might say, since there are few peoples [*gentes*]
who obey the Roman empire, it therefore appears that the Roman people
is rather small. I answer that there are certain peoples [*gentes*] which obey
the Roman empire and they are without doubt part of the Roman people. There are some which do not obey the Roman empire in all respects
but in some they do obey, such as those who live according to the law of
the Roman people, such as the cities of Tuscany, Lombardy, and the like,
and they also belong to the Roman people. For since the Roman people
exercises jurisdiction over them in some particular respect, it retains all
jurisdiction: *Dig.* 39.3.17 with similar passages and what is noted there.[141]
There are some peoples who do not obey the emperor at all, nor live by
those laws, and they say they do this on the strength of a privilege from
the emperor, as the Venetians do, and they similarly belong to the Roman
people. For they say they have that liberty from the emperor, and hold it
from him by a privilege which is in a certain sense precarious, and he could
revoke that privilege when he wished, since he is permitted to change his
mind: *Dig.* 32.22.[142] Moreover, that privilege which has been granted to
them ought to be to their advantage, such that they are not deprived of
their Roman citizenship, by argument from *Dig.* 49.15.12.7.[143] There are
some peoples who do not obey the emperor, yet claim to possess a liberty from him on the basis of some contract, such as the provinces held
by the Roman church which were donated by Emperor Constantine to
the Roman church; assuming as a certainty that the donation was valid
and that it could not be revoked, to that degree I say they belong to the
Roman people. For the Roman church exercises jurisdiction over those
lands which used to belong to the Roman empire and this they admit;
therefore they do not cease to belong to the Roman people; rather, the
administration of those provinces has been granted to somebody else.

---

[139] *Dig.* 49.15.7 notes that allies and free peoples (*foederati et liberi*) are 'foreigners to us'.

[140] See Accursius's gloss *vel praedones*; *Dig.* 50.1.33 states in the context of municipal
citizenship within the Roman empire that 'Rome is the common *patria* of us all.'

[141] Bartolus seems to have in mind the gloss *Plures sunt*, where Accursius explains that one
does not lose the right of drawing water by night if one only draws it by day, so long as
both rights are included in the same servitude. By using a part, the holder of the servitude
retains the whole.

[142] *Dig.* 32.22 explains that a testator can change his mind about the legacies he wishes to
leave.

[143] *Dig.* 49.15.12.7 explains that someone who buys a slave captured by the enemy becomes
the owner until he is reimbursed.

See in a similar case: jurisdiction over the clergy has been granted in its entirety to the pope; do they for that reason cease to be Roman citizens? Certainly not, as is apparent from the fact that they retain the right of succession: *Cod.* 1.3.54.5.[144] And I say the same of those other kings and princes who deny that they are subject to the king of the Romans, such as the king of France, the king of England, and others like them. For if they admit that he is the universal lord, even though they withdraw themselves from that universal lordship thanks to a privilege or prescription[†] or something similar, they do not cease to be Roman citizens, on the basis of what has been said above. And on this reasoning virtually all peoples [*gentes*] who obey holy mother church belong to the Roman people. And perhaps if someone were to say that the lord emperor was not the lord and monarch of the whole word, he would be a heretic, because he would be speaking against the interpretation of the church, against the text of the holy gospel, when it says 'There went out a decree from Caesar Augustus that all the world should be taxed ...' as we have in *Luke* 2, 1. Thus Christ also recognized the emperor as lord. What has been said is true, unless a public war were to be declared against certain of them, for then they would be made enemies because of the declaration of war, as I shall say below.

Secondly, I have said that other peoples are foreigners; and strictly speaking peoples are foreign who do not admit that the Roman emperor is universal lord, like the Greeks, who do not believe the Roman emperor is universal lord but say the emperor of Constantinople is the lord of all the world. Then there are the Tartars, who say the Great Khan is universal lord; and the Saracens who say their lord is lord of all the world. It is the same with the Jews. But there is a difference between them, because some of them are allied with us, as the Greeks were allied with us against the Turks. There are some with whom we are at peace, such as the Tartars, for our merchants travel to them, and they to ours. There are some with whom we are neither at peace nor at war, nor do we have anything to do with them, such as those in India. There are some with whom we are in open war, as we are with the Saracens, and nowadays with the Turks, but those outside are of small concern to us.

---

[144] A constitution of Justinian of 533 or 534 protecting children who choose to join a monastery or the clergy from disinheritance by their parents.

With this established in advance, let us see who can declare war and what the effects of a declaration of war are.¹⁴⁵ [...]

Further, anyone with jurisdiction may declare a just war in order to exercise his jurisdiction: *Dig.* 6.1.68,¹⁴⁶ *Dig.* 50.17.176,¹⁴⁷ *Dig.* 43.4.3,¹⁴⁸ and although this war is legal it is nevertheless not public in the sense in which the term is used here, and therefore the things taken there do not become the property of those who take them, nor are the captives made slaves, unless a law has been passed about this by that duke, prefect, or king who declares the war. And this is Innocent's opinion at *Extra* 2.13.12¹⁴⁹ and *Extra* 2.24.29.¹⁵⁰ And on this reasoning I say that if a governor in the duchy [of Spoleto] or the March [of Ancona] declares war against some place,¹⁵¹ the things taken are not made the property of those who take them and captives are not made slaves unless a constitution or court sentence about this has been passed beforehand. Here, however, it appears that if someone is a rebel against an officer or governor [installed by] the church, he is a rebel against the entire church which occupies the position of the empire in those areas, but I will answer [this] below. A public war is declared in a third manner when it is declared by the Roman people or the emperor, to whom all the jurisdiction of the Roman people has been transferred, as here,¹⁵² and *Dig.* 50.16.118.¹⁵³ And I therefore think that the cities of Italy on which the emperor has declared war, such as the city

---

¹⁴⁵ In the next section, omitted here, Bartolus allows the right to declare war to private citizens who fight in self-defence, who assemble a posse to fight for the immediate recovery of their goods, and who do so after a delay, so long as they have no access to a judge.

¹⁴⁶ *Dig.* 6.1.68 allows a judge to use armed force against a person refusing to comply with the court's order to restore property.

¹⁴⁷ Individuals are prohibited from doing what a judge can do publicly, lest tumult result.

¹⁴⁸ When someone has been put into possession by a magistrate but is prevented, the magistrate may use force to get him in.

¹⁴⁹ Innocent IV, *Apparatus super quinque libris decretalium*, fo. 231vb, sets out several cases where a prelate may use armed force in the exercise of his jurisdiction.

¹⁵⁰ Innocent IV's commentary on the decretal *Sicut* of Innocent III sets out this principle in slightly less specific terms. If the war is decreed by a holder of jurisdiction, he may pass a statute making whatever is taken the property of those who take it; see Innocent IV, *Apparatus super quinque libris decretalium*, fo. 287va.

¹⁵¹ Latin: *terrae*.

¹⁵² That is, *Dig.* 49.15.24, the law he is currently commenting on, which defines as enemies those on whom the Roman people has publicly declared war, or those who have done so on the Roman people.

¹⁵³ *Dig.* 50.16.118 virtually repeats the last passage cited, but uses the first person plural instead of referring to the Roman people.

of Florence and others like it,[154] are truly enemies of the empire and captives become slaves, and the things which are captured there become the
property of the captors; you should not understand this to mean the persons of the captors in a simple sense because sometimes they are seized
[by the emperor], as I shall say below at *Dig.* 49.15.28.[155] Concerning what
has been said I ask: what if some city or place [*terra*] resists some officer
of the lord emperor or the supreme pontiff in the lands in which he holds
imperium†? Are they because of this truly said to be enemies? I answer:
sometimes someone rebels against an officer not because of the officer but
because of the emperor; so because he will not obey the emperor then he
appears to rebel against the emperor and declare war on the emperor, and
this is what the aforesaid constitution by Henry says,[156] and by argument
from *Dig.* 39.3.25.[157] A certain decretal provides particularly strong support for this: *Sext.* 1.14.14,[158] which says that if there is an appeal from a
subdelegate judge for a reason relating to the person of the subdelegating
judge, the appeal should be made to the first ordinary judge; but if the
appeal is made for a reason relating to the person of the subdelegate the
appeal is made to the subdelegating judge himself. But if someone were
to rebel against a governor [*rector*] because of something the governor
himself does, because he mistreats them,[159] as the cities of the Duchy of
Spoleto and the March [of Ancona] do, then they would not be called

---

[154] W. M. Bowsky, *Henry VII in Italy: The Conflict of Empire and City-State, 1310–1313*
(Lincoln, NE 1960), p. 180: in September 1312 Emperor Henry VII laid siege to Florence;
the following February he condemned over 600 inhabitants of the city and its *contado*† to
death as rebels.

[155] Latin: *publicari*, the sense of which Bartolus explains in *In secundam Digesti Novi partem
commentaria* (Turin 1574), fo. 228va, where he argues that immovable goods captured in
war become the property of the commonwealth – *res publica*† – which has declared the
war, while immovables are consigned – again: *publicari* – to the victorious general who
then distributes or sells them among his troops.

[156] 'Frederick' in the text is manifestly a scribal error – *Henrici* has become *Frederici*. Bartolus
refers to Emperor Henry VII's constitution *Quoniam nuper*, promulgated at Pisa on 2
April 1313: those who machinate against imperial officers performing their duties are
rebels (MGH, *Constitutiones et acta publica imperatorum et regum*, ed. J. Schwalm, iv, pt. 2
(Hanover 1909–11), nos. 931–2, pp. 966–8).

[157] *Dig.* 39.3.25: when damage is done to a right of way leading to a piece of land and owed as
a servitude to it, the land itself is deemed to be damaged. Bartolus found this an inspiring
passage, applicable in many contexts ('*Facit ad multa*'). He does not mention rebellion in
his commentary on it: *In primam Digesti Novi partem*, fo. 49rb, but does use it to explore
aspects of appeal from city courts to that of the emperor.

[158] *Sext.* 1.14.14 is the decretal *Si a subdelegato* of Boniface VIII.

[159] The change from singular to plural is in the original; Bartolus means those subject to the
jurisdiction of the governor.

106

rebels against the emperor or supreme pontiff, but against the governor. And this is what the aforementioned passages say. I ask further, what of those wars which are fought between city and city: are these said to be enemies to one another such that the right of captivity and *postliminium*† applies, as when there is hostility between the Roman people and the Saracens? Briefly, I say when there is hostility between certain cities which are beneath the same lord, then the right of captivity and *postliminium* does not apply: *Dig.* 49.15.21.1.[160] Sometimes there is hostility between two cities which do not recognize a superior, such as between the city of Florence and the city of Pisa, and say – to remove all doubt – that each of these is an enemy of the empire: certainly according to the law of nations [*ius gentium*†] introduced by ancient customs the right of captivity and *postliminium* should apply: *Dig.* 49.15.19.*pr.*,[161] and here. But according to the customs of the modern age, and the custom observed since antiquity among Christians, we do not observe the rights of captivity and *postliminium* in relation to people's persons. They are neither sold, nor are captives held as slaves; but in relation to their property we do observe those rights. Which custom should be obeyed: *Dig.* 49.15.19.*pr.*[162] However, how and by what right war should be declared against the Saracens, you should say according to what Innocent says at *Extra* 3.34.8.[163]

Dig. 50.9.4[164]

Further,[165] it is said here that decrees [of the decurions] should be rescinded; I ask by whom, and at whose petition? I answer: they should be

---

[160] See above, *On Guelfs and Ghibellines*, p. 6. The point is that for Bartolus, such cities all belong to the same *res publica*,† the Roman empire.

[161] The beginning of *Dig.* 49.15.19 describes the right of *postliminium* as a right 'established by customs and laws' and introduced by natural justice, not specifically by the *ius gentium*. There is no obvious support in the current law, which Bartolus cites next, for this association either.

[162] See preceding note.

[163] Innocent IV's commentary on Innocent III's decretal *Quod super his*: *Apparatus super quinque libris decretalium*, fos. 429vb–430vb. It established the main categories of canon law debate about crusading against Muslims and, later, Slavs. There is a partial English translation in B. Tierney, *The Crisis of Church and State 1050–1300* (Englewood Cliffs, NJ 1964), pp. 155–6.

[164] Ed. cit., fo. 239va–b.

[165] *Dig.* 50.9 is another title about decurions.† The passage Bartolus has in mind from *Dig.* 50.9.4 begins by nullifying decrees made by decurions favouring some individual, and instances grants of public estates or houses. We give here the last two-thirds of Bartolus's commentary.

rescinded by the superior, if there is one, such as the governor [*praeses*], or if there is no governor I think they can be rescinded by the great council of the city: *Dig.* 26.5.19.[166] And I have talked about this above at *Dig.* 50.1.2.[167] And this should be done at the petition of anyone belonging to the people [by recourse to] the legal remedy offered by this law,[168] or to the discretionary duty of the judge, as is noted by Innocent at *Extra* 1.31.16[169] and at *Extra* 1.33.[170] I ask, taking it as established that the decurions† themselves cannot make gifts, as has been said, whether the entire people could make a gift? I think it could, which is evident, because it can pass a law on making gifts: *Dig.* 43.24.3.4,[171] and I have said there that this undoubtedly occurs in those cities which *de facto* do not recognize a superior and so have *imperium*† over themselves.[172] Concerning the subject covered by the present law, since in many cases decurions and the governing orders of cities have discretionary powers, and since it is very commonly asked to what matters the said discretionary powers extend, let us consider a few things concerning this. And sometimes it is normal for them to have discretionary power over the good and peaceful condition of

---

[166] Bartolus cites *Dig.* 26.5.19, which is in a title about the appointment of tutors† by various civil authorities, in his commentary on *Dig.* 1.1.9; see above, p. 78. The passage allows decurions to appoint tutors in the absence of those who would normally do so, so long as the majority agree.

[167] Actually *Dig.* 50.1.3 (ed. cit., fo. 231rb), where Bartolus makes the slightly different point that, unless there are no other judges, decurions may only appoint tutors when they have been specially commissioned to do so. He adds that where there are no judges of appeal a sentence passed by the *podestà*† can be appealed before the *priori*† of the city.

[168] Bartolus means *Dig.* 50.9.4, the law on which he is commenting here.

[169] Innocent IV, *Apparatus super quinque libris decretalium*, fo. 153ra, argues that a monastery should be allowed to implead a bishop by appeal to the *officium iudicis* – which we translate here as the discretionary duty of the judge – because for various reasons other legal remedies of a more formal nature do not fit the circumstances.

[170] Innocent IV, *Apparatus quinque libris decretalium*, fo. 158ra; actually *Extra* 1.33.8.

[171] Above, n. 54.

[172] Bartolus does not mention such cities in his commentary on *Dig.* 43.24.3.4 (*In primam Digesti Novi partem*, fo. 162va). Nevertheless, he highlights its implicit recommendation that, before selling anything belonging to a *res publica*,† 'You first make the city pass a statute about this, and, with the statute made, you will be able to sell according to the formulation of the statute.' He adds that a statute allowing the alienation of public property to the city's tyrant is invalid. In his commentary on *Cod.* 10.47(46).1 (Bartolus, *In tres libros Codicis commentaria* (Turin 1574), fo. 22vb), which with certain exceptions prohibits decurions from granting immunity from municipal dues and services, Bartolus refers to this commentary on *Dig.* 50.9.4, when he asks who is permitted to grant such immunity? Accursius's gloss *cura funguntur* reserves this power to the emperor alone (*solus princeps*), to which Bartolus adds: 'I think the same [goes for] the Great Council and the General Assembly [*consilium magnum et adunantia generalis*], because perhaps it is a city which recognizes no superior.'

the city, sometimes over a superabundance in the city, sometimes over the defence of the city. Sometimes they are accustomed to have discretionary power to ensure that money reaches the commune [*commune*], and over many other matters which the variety of circumstances throws up. So it should be known that on the strength of the said discretionary power, or one of them, they cannot readmit to civic rights those who have been banished, unless this has been expressly permitted by the people, which is said to be the emperor in its own city: *Dig.* 48.19.4,[173] and by argument from *Dig.* 1.19.3.[174] They can, however, readmit banished persons for one reason, namely if [these] apprehend and denounce many other banished persons: *Dig.* 49.16.5.[175] They can issue a licence to return to the city for legitimate cause according to what I have said at *Dig.* 48.1.5.[176] Further, they cannot nullify any condemnatory judicial sentence: *Dig.* 48.18.1.27[177] and *Dig.* 3.1.1.10.[178] Further, they cannot suspend execution of any sentence beyond a period of three months, as in *Dig.* 49.14.45.10.[179] And so it is apparent that decurions† who sometimes suspend execution of sentence for longer periods are not acting according to law; the whole people, however, which takes the place of the emperor regarding penalties which it has itself imposed, could do this, as in the said *Dig.* 49.14.45.10. Further, they cannot, on the strength of the aforementioned discretionary power, or any of them, change the ruling orders and governmental organs of cities, by argument from *Dig.* 49.14.8, 30 and 46 section 7.[180] For the discretionary power they have over the good and peaceful condition of the city is understood to refer to the current dispensation – *Dig.* 34.2.7[181] and by

---

[173] Above, p. 99.

[174] *Dig.* 1.19.3 forbids imperial procurators† from readmitting people to imperial estates whom they have already ejected as troublesome.

[175] The text, from the title on military law, is about deserters from the Roman army who are later caught. It cautions that the punishment of such persons will depend on a variety of further considerations, although there is no close analogy to the caveat Bartolus mentions here.

[176] Bartolus says there (*In secundam Digesti Novi partem*, fo. 152va–b) that a judge may readmit a banished person to the city in order for the latter to answer fresh charges.

[177] The text rules that a provincial governor may not revoke a sentence he has passed.

[178] See above, p. 91.

[179] A judge may grant debtors to the fisc a delay of three months before paying.

[180] These three laws from the title on the law of the fisc all prohibit the sale by fiscal procurators of the slaves put in charge of goods claimed by the fisc. The chasm dividing Bartolus's point and the authorities he fields in support is obvious, and shows the difficulty in finding credible passages in the law by means of which to articulate the fundamentals of contemporary civic political propriety.

[181] A legacy is interpreted with reference to what the testator owns at that moment.

argument from it – but to revoke or change the ruling orders and governmental organs would be to pass a new statute,[182] therefore, etc. What has been said is true unless this has been specifically permitted to them. Further, they cannot alienate the immovable property of the city unless this is specifically permitted to them: *Cod.* 11.32(31).3[183] and the aforementioned *Dig.* 43.24.3.4.[184] Further, on the strength of the said discretionary power they cannot establish anything against the statute and ruling order established by the whole people from which they have their authority, unless a new reason were to arise, or an ancient one which manifested itself afresh, which was unknown to the people at the time the law was passed: *Dig.* 17.1.30.[185] Further, on the strength of the said discretionary power, or one of them, they cannot pass a statute by which a private right already acquired by someone may be removed. For although the whole people could do this – *Dig.* 8.4.13.1,[186] and *Dig.* 42.5.37,[187] and I have said so at *Dig* 50.12.6[188] – nevertheless, when discretionary power is granted to someone it is understood to be granted without injury to another: *Dig.* 43.8.2.10 and 16[189] and so on the strength of such discretionary power they could not free debtors of anyone from their obligation. [...]

Further, could new taxes or excise duties be imposed in that city on the strength of some discretionary power among those mentioned above? And I understand the aforesaid question taking it as a principle that the city itself or the people could, as we see being done every day, even though according to the common law it could not: *Cod.* 4.62.2.[190] I answer: if indeed taxes and excise duties are not accustomed to be imposed in that city, the government [*ordo*] will not be able to impose them, unless this

---

[182] In the singular *statutum* could mean both a single statute among many others, and the entire statute book of the city; to alter the *statutum* in this second sense would be to rewrite the constitution.

[183] *Cod.* 11.32(31).3 permits decurions† to sell certain assets of their city, provided that they observe certain rigorous formalities.

[184] Above, n. 54.

[185] *Dig.* 17.1.30 provides that a procurator† may become aware of a good reason for countermanding a mandate issued by his principal.

[186] Nobody who is not entitled to do so may quarry stone on another person's land, whether in a private or public capacity, unless custom permits it.

[187] A statute of Antioch gives the city precedence over other creditors of a dead debtor.

[188] *In secundam Digesti Novi partem*, fo. 242ra. Bartolus argues here that those granted discretionary authority by a city may not violate the rights of others, whereas the city itself, by passing a statute, can.

[189] Imperial permission to build in public places is subject to the caveat that nobody else sustains damage.

[190] *Cod.* 4.62.2 rules that cities cannot decree new taxes.

is specifically permitted to them, for this is a case which is reserved to the people which has *imperium*† in its city, or occupies the place of the emperor, just as it is reserved to the universal emperor by the cited law.

Cod. 2.3.28[191]

You know that the cities of Italy generally do not possess *merum imperium*† but have usurped it. Nevertheless, I say that, if a city wished to defend itself and exercise *merum imperium*, it would have of necessity to cite a grant by the emperor; further, a very long period during which the said city has been exercising *merum imperium*, it being assumed in this case that there were no proof of a grant from the emperor. Nevertheless, if it proved that it has been exercising *merum imperium*, then [the claim] is valid.

Cod. 3.5.1[192]

The rubric summarizes the law.[193] Understand this to be true except of judges who recognize no superior, for then they themselves judge in their own cases, as in *Dig.* 28.5.42(41).[194] And so we see *de facto* in cities which do not recognize a superior. And the gloss to *Dig.* 43.24.7.3 supports this interpretation.[195]

Cod. 10.32(31).2[196]

Further, note that by the common law it pertains to the council of the city to run elections of officials and syndics:† *Cod.* 10.32(31).30 is relevant,[197] and so there will be no need for the *arenga*[198] or general assembly. Nevertheless, it is for the *arenga* or parliament, where there is no super-

---

[191] *Bartoli a Sassoferrato in primam Codicis partem commentaria* (Turin 1574), fo. 50va.

[192] Ed. cit., fo. 102ra.

[193] The rubric of *Cod.* 3.5 is 'No one shall be judge in his own case or pass judgment on himself.'

[194] The passage describes a judgment given by Emperor Tiberius in which his own rights were at stake.

[195] See the gloss *Ex magna*, where Accursius follows the text of the *Digest*† in allowing a private citizen to use force or stealth to demolish a house which has been built by force or stealth (*vi aut clam*), but only for good and sufficient cause, adding as an example the case where there is no judge to take care of the matter.

[196] *Bartoli a Sassoferrato in Tres libros Codicis commentaria* (Turin 1574), fo. 16ra.

[197] *Cod.* 10.32(31).30 states that procurators† of a municipality† should use the popular actions. Their object was the punishment of crimes, and thus to protect the public interest.

[198] *Arenga* was the common term for the main assembly of the citizens in the Italian city-states.

ior, to elect the council in the first place, as in *Dig.* 1.2.2 towards the beginning.[199] Thus elected, this council then represents the whole people, as is noted at the rubric of *Cod.* 8.52(53).[200]

Cod. 10.32(31).61[201]

This law[202] supports the claim that Perugia is not subject to the church or the empire. And if you said that whatever is not subject to the empire is subject to the church, I concede that, unless some city is not subject to the church on the strength of a privilege granted it; but the city of Perugia is in this category because the emperor gave it to the church or swapped it with the church, and the church liberated it by a privilege.

Cod. 11.32(33).3[203]

Note from the second section that in both Romes[204] imperial authorization is required for the sale [of civic property]. And on this basis I say that in cities which recognize no superior in temporalities, such as the city of Perugia – and so the people is free, as is noted at *Dig.* 49.15.24[205] – the sale of immovable goods could be done on the authority of its council, where all power resides. For it represents the emperor in that city.

---

[199] The target of this reference is not obvious; Bartolus seems to be thinking of §4, where the *Decemviri* responsible for creating Rome's first laws after the expulsion of the kings are said to have been appointed 'by public authority'.

[200] *Cod.* 8.52(53) concerns long-established custom (*consuetudo*†). In his gloss to the rubric, Accursius notes that two repetitions suffice to found a custom, so long as the people, or the council which represents the people, approves.

[201] Ed. cit., fo. 18vb.

[202] *Cod.* 10.32(31).61 is a privilege exempting those who belong only by maternal descent to the council of Antioch from the obligation to serve as decurions.†

[203] Ed. cit., fos. 35vb–36ra.

[204] The text – *Cod.* 11.32(33).3 – refers to Constantinople, the New Rome; Bartolus extends it to Old Rome as well. It allows the civic authorities in Constantinople to sell bequests for proper civil purposes, with the proviso that imperial authorization is given. In the provinces, by contrast, the order of decurions and certain others must observe certain formalities before making such a sale.

[205] Above, pp. 92, 96.

Index of Legal Citations

General Index

abbot, 42

Accursius, xi, xx, xxxiv, xlv, xlviii, xlix, lvii, lxi, 6n., 8n., 23, 30n., 37n., 40n., 41n., 43n., 46n., 47n., 48n., 50n., 51n., 52n., 58n, 59n., 69n., 70n., 71 n.,72n., 74n., 75n., 77n., 81n., 83n., 86n., 87n., 88n., 89n., 93n., 95n., 99n., 100n., 101n., 103n., 108n., 111n., 112n.

adoption, 20n.

aedile, 51 n 100

affectio, xliii, 3, 15

Africa, 56n., 131

Albericus de Rosate, 35

Albornoz, Gil, Cardinal, xv, lviii, 57 and n.

Alexander III, Pope, 4n., 31n., 41n., 45n., 49n., 59n.

allies, 95, 103n., 104

alluvial deposit, xiii, xvi

Ancona, March of, xi, xvii, 57, 72, 105, 106

animals, xlix, 71, 83n., 100n.

antianus, xliv, xlvii, liv

Antioch, 73n., 112n.

anti-pope, 45n., 49n.

anziano, see *antianus*

Apocalypse, xxix

appeal, xxxii, xlvii, li, 28n., 102, 106 and n., 108n.

Aquinas, Saint Thomas, lvii, 9 and n., 24n., 27n.

arenga, 111 and n., 112

aristocracy, xiii, xxiii, xxx, xxviii, 17

Aristotle, lviii, 9n., 16 and n., 17, 18, 19 and n., 20 n., 21 and n., 26, 27 and n., 53 and n.; *Nicomachean Ethics*, 27; *Politics*, 16, 53

army, xxvii, 9, 43 and n., 109n.; Roman, 109n.

assembly: general assembly of city, xvii, xxxii, 39, 53, 54, 108n., 111 and n.; of *municipium*, l

Associations of Mercy, 94

Athens, 73 and n.

Augustine, Saint, 8n., 32 and n., 44n.

Augustus, Caesar, liv, 104

Authenticum, xiv, xliii, xliv, xlvi, xlviii, xlix, l, lvi, lix

authorization, xxxi, 12n., 68, 112 and n.

Azo, lvii, 77n., 90 and n.

Babylonians, 83

Baldus de Ubaldis, xxxv, li

banishment, xviii, 79 n., 97, 100n., 109 and n.

baron, 35, 56, 91, 95 and n., 96

Bartholomaeus Brixiensis, xlvii, 49n.

Bartolus of Sassoferrato: and Aristotelian political science, xxi, xxviii; and Giles of Rome, xxi-xxii; biography, xi; *de facto/de iure* distinction, xvi, xxx, xxxv; death before completion of treatises, xv, xl; definition of city, xlvii; influence, xi-xii; on aristocracy, xxiii; on artificial personhood, xxxiii; on *civitas sibi princeps*, xxx, xxxiii, xxxiv; on collective action against tyrannical government, xx; on common good, xix, xx, xxi; xxiv; xxv, xxvii; on kings, xxxii; on legal personality, xxxiii-xxxiv; on legality of factional names, xx-xxi; on legisla-

CAMBRIDGE TEXTS IN THE HISTORY OF POLITICAL THOUGHT

Titles published in the series thus far

Albert Venn Dicey *Writings on Democracy and the Referendum* (edited by Gregory Conti)

Diderot *Political Writings* (edited and translated by John Hope Mason and Robert Wokler)

The Dutch Revolt (edited and translated by Martin van Gelderen)

Early Greek Political Thought from Homer to the Sophists (edited and translated by Michael Gagarin and Paul Woodruff)

The Early Political Writings of the German Romantics (edited and translated by Frederick C. Beiser)

Emerson *Political Writings* (edited by Kenneth S. Sacks)

The English Levellers (edited by Andrew Sharp)

Erasmus *The Education of a Christian Prince with the Panegyric for Archduke Philip of Austria* (edited and translated by Lisa Jardine; translated by Neil M. Cheshire and Michael J. Heath)

Fénelon *Telemachus* (edited and translated by Patrick Riley)

Ferguson *An Essay on the History of Civil Society* (edited by Fania Oz-Salzberger)

Fichte *Addresses to the German Nation* (edited by Gregory Moore)

Filmer *Patriarcha and Other Writings* (edited by Johann P. Sommerville)

Fletcher *Political Works* (edited by John Robertson)

Sir John Fortescue *On the Laws and Governance of England* (edited by Shelley Lockwood)

Fourier *The Theory of the Four Movements* (edited by Gareth Stedman Jones; edited and translated by Ian Patterson)

Franklin *The Autobiography and Other Writings on Politics, Economics, and Virtue* (edited by Alan Houston)

Gramsci *Pre-Prison Writings* (edited by Richard Bellamy; translated by Virginia Cox)

Guicciardini *Dialogue on the Government of Florence* (edited and translated by Alison Brown)

Hamilton, Madison, and Jay (writing as 'Publius') *The Federalist with Letters of 'Brutus'* (edited by Terence Ball)

Harrington *The Commonwealth of Oceana and A System of Politics* (edited by J. G. A. Pocock)

Hegel *Elements of the Philosophy of Right* (edited by Allen W. Wood; translated by H. B. Nisbet)

Hegel *Political Writings* (edited by Laurence Dickey and H. B. Nisbet)

Hess *The Holy History of Mankind and Other Writings* (edited and translated by Shlomo Avineri)

Hobbes *Leviathan* (edited by Richard Tuck)

Hobbes *On the Citizen* (edited and translated by Michael Silverthorne and Richard Tuck)

Hobhouse *Liberalism and Other Writings* (edited by James Meadowcroft)

Hooker *Of the Laws of Ecclesiastical Polity* (edited by A. S. McGrade)

Hume *Political Essays* (edited by Knud Haakonssen)

King James VI and I *Political Writings* (edited by Johann P. Sommerville)

Jefferson *Political Writings* (edited by Joyce Appleby and Terence Ball)

John of Salisbury *Policraticus* (edited by Cary J. Nederman)

Kant *Political Writings* (edited by H. S. Reiss; translated by H. B. Nisbet)

Knox *On Rebellion* (edited by Roger A. Mason)

Kropotkin *The Conquest of Bread and Other Writings* (edited by Marshall Shatz)

Kumazawa Banzan *Governing the Realm and Bringing Peace to All below Heaven* (edited and translated by John A. Tucker)

Lawson *Politica Sacra et Civilis* (edited by Conal Condren)

Leibniz *Political Writings* (edited and translated by Patrick Riley)

Lincoln *Political Writings and Speeches* (edited by Terence Ball)

Locke *Political Essays* (edited by Mark Goldie)

Locke *Two Treatises of Government* (edited by Peter Laslett)

Loyseau *A Treatise of Orders and Plain Dignities* (edited and translated by Howell A. Lloyd)

Luther and Calvin on Secular Authority (edited and translated by Harro Höpfl)

Catharine Macaulay *Political Writings* (edited by Max Skjönsberg)

Machiavelli *The Prince, Second Edition* (edited by Quentin Skinner and Russell Price)

Joseph de Maistre *Considerations on France* (edited and translated by Richard A. Lebrun)

Maitland *State, Trust and Corporation* (edited by David Runciman and Magnus Ryan)

Malthus *An Essay on the Principle of Population* (edited by Donald Winch)

Marsiglio of Padua *Defensor minor and De translatione Imperii* (edited by Cary J. Nederman)

Marsilius of Padua *The Defender of the Peace* (edited and translated by Annabel Brett)

Marx *Early Political Writings* (edited and translated by Joseph O'Malley)

Medieval Muslim Mirrors for Princes: An Anthology of Arabic, Persian and Turkish Political Advice (edited and translated by Louise Marlow)

James Mill *Political Writings* (edited by Terence Ball)

J. S. Mill *On Liberty and Other Writings* (edited by Stefan Collini)

Milton *Political Writings* (edited by Martin Dzelzainis; translated by Claire Gruzelier)

Montesquieu *The Spirit of the Laws* (edited and translated by Anne M. Cohler, Basia Carolyn Miller, and Harold Samuel Stone)

More *Utopia* (edited by George M. Logan and Robert M. Adams)

Morris *News from Nowhere* (edited by Krishan Kumar)

Nicholas of Cusa *The Catholic Concordance* (edited and translated by Paul E. Sigmund)

Nietzsche *On the Genealogy of Morality* (edited by Keith Ansell-Pearson; translated by Carol Diethe)

For EU product safety concerns, contact us at Calle de José Abascal, 56–1°, 28003 Madrid, Spain or eugpsr@cambridge.org.

www.ingramcontent.com/pod-product-compliance
Ingram Content Group UK Ltd.
Pitfield, Milton Keynes, MK11 3LW, UK
UKHW020428240426
470322UK00017B/407